Cases Without Controversies

Cases Without Controversies

Uncontested Adjudication in Article III Courts

JAMES E. PFANDER

OXFORD
UNIVERSITY PRESS

OXFORD
UNIVERSITY PRESS

Oxford University Press is a department of the University of Oxford. It furthers the University's objective of excellence in research, scholarship, and education by publishing worldwide. Oxford is a registered trade mark of Oxford University Press in the UK and certain other countries.

Published in the United States of America by Oxford University Press
198 Madison Avenue, New York, NY 10016, United States of America.

Library of Congress Cataloging-in-Publication Data

Names: Pfander, James E., author.
Title: Cases without controversies : uncontested adjudication in
Article III courts / James E. Pfander.
Description: New York : Oxford University Press, [2021] | Includes index.
Identifiers: LCCN 2020048201 | ISBN 9780197571408 (hardback) |
ISBN 9780197571415 (UPDF) | ISBN 9780197571422 (EPUB) | ISBN 9780197571439 (Digital-Online)
Subjects: LCSH: Courts—United States. | Jurisdiction—United States. |
Judicial power—United States, | Administrative procedure—United States. |
United States. Supreme Court. | Same-sex marriage—Law and legislation—United States.
Classification: LCC KF8719.P43 2021 | DDC 347.73/282—dc23
LC record available at https://lccn.loc.gov/2020048201

DOI: 10.1093/oso/9780197571408.001.0001

1 3 5 7 9 8 6 4 2

Printed by Integrated Books International, United States of America

Note to Readers

This publication is designed to provide accurate and authoritative information in regard to the subject matter covered. It is based upon sources believed to be accurate and reliable and is intended to be current as of the time it was written. It is sold with the understanding that the publisher is not engaged in rendering legal, accounting, or other professional services. If legal advice or other expert assistance is required, the services of a competent professional person should be sought. Also, to confirm that the information has not been affected or changed by recent developments, traditional legal research techniques should be used, including checking primary sources where appropriate.

(Based on the Declaration of Principles jointly adopted by a Committee of the American Bar Association and a Committee of Publishers and Associations.)

Contents

Foreword

This book owes much to my student, faculty, and library colleagues at Northwestern University Pritzker School of Law, where I have been happily professing law for nearly fifteen years. I worked out many of the ideas in this book in a series of law review articles—often in the course of senior research collaborations with Northwestern law students. Uniquely among major law schools, Northwestern encourages third-year students to work closely with professors in the development of scholarly ideas. I owe thanks to Daniel Birk, Emily Damrau, and Michael Downey, all of whom joined me in senior research projects aimed at understanding the mysteries of uncontested adjudication. Thanks as well to the students in my federal jurisdiction classes for wrestling productively with the words of Article III of the U.S. Constitution and to the editors of the law reviews where some pieces of this work first appeared in a less well-integrated form.[1]

Northwestern Pritzker has a superb faculty and an inclusive and engaging scholarly community, with first-rate library and staff support. I have been, if anything, only too willing to take advantage of these resources. A series of workshops and conversations with my public law colleagues—Steve Calabresi, Zach Clopton, Erin Delaney, Paul Gowder, Heidi Kitrosser, Andy Koppelman, John McGinnis, Jide Nzelibe, Marty Redish, Jim Speta,

1. Thanks in particular to the law reviews who published the following pieces, all of which I have drawn upon with their permission in the course of this book. *Standing, Litigable Interests, and Article III's Case-or-Controversy Requirement*, 65 UCLA L. Rev. 170 (2018); *Adverse Interests and Article III: A Reply*, 111 Nw. U.L. Rev. 1067 (2017) (with Daniel D. Birk); *Standing to Sue: Lessons from Scotland's Actio Popularis*, 66 Duke L.J. 1493 (2017); *Scalia's Legacy: Originalism and Change in the Law of Standing*, 6 Brit. J. Am. Legal Stud. 85 (2017); *A Non-Contentious Account of Article III's Domestic Relations Exception*, 92 Notre Dame L. Rev. 117 (2016) (with Emily Damrau); *Article III Judicial Power, the Adverse-Party Requirement, and Non-Contentious Jurisdiction*, 124 Yale L.J. 1346 (2015) (with Daniel D. Birk); *In Search of the Probate Exception*, 67 Vand. L. Rev. 1533 (2014) (with Michael Downey). This material is republished here in a modified form by special permission of the Northwestern Pritzker School of Law and the *Northwestern University Law Review*.

and Deb Tuerkheimer—have challenged and sharpened my thinking. My colleagues in legal history, Charlotte Crane, Emily Kadens, and Ajay Mehrotra, remind me to read my sources one more time. Tom Gaylord and the Pritzker Legal Research Center team prove that cheerful and unstinting help in locating those sources remains possible in the digital age. My assistant, Jane Brock, impresses me every day with her calm and sophisticated professionalism. Kristi Lew provided indispensable editorial and research assistance.

I feel especially fortunate to have had the opportunity to share these ideas with my colleagues in history and public law across the country and, indeed, around the world. Akhil Amar, Dick Fallon, Tara Grove, Henry Monaghan, Bob Pushaw, and Amanda Tyler have been spirited, if geographically distant, interlocutors. Special thanks to Caleb Nelson and Ann Woolhandler for their willingness to test these ideas and to share the litigable interest construct on which this book draws. Faculty workshops at the law schools at Cornell, Duke, Michigan, North Carolina, Pennsylvania, and Vanderbilt encouraged me to think more deeply about the social forces that drove the changes I recount; participants in meetings of the American Society of Legal History gave me a better feel for the Roman law precursors of uncontested proceedings; and the members of the Tel Aviv University legal workshop, the British Legal History conference in St. Andrews, and the Scottish Legal History Group in Edinburgh displayed a remarkable tolerance for one American's gloss on a set of ideas that civilians may find only too familiar. Mary Bilder generously helped me modulate my voice and consider my auditors but bears no responsibility for any discordant notes that remain.

A brief word about the editorial apparatus. The endnotes in this book refer to sources—other books, articles, and judicial decisions—that appear in tables of cases and authorities in the back. Endnote references to books and articles in each part will, after a full initial reference, identify only the author(s), page number, and perhaps a brief title to distinguish among multiple works by a single author. Endnote references to decisions of the Supreme Court of the United States will, after a full initial citation, identify the case by first party name, reporter, and page number; abbreviated endnote references to other judicial decisions will also identify the court.

My family continues to provide me with just the right mix of loving support and provocative distraction, reminding me that there's more to life than endnotes. In our interactions and discourse, we resemble the federal courts in that we rely on both contentious and non-contentious forms. Whether immediate (Laurie, Sarah, Sam, and Ben) or extended (Margaret, Bill, Michael, and Geoff), family life has bound me more closely to the world and borne me up. It has made this book, and many other things, possible.

Introduction

For students of the federal judiciary, the Supreme Court's 2013 encounter with the adverse-party requirement in the Defense of Marriage Act (DOMA) case, *United States v. Windsor*, was disappointing. The Court has rather dogmatically insisted that federal courts can hear only "definite and concrete" controversies that touch upon "the legal relations of parties having adverse legal interests." But the Court has failed to provide a coherent account of the adverse-party requirement or of how such a requirement can coexist with a variety of clearly non-adverse or ex parte proceedings that have worked their way onto the docket of the federal courts. Since the 1790s, Congress has assigned pension claims, warrant applications, naturalization proceedings, and a surprisingly broad range of other ex parte matters to the federal courts. Even today, the Foreign Intelligence Surveillance Act, a subject of some controversy, requires the government to obtain an ex parte federal court order to conduct certain kinds of electronic surveillance. Aside from a decision nearly one hundred years ago addressing the power of the federal courts to naturalize aliens, and a few relatively uninformative decisions thereafter, the Court has failed to wrestle with the tension between adverse-party rhetoric and ex parte reality.[1]

Windsor did little to clarify matters. Doubts as to the presence of truly adverse parties had arisen early on, when the government insisted on enforcing DOMA but agreed with its nominal opponent, Edith Windsor, that the law violated her constitutional rights by denying her the beneficial federal tax treatment she would have received had she been the surviving spouse of a man instead of a woman. Yet the opinion by Justice Anthony Kennedy for a five-Justice majority announced that the disappearance of adverseness did not deprive the Court of power to reach the merits. For the majority, the adverse-party requirement was a prudential element of standing doctrine, appropriately informing the Court's discretion but not inflexibly compelling party opposition as a jurisdictional prerequisite at every stage of every case. The Court did not offer much by way of support for its conclusion that such a requirement existed or, if it did, why it was merely a matter of prudence;

Cases Without Controversies. James E. Pfander, Oxford University Press.
DOI: 10.1093/oso/9780197571408.003.0001

certainly the Court took no notice of the many instances in which the federal judiciary, without first consulting prudential considerations, proceeds in the absence of party adverseness.[2]

Justice Antonin Scalia's sharply worded dissent also added little to our understanding of the adverse-party requirement. To be sure, Justice Scalia viewed the rule as an "essential element of an Article III case or controversy," not as a prudential requirement "that we have invented." Moreover, Justice Scalia attempted to connect the adverse-party restriction to the text of Article III, placing some emphasis on the fact that the term "controversy" connotes a live dispute between opposing parties. But the Justice did not address the meaning of Article III's grant of "judicial power" or of its reference to "cases"; both terms have suggested to other readers, including Chief Justice John Marshall and Justice Joseph Story, that federal jurisdiction encompasses more than disputes between adversaries.[3]

As for history, Justice Scalia depicted Article III's case-or-controversy limits as reflecting the traditional forms of adjudication inherited from early Americans and our "English ancestors," an echo of an earlier claim that the federal judicial power extends only to the forms and actions of the English courts at Westminster. This emphasis on England and the practice of the courts at Westminster, however, overlooks the fact that the English courts exercised jurisdiction over certain ex parte and non-adverse matters. It also tends, in its focus on the common law, to obscure the alternative forms of adjudication on which the Framers were to draw in crafting Article III. It was mainly in the equity, admiralty, and probate courts of the eighteenth century, where judges rather than juries bore primary responsibility for fact-finding, that the Framers were to encounter the range of ex parte proceedings that made their way onto federal court dockets in the early Republic. *Windsor* thus brought us little closer to resolving the tension between the theory and reality of the adverse-party requirement.[4]

Five years later, in 2018, the Court tackled another instance of non-adverse adjudication and again failed to offer any real insight into the nature of the adverse-party requirement. The Court agreed to hear *Ayestas v. Davis* to clarify the standard of review that governs funding requests by capital habeas petitioners under a federal statute that authorizes payment of investigative costs. Opposing review, the State of Texas argued that the funding application had been submitted in a non-adversarial ex parte context and thus called for an administrative, rather than a judicial, determination. Texas accordingly urged that the habeas petitioner's appeal from denial of the funding application was not a "case" within the meaning of federal appellate jurisdiction. But the Court rejected that claim, holding that such matters could qualify as cases for judicial determination and noting that Texas vigorously contested the funding request. While the Court cited a handful of its earlier decisions, it offered no considered justification for its suggested distinction between administrative and judicial matters.[5]

Like the Court itself, few scholars have explored the textual and historical underpinnings of the adverse-party requirement. Fewer still have assessed the requirement in light of the ex parte practices of the federal courts. To be sure, some students of constitutional history have called attention to certain ex parte proceedings that appear very much at odds with an adverse-party requirement. Others have identified modern examples of seemingly curious departures from our adversary ideal, such as bankruptcy administration. Still others have attempted to justify particular ex parte practices, such as search and arrest warrants, by highlighting the possibility that related adverse-party litigation might ensue. Yet these scholars have not offered a comprehensive account of how such practices fit into the broader framework of Article III adjudication. Instead of attempting to develop a theory that can account for the federal courts' willingness to hear both adverse-party disputes and ex parte proceedings, scholars tend to treat ex parte practices as aberrational vestiges of an earlier day, or as anomalies that have become too entrenched to question.[6]

Beneath the surface of this judicial and scholarly neglect lies a deeply ingrained set of assumptions about the adversarial character of the judicial system of the United States. In an adversary system, the parties maintain substantial control over the development of the legal issues and evidence bearing on the resolution of their dispute. Judges play a more passive role as neutral arbiters of disputes presented to them by the parties. This passivity contrasts with the more active judicial role practiced in European and other civil law inquisitorial systems. There, judges develop the factual record of the case and enjoy some control over the legal issues to which they will most closely attend. The attorneys stay somewhat on the sidelines, particularly during the fact-finding process.[7]

Although the contrast between the Anglo-American adversary system and the inquisitorial systems of continental Europe may be slightly overdrawn, American lawyers and judges have been steeped in the adversarial ideal. In a paper cautiously celebrating the inquisitorial features of developments in the management of mass tort litigation, one commentator recognized that the culture of American adjudication remains decidedly adversarial and may not easily support a shift to a more inquisitorial model. Indeed, one can sense that the adversary ideal has come to be seen as yet another feature of American procedural exceptionalism, that is, as a deliberate departure from the practice of European countries of which Americans should be justly proud. As another commentator noted, inquisitorial judging has become something of an "epithet among American judges," with the consequence that most seek to avoid even a "whiff of its judge-dominated procedures."[8]

Coupled with neglect of the issue by the Court, scholarly devotion to the adversary tradition tends to encourage strong statements of the adverse-party requirement and to cast doubt on the power of federal courts to entertain ex parte proceedings. After all, in many ex parte proceedings, the courts preside over applications for benefits in somewhat the same way administrative agencies might hear benefit claims. To rule on a petition or application, the judge must investigate the factual and legal justification for the relief sought. Such uncontested proceedings present a challenge, especially for federal judges who may lack the training, administrative support, and inclination to conduct their own investigations. Modern observers justifiably view such ex parte practices as inconsistent with the adversary ideal. Consider, for example, the thorough critique of settlement class actions by Martin Redish and Andrianna Kastanek. The two authors argue that settlement class actions violate Article III's adverse-party requirement, which they view as a "logical outgrowth of the nation's commitment to an adversary system."[9]

This book tackles the puzzle of how federal courts, limited by Article III's reference to cases and controversies and by the adversary ideal that animates so much of American procedural exceptionalism, may entertain ex parte proceedings. The key lies in recovering the lost history of the American acceptance of uncontested forms of judicial process. One can best reclaim that history by considering the distinction drawn by civilian lawyers between "contentious" and "non-contentious" jurisdiction. Following Roman law, civilians use the term "contentious" jurisdiction to describe the contests between opposing parties that lie at the heart of the adversary system. They use the terms "voluntary" or "non-contentious" jurisdiction to describe a collection of ex parte proceedings in which petitioners seek a judicial decree confirming that they enjoy a new right or status under applicable law. Civilian systems typically authorize their courts to handle both contested and uncontested adjudication.[10]

History shows that the American colonies followed England in relying on both contentious and non-contentious forms of adjudication. Proceedings in probate and admiralty jurisdiction in England and the colonies were governed by civil law; both proceedings were understood as in rem, and both featured elements of uncontested adjudication. An outgrowth of estate administration by the courts of equity, bankruptcy includes ex parte proceedings that do not invariably feature adverse parties. Blackstone's *Commentaries* described uncontested forms of practice, distinguishing "voluntary" from "contentious" jurisdiction in the probate of wills and granting of administration. Justices of the peace, the workhorses of early modern adjudication, resolved disputes and handled a range of legislative and administrative chores at the county level. All these forms of uncontested adjudication were part of the complex legal world in which lawyers of the early Republic practiced law, and some similar proceedings would find their way onto the dockets of the first federal courts.[11]

Indeed, evidence from the early Republic suggests that the Framers viewed the "judicial power" with which Article III courts were invested (and to which they were limited) as capacious enough to encompass forms of uncontested adjudication. In one of the clearest examples, Congress adopted a naturalization statute in 1790 that called upon federal courts to entertain petitions for naturalized citizenship on an ex parte basis. Federal and state courts alike heard such petitions throughout the nineteenth century without questioning their propriety, despite the fact that the claimants did not (as required by latter-day statements of Article III standing requirements) seek redress for an injury inflicted by an opposing party. Such leading early exponents of federal jurisdiction as Chief Justice Marshall and Justice Story recognized the power of federal courts to pass on naturalization claims; they viewed the resulting naturalization decrees as judgments of record that were entitled to preclusive effect and immunity from collateral attack.

One can best make sense of this acceptance of ex parte adjudication by better understanding Article III's extension of the judicial power to "cases" and "controversies." While modern readers have been taught to view the terms as essentially synonymous, nineteenth-century lawyers and jurists perceived them as quite different. "Controversies" arose between specified opposing parties and were thought to require contestation. But "cases" could include uncontested petitions to secure a right under federal law. Both

Marshall and Story couched their canonical definitions of the term "case" in terms broad enough to encompass ex parte matters. Listen first to the familiar words of Marshall's opinion in *Osborn v. Bank of the United States*:

> This clause [extending jurisdiction to federal question "cases"] enables the judicial department to receive jurisdiction to the full extent of the constitution, laws, and treaties of the United States, when any question respecting them shall assume such a form that the judicial power is capable of acting on it. That power is capable of acting only when the subject is submitted to it by a party who asserts his rights in the form prescribed by law. It then becomes a case, and the constitution declares, that the judicial power shall extend to all cases arising under the constitution, laws, and treaties of the United States.

Story's *Commentaries on the Constitution* adopted the same formulation:

> A case, then, in the sense of this clause of the Constitution, arises when some subject touching the Constitution, laws, or treaties of the United States is submitted to the courts by a party who asserts his rights in the form prescribed by law.

By distinguishing between cases and controversies and defining cases to encompass claims of right under federal law by a single party, these nineteenth-century thinkers imagined a much wider range of federal adjudication than jurists do today.

To be sure, the Marshall-Story definition of "cases" allows federal courts, where the matter arises under federal law, to exercise jurisdiction over a contested claim, one in which a party demands a remedy from an opposing party for the alleged violation of a federal right. Such a claim for redress of violations would clearly qualify as an assertion of one's rights within the Marshall-Story paradigm. Yet the Marshall-Story definition would also encompass uncontested federal question claims. Their definition requires only the assertion of claims by a single "party" and says nothing about the joinder of an opposing party. In addition, the formulation requires only the assertion of one's "rights," and thus extends to claims in the nature of ex parte applications for pension benefits, naturalized citizenship, and other legal entitlements conferred by law. As both Marshall and Story understood, naturalization and other ex parte petitioners were empowered to assert federal claims of right in an ex parte proceeding that did not entail any demand for redress from an opposing party.[12]

For modern readers, the power of federal courts to exercise authority over contested and uncontested "cases" might seem both illuminating and unsettling. On the illuminating side of the ledger, the recognition of judicial power over uncontested claims provides a solution to a serious problem of coherence in the workaday world of the Article III judiciary by explaining how such courts can hear both adversary disputes and certain ex parte and non-adverse proceedings. By recognizing ex parte proceedings as cases under federal law, the account of judicial power proposed in this book fits well with the text, structure, and history of Article III and maps onto the practice of the courts of admiralty and equity at the time of the framing. In addition, formulating a workable theory for the ex parte proceedings already heard by federal courts helps to situate those proceedings within the bounds of Article III and to provide a framework for evaluating their compliance with other applicable jurisdictional prerequisites.

On the other, more unsettling side of the ledger, few notions seem more central to our conception of Article III courts than that they serve as tribunals for the resolution of concrete disputes between adverse parties and perform their law-exposition functions best in that setting. Recognition of uncontested adjudication challenges this familiar conception of the Article III judiciary and forces courts and scholars to confront the inability of current doctrines, such as the adverse-party requirement and the injury-in-fact test for standing, to make room for uncontested, ex parte practices. Naturalization petitioners, after all, were not seeking redress for an injury inflicted by an opposing party, as standing law has come to require. In addition, the recognition of uncontested adjudication poses a potential risk to the rights of third parties, necessitating a cautious approach to such proceedings. Finally, one might worry that the formal recognition of the propriety of uncontested adjudication could encourage Congress to assign more such chores to the federal courts, burdening them with matters that would be better handled by administrative agencies and other non–Article III actors.

In accounting for uncontested proceedings and proposing to make a place for them on the docket of the federal courts, this book proposes to achieve greater coherence without calling for an unsettling transformation of the work of the Article III judiciary. Greater coherence starts with a clear conceptual distinction between the operative assumptions of contested and uncontested adjudication. Unlike ordinary litigation to resolve a dispute between the parties over the application of (potentially contested) law to (potentially contested) fact, uncontested adjudication seeks to bring a new set of legal rights or legal status into being. This book will sometimes refer to the orders that emerge from uncontested adjudication as *constitutive* to describe their operation in creating a new legal relationships or investing parties with new legal rights. Consider judicial decrees that uphold an application for naturalized citizenship or that declare a formerly married couple to have been divorced in the eyes of the law. Such decisions usher into existence a new set of legal rights and relationships, transforming the individuals for legal purposes from a foreign national into a citizen and from members of a marital union into single persons. Applications for bankruptcy (and probate), if approved, similarly create or constitute a new legal entity, the bankruptcy (or decedent's) estate. Moreover, such decrees may identify the trustee or executor of the estate—a party newly invested with certain rights and fiduciary responsibilities under the law. Much uncontested adjudication, in both state and federal courts, seeks to produce these constitutive results.[13]

A moment's reflection reveals the difference between litigation that seeks to resolve a dispute over the scope or meaning of rights elsewhere conferred and uncontested adjudication that seeks to constitute or invest a party with a set of new legal rights. That distinction, though not entirely airtight, has proven helpful in clarifying the role of Article III courts in such cases as *Spindel v. Spindel*. There, the plaintiff brought suit alleging that her former husband induced her to marry him and then fraudulently procured a Mexican divorce. While the action, if successful, would deny legal effect to the Mexican divorce, the suit was not brought to secure a divorce (a constitutive decree). Rather, the point of the litigation was to test the validity of a legally significant act that had been performed under the laws of Mexico. The parties, in short, were in court to litigate their jural relationship, which was contested, rather than to alter that relationship through a constitutive act. The federal district court in New York accordingly agreed to hear the case as a contested proceeding within the court's diversity jurisdiction.[14]

The distinction between contested matters and uncontested applications for the issuance of constitutive decrees provides an important key to federal judicial power. When the matter arises under federal law, federal courts can both resolve disputes and conduct uncontested proceedings with a view toward the issuance of constitutive decrees. Naturalization decrees and search warrants, and a wide range of antebellum federal proceedings, were understood to alter the legal status quo and invest the parties with new legal rights often on an uncontested basis. As to matters of state law, by contrast, Article III limits the federal courts to the adjudication of controversies between specified opposing parties; that means the federal courts lack power to entertain uncontested state law applications for constitutive or investitive decrees. The district court in *Spindel* was applying this distinction, disclaiming any power to issue a state law divorce decree but reaffirming federal power to hear a diverse-party dispute over the *validity* of a decree issued by another tribunal.[15]

How, then, can we best incorporate the uncontested constitutive work of the federal judiciary into a jurisprudential framework that has grown increasingly focused on dispute resolution? Federal courts might continue to insist that, in matters governed by the rules of contentious jurisdiction, the parties present concrete disputes between genuine adversaries. But when Congress has acted within its Article I powers in assigning them uncontested matters to adjudicate, federal courts should follow a different set of guidelines or best practices. To be sure, courts should continue to apply elements, some familiar, some adapted, of the modern law of justiciability. Thus, while no adverse party need appear, the federal courts should exercise uncontested jurisdiction only if the party invoking federal power has a concrete interest in the recognition of a legal claim. The courts should do so, moreover, only where they have been called upon to exercise judicial judgment in the application of federal law to the facts and only where their decisions will enjoy the finality essential to the federal judicial role. Drawing on the Marshall-Story definition, this book uses the term "litigable interest" to describe the universe of contested and uncontested claims of right that qualify for Article III adjudication. Derived from practice, the litigable interest construct should help courts and scholars evaluate and refine our understanding of the judicial role in contested and uncontested proceedings. Chapter 11 provides a primer, exploring in greater detail the modern elements of uncontested adjudication.[16]

A word about methodology. This book begins by exploring the origin and early development of uncontested proceedings on the dockets of the federal courts. Subsequent chapters describe the surprisingly widespread presence of uncontested litigation on those dockets today. Having offered a catalog of uncontested proceedings, this book explains how Article III extends federal power to adjudicate such matters. In brief, this book distinguishes between "cases" and "controversies," arguing that, as a matter of text and history, the provisions of Article III permit the adjudication of uncontested matters only when (as with naturalization petitions) they arise as "cases" under federal law. If Article III cases do not invariably require contestation, controversies do. Indeed, Article III defines controversies by reference to the alignment of the adversaries; it provides a neutral federal forum for disputes between opponents, one of whom might face a risk of partiality if consigned to state court. Party opposition and contestation, in short, define federal jurisdiction over controversies. This book thus shows that while Congress can assign federal courts power to adjudicate matters of federal law on an ex parte or uncontested basis, uncontested adjudication of issues of state law must remain in the state courts.

In proposing a theory of Article III adjudication, this book takes account of what we know about the history and current practice of Article III courts. Among its striking implications, the proposed distinction between cases and controversies may help to explain two of the most puzzling features of federal jurisdictional law: the so-called domestic relations and probate exceptions to Article III. The subject of countless articles and judicial opinions, these exceptions posit that certain matters of state law lie beyond the judicial power of the federal courts. Today these exceptions primarily serve to limit the power of federal courts sitting in diversity, a disposition broadly consistent with this book's proposed distinction between cases and controversies. Matters of domestic relations and probate arise under state law, often in connection with uncontested applications for constitutive rulings, such as the appointment of an estate administrator, or the adoption of a child. Without a controversy between properly aligned adversaries, federal courts have no power to adjudicate such state law matters. Chapters 3 and 4 explore the antebellum origins of the probate and domestic relations exceptions to Article III, suggesting that the absence of contestation may help explain their judicial recognition.

In the course of responding to critics, this book offers a new synthesis of the rules that govern access to federal court. The brute fact that federal courts have long entertained uncontested applications under federal law reveals serious problems with strict versions of the adverse-party and injury-in-fact rules that now govern the standing of plaintiffs to pursue claims in federal court. In keeping with its recognition that well-established historical practice can be "well-nigh conclusive" of the legitimate reach of judicial power, the Supreme Court should limit its adverse-party rhetoric and its standing doctrine to contested matters and rely instead on the more nuanced construct of the litigable interest to measure the right of parties to invoke the jurisdiction of the federal courts. By allowing access to court for those who pursue a claim of right in the form prescribed by law, such a litigable interest construct would encompass the claims of both the injured plaintiff, seeking redress, and the ex parte petitioner. By capturing the full extent of federal judicial power, the litigable interest construct would also call for greater deference to congressional choices about what kind of litigation to assign to the federal courts.[17]

Finally, this book reflects on what the story of uncontested adjudication reveals about the way constitutional meaning changes over time. For much of the nineteenth century, courts and commentators accepted that federal courts could hear uncontested matters under laws adopted by Congress. In the late nineteenth and early twentieth centuries, seeking to narrow the role of the federal courts, jurists gave voice to the idea that the "case-or-controversy" requirement of Article III serves to limit congressional power. Today, many observers view the words of Article III through the eyes of those twentieth-century jurists, a viewpoint that, as this book makes clear, poses a threat to much of the uncontested work of the federal judiciary. Indeed, modern critics often embrace the now-conventional case-or-controversy wisdom as they criticize non-contentious practices.

Chapter 12 reflects on the interpretive significance of this narrative of changed meanings. It appears that, with vague references to history, tradition, and the practices of the courts at Westminster, the Court and its originalist jurists have played a surprisingly active role in forging a body of constitutional law that has little connection to the original meaning of Article III. No one did more than Justice Scalia to rewrite the law of justiciability, invoking a case-or-controversy doctrine that first appeared in a circuit court opinion one hundred years after Article III became law. Such lapses from interpretive consistency do not necessarily disprove the project of originalism, but they do perhaps reveal the complexity of the task of constitutional interpretation. The challenge lies in articulating a constructive or synthetic form of constitutionalism that can take account of the old and the new. The idea of a litigable interest may help bridge the gap between yesterday and today, accommodating both the historical reality of uncontested adjudication and preserving much of what modern jurists have had to say about the (changing) nature of the judicial power.

This book proceeds in three parts. Part I recounts the history of uncontested adjudication in the federal courts. Drawing on a practice rooted in Roman law, Congress assigned various forms of uncontested or non-contentious jurisdiction to the federal courts in antebellum America. A key feature of such jurisdiction was its provision for federal courts, perhaps acting on an ex parte basis, to issue constitutive rulings—rulings that changed the legal status quo and recognized the existence of a new set of legal rights. Such rulings included naturalization decrees, which established a new status of citizenship, as well as prize decrees (ordering a change in the ownership of property), warrants (legalizing an arrest, a search, or a seizure of property), and a host of other proceedings. Antebellum legal thinkers viewed these matters as uncontested "cases" arising under federal law and distinguished them from "controversies" between opposing parties that turned on principles of general common law. Building on the distinction between cases and controversies, nineteenth-century Americans understood, for example, that federal courts could hear uncontested matters of federal law (in bankruptcy) but lacked power to enter uncontested constitutive rulings as to matters of state law.

Part II tells a story of change. Beginning in the late nineteenth century, jurists and scholars reformulated the meaning of cases and controversies to introduce an across-the-board requirement of contestation. After this idea took root in the doctrine of the day, it became embedded in modern restatements of judicial power and came to threaten many settled forms of adjudication. These threats deserve to be taken seriously; scholars and jurists have questioned the constitutionality of a range of traditional adjudicative forms, including naturalization petitions, warrant proceedings, habeas petitions, bankruptcy proceedings, consent decrees, class action settlements, and petitions seeking forfeiture of certain property or the waiver of fees. Part II shows that, for these and other matters, the idea of contestation implicit in modern restatements of the case-or-controversy requirement serves as the basis for challenging the legitimacy of many longstanding forms of uncontested federal adjudication.

Part III offers a constructive new account of federal judicial power that seeks to harmonize the world of antebellum adjudication with the concerns that seemingly led to the modern case-or-controversy requirement. In place of the modern rules of standing to sue, which call for the identification of an injury inflicted by an opponent, part III would substitute the construct of a "litigable interest" to describe what a plaintiff must show to mount a claim in federal court. Importantly, though, by defining the litigable interest broadly enough to encompass uncontested claims of right by parties who seek a constitutive ruling, part III calls for some rethinking of the modern standing and adverse-party requirements. Having proposed a new approach, part III responds to critics who continue to defend a watered-down version of the adverse-party requirement on historical grounds. These responses set the stage for a concluding reflection on what we can learn about constitutional interpretation from this book's account of how a nineteenth-century practice of uncontested adjudication came to be seen as in conflict with modern jurisprudential commitments.

Two lessons stand out. First, the project of reclaiming the original understanding of our eighteenth-century Constitution must consider the words in light of the practices of the day. Parsing the words alone, however much one applies modern linguistic tools to their proper interpretation, cannot always recapture the understood operation of old provisions. Arguments that attempt to justify the modern case-or-controversy requirement by pointing to the language of Article III have little to recommend them. Second, the project of modern constitutional interpretation requires a measure of epistemic humility, a recognition that we have much to learn from the way practices have developed since the framing. Such humility calls for fair consideration of both the nineteenth-century practices that underlie uncontested adjudication and the twentieth-century concerns that led to the rise of the modern case-or-controversy dispensation. This book ultimately calls upon the Supreme Court to find a middle way, using the construct of the litigable interest to accommodate both the old and new worlds in a synthesis of the law governing access to federal courts. Even if the Court fails to embrace the proposed synthesis in terms and chooses instead to muddle through, as it has done in recent cases, this book offers a framework that can better explain the choices the Court faces, the conclusions it reaches, and the duties that uncontested adjudication properly casts on federal courts.

Notes

1. *See* United States v. Windsor, 570 U.S. 744, 757–60, 773–75 (2013) (invalidating Section 3 of the Defense of Marriage Act, 110 Stat. 2419, but rejecting the argument that the proceeding lacked the necessary adversarial quality to permit federal court adjudication). The quote appears in Aetna Life Ins. Co. of Hartford, Conn. v. Hayworth, 300 U.S. 227, 240–41 (1937). On the operation of ex parte proceedings before the FISA court(s), *see In re* Sealed Case, 310 F.3d 717, 737–41 (FISA Ct. Rev. 2002); Note, *Shifting the FISA Paradigm: Protecting Civil Liberties by Eliminating Ex Ante Judicial Approval*, 121 Harv. L. Rev. 2200, 2206–07 (2008). For the decision

upholding ex parte practice in naturalization proceedings, *see* Tutun v. United States, 270 U.S. 568 (1926).

2. Recognizing that party agreement posed a jurisdictional hurdle, the Court appointed an amicus curiae to argue that the United States had no standing to appeal from the decision below once it concluded, in agreement with Windsor, that DOMA was unconstitutional. But the Court rejected that argument. *See Windsor*, 570 U.S. at 757–60.
3. Quoted language appears in *Windsor*, 570 U.S. at 786 (Scalia, J., dissenting). *Id.* at 785 ("The question here is not whether, as the majority puts it, 'the United States retains a stake sufficient to support Article III jurisdiction,' the question is whether there is any controversy (which requires *contradiction*) between the United States and Ms. Windsor." (internal citation omitted)). For the views of Marshall and Story, *see* chapter 4.1. *See also* Robert J. Pushaw Jr., *Article III's Case/Controversy Distinction and the Dual Functions of Federal Courts*, 69 NOTRE DAME L. REV. 447 (1994).
4. *Windsor*, 570 U.S. at 780 (Scalia, J., dissenting). *See also* Coleman v. Miller, 307 U.S. 433, 460 (1939) (Frankfurter, J.) ("courts of Westminster"); Willing v. Chi. Auditorium Ass'n, 277 U.S. 274, 290 (1928) (Brandeis, J.) ("English . . . courts"). *See* James E. Pfander & Daniel D. Birk, *Article III and the Scottish Judiciary*, 124 HARV L. REV. 1613 (2011) (arguing that the focus of American legal scholars on Blackstone and the horizontal structure of the English judiciary may have obscured the extent to which the hierarchical structure of the Scottish judicial system influenced the structure of the Article III judicial system). Although the High Court of Chancery, which exercised the equitable jurisdiction of the Crown, sat in Westminster Hall, along with the courts of King's Bench and Common Pleas, most civil law courts sat outside Westminster. Thus, the High Court of Admiralty, which followed civil law forms of action, sat at Doctors' Commons in London, at least during the eighteenth century, and heard claims by civil lawyers trained at universities and admitted to the College of Advocates. *See* 1 WILLIAM S. HOLDSWORTH, HISTORY OF ENGLISH LAW 547 (1926). The ecclesiastical courts, which handled probate and family law matters in the first instance, sat in dioceses throughout the realm. *See* R.H. HELMHOLZ, THE OXFORD HISTORY OF THE LAWS OF ENGLAND: THE CANON LAW AND ECCLESIASTICAL JURISDICTION FROM 597 TO THE 1640S, at 396–97 (2004) (describing "widely dispersed" jurisdiction over probate matters, with records held by "rural deans, archdeacons, and cathedral prebendaries").
5. Ayestas v. Davis, 138 S. Ct. 1080 (2018). Chapter 7 treats *Ayestas* at greater length.
6. *See* Martin H. Redish & Andrianna D. Kastanek, *Settlement Class Actions, the Case-or-Controversy Requirement, and the Nature of the Adjudicatory Process*, 73 U. CHI. L. REV. 545, 548, 552 (2006) (noting that neither courts nor scholars have devoted sustained attention to the theoretical underpinnings of the adverse-party requirement and describing the analysis of the foundations of the adverse-party requirement as one that had not been previously "undertaken by jurist or scholar"). On departures from the adversary ideal in bankruptcy, *see* Ralph E. Avery, *Article III and Title 11: A Constitutional Collision*, 12 BANKR. DEV. J. 397, 417 n.137, 449–50 (1996). Scholarly treatment of ex parte proceedings as entrenched and anomalous can be found in Redish & Kastanek, at 587 n.157. *See also* Michael T. Morley, *Non-Contentious*

Jurisdiction and Consent Decrees, 19 U. Pa. J. Const. L. Online 1 (2016); Michael T. Morley, *Consent of the Governed or Consent of the Government? The Problems with Consent Decrees in Government-Defendant Cases*, 16 U. Pa. J. Const. L. 637 (2014). Richard J. Fallon Jr. et al., Hart & Wechsler's Federal Courts and the Federal System 86 (7th ed. 2015) [hereinafter Hart & Wechsler 7th] (expressing doubt as to the constitutionality of the ex parte practice of naturalization).

7. Lon Fuller, the scholar perhaps most closely associated with the adversary conception of the judicial role, explained that the system works best when the judge bases her decision "wholly on the proofs and argument actually presented to [her] by the parties." Lon L. Fuller, *The Forms and Limits of Adjudication*, 92 Harv. L. Rev. 353, 388 (1978). *See also* Stephan Landsman, Readings on Adversarial Justice: The American Approach to Adjudication (1988); Judith Resnik, *Managerial Judges*, 96 Harv. L. Rev. 374 (1982). For a classic endorsement of inquisitorial civil procedure, *see* John H. Langbein, *The German Advantage in Civil Procedure*, 52 U. Chi. L. Rev. 823 (1985).
8. The Court most frequently celebrates the adversary ideal in the context of criminal procedure. *See* Greenlaw v. United States, 554 U.S. 237, 243 (2008) (declaring the norm of the adversary system in civil and criminal cases to be one of reliance on the parties "to frame the issues for decision" and on courts to play "the role of neutral arbiter"); United States v. Burke, 504 U.S. 229, 246 (1992) (Scalia, J., concurring) (implying that the rule imposing a procedural default may have a constitutional underpinning in that it distinguishes "our adversary system from the inquisitorial one"). *Cf.* Sims v. Apfel, 530 U.S. 103, 110–12 (2000) (distinguishing the adversary proceedings of courts from the inquisitorial approach of benefit agencies, such as the Social Security Administration, at which no party opposes the claim for benefits). One important exception—and one in some tension with the adversary ideal in criminal procedure—is plea bargaining, which disposes of 95 percent of federal criminal cases, and in which the prosecutor serves as the de facto judge of guilt or innocence. On the ex parte nature of guilty pleas, *see* chapter 2.5.3. *See generally* Howard M. Erichson, *Mass Tort Litigation and Inquisitorial Justice*, 87 Geo. L.J. 1983, 2010–15 (1999). Two exceptional features, American devotion to the jury trial and punitive damages, remain a sore spot for European countries confronting suits to recognize and enforce sizable American judgments. A third, the exercise of "doing business" jurisdiction over firms with their corporate seat elsewhere, was curtailed in *Daimler AG v. Bauman*, 571 U.S. 117 (2014). Quoted text appears in Amanda Frost, *The Limits of Advocacy*, 59 Duke L.J. 447, 460 (2009).
9. Redish & Kastanek at 587 n.157. Supporting their position with evidence from the practice of litigation as it has developed in the courts of the United States, Redish and Kastanek explain that party adverseness ensures a "well-developed record" on which to base a decision and conforms to a liberal democratic model of litigation that presupposes private control of the litigation process. *Id.* at 572 (describing party adverseness as part of the "DNA" of the adversary system of litigation in the United States). As a powerful restatement of the adverse-party requirement, the authors' work has proven extremely helpful.

10. *See* chapter 1.2.
11. 3 WILLIAM BLACKSTONE, COMMENTARIES ON THE LAWS OF ENGLAND *98. *See* SAMUEL BAYARD, AN ABSTRACT OF THOSE LAWS OF THE UNITED STATES WHICH RELATE CHIEFLY TO THE DUTIES AND AUTHORITY OF THE JUDGES OF THE INFERIOR STATE COURTS AND JUSTICES OF THE PEACE THROUGHOUT THE UNION (1804) (describing both ministerial and judicial functions). Chapter 2 describes ex parte practice in the early Republic.
12. Osborn v. Bank of the U.S., 22 U.S. 738, 819 (1824); *see also* Weston v. City Council of Charleston, 27 U.S. 449, 464 (1829) (explaining that the term suit encompasses "any proceeding in a court of justice by which an individual pursues that remedy . . . which the law affords him"); Cohens v. Virginia, 19 U.S. 264, 408 (1821) (defining the term suits to include "all cases were [*sic*] the party suing claims to obtain something to which he has a right"). The quotation appears in JOSEPH STORY, 3 COMMENTARIES ON THE CONSTITUTION 436 (Thomas M. Cooley ed., 4th ed. 1873). The Marshall-Story definition encompasses contested "cases" seeking redress but is not limited to them. *Cf.* Redish & Kastanek, at 565 n.71.
13. Chapter 3 explores the constitutive features of some uncontested litigation.
14. Spindel v. Spindel, 283 F. Supp. 797 (E.D.N.Y. 1968).
15. *Spindel*, 283 F. Supp. at 810; *see* Barber v. Barber, 62 U.S. 582, 584 (1858) (distinguishing between the initial issuance of a divorce or alimony decree and litigation to enforce the judgment).
16. For the term litigable interest, *see* Ann Woolhandler & Caleb Nelson, *Does History Defeat Standing Doctrine?*, 102 MICH. L. REV. 689, 708 (2004).
17. Vt. Agency of Nat. Res. v. United States *ex rel.* Stevens, 529 U.S. 765, 777 (2000) ("We think this history well-nigh conclusive.").

PART I

THESIS: UNCONTESTED ADJUDICATION IN THE EARLY FEDERAL COURTS

Two depictions of St. Ives, a civil law judge in thirteenth century France and later the patron saint of lawyers. On the left, St. Ives administers equal justice to rich and poor, acting as the arbiter of a contest between opposing parties. On the right, St. Ives reviews a scroll as he might have done in the course of uncontested adjudication.
Photo Credit: Annie O'Neill.

The history of uncontested adjudication begins with Roman law. Although the Romans viewed the resolution of legal disputes as a crucial judicial function, they also recognized a role for the judicial exercise of what has come to be known as voluntary or non-contentious jurisdiction. Quite in contrast to some modern formulations of the judicial power conferred in Article III, the Romans held that courts had power both to adjudicate contests between opposing parties (in the exercise of contentious jurisdiction) and to register and record claims to a new legal right or new legal status (in the exercise of voluntary or non-contentious jurisdiction).

Building on the Roman example, European civilians also embraced both contested and uncontested forms of adjudication. In time, uncontested forms were incorporated into the practice of the courts of Great Britain and eventually made their way to British North America. Part I tells this story, concluding with an examination of the way uncontested adjudication became an accepted part of antebellum conceptions of federal judicial power. As we shall see, leading figures on the federal bench oversaw uncontested adjudication and regarded the exercise of such authority as entirely consistent with the demands of Article III.

1

The Origins of Uncontested Adjudication

To modern students of the federal judicial power in the United States, the provision for the entry of a decree in the absence of an adverse-party dispute can appear quite anomalous. But as this chapter explains, antebellum jurists viewed uncontested proceedings—applications for a warrant or a grant of naturalized citizenship—as well-accepted instances of what European lawyers have long known as non-contentious or voluntary jurisdiction, a form that dates to Roman times. While common law forms of action were available to resolve disputes, uncontested forms of adjudication also flourished on the state and federal dockets of antebellum America.

1.1 The Roman Law Conception of Non-Contentious Jurisdiction

Although it did not leave much of an impression on the common law of England, non-contentious jurisdiction has a rich grounding in the history of civil law. Its origins lie in the law of ancient Rome, which divided judicial actions into two forms: *iurisdictio contentiosa* and *iurisdictio voluntaria*, or contentious and voluntary jurisdiction. Contentious jurisdiction was "[j]urisdiction in cases involving a legal controversy between the parties to [a] trial" designed to resolve a conflict of legal or personal interests. Voluntary jurisdiction, by contrast, was "the intervention of a magistrate in matters in which there [was] no quarrel between the parties and the fictitious trial serve[d] only as a way of performing certain legal acts or transactions."[1]

Voluntary proceedings abounded. They included *in iure cessio* (the conveyance of property in the form of a feigned case, which resulted in a consent judgment sanctioning the conveyance), *emancipatio* (the emancipation of minors), *adoptio* (adoption), and *manumissio* (the manumission of slaves), as well as the "cooperation of officials in guardianship matters and legal acts for the validity of which a permission of the competent authority is required." The court's function in such matters was limited to sanctioning, ratifying,

Cases Without Controversies. James E. Pfander, Oxford University Press. © James E. Pfander 2021.
DOI: 10.1093/oso/9780197571408.003.0002

legitimizing, or collaborating in the creation of a legal act or relationship that was agreed to by the parties in advance and that did not prejudice the rights of third parties not before the court. As such, whenever it appeared that the interest of the parties was no longer aligned, the proceedings would become contentious in character.[2]

As this brief summary reveals, matters within *iurisdictio voluntaria* arose not from a concrete dispute of law or fact among the parties, but from the desire of those parties to secure a conclusive legal recognition of their claim to a new status or to obtain formal approval of "certain legal acts or transactions." Indeed, many of the invocations of voluntary jurisdiction described above were similar to petitions for naturalization in federal courts—in that the law provided a procedure by which parties could alter their legal status through ex parte applications for judicial action. For example, *emancipatio*, or the voluntary release of a son or daughter from paternal power, could, under the law of Justinian, "be performed by a simple declaration before a competent official."[3]

Other invocations of non-contentious jurisdiction took the form of feigned controversies. Notably, *in iure cessio* ("a surrender in court"), would secure a change in property ownership through "a collusive or fictitious suit whereby the person to whom the property right was to be conveyed claimed in open court to be the owner. Thereupon, the magistrate asked the other party, the present owner, whether he also claimed it. Upon the denial or silence of such other party, the magistrate gave judgment (*addicit*) in favor of the claimant." Parties relied upon proceedings *in iure cessio* "for a number of legal transactions," such as the transfer of property, the formalization of adoption and emancipation, and "the creation of servitudes."[4]

According to Professor Antonio Fernandez de Bujan, voluntary jurisdiction in Roman law occupied an "autonomous" zone on the border between the judicial and administrative powers and as a result has posed challenges for historians attempting to classify or describe its precise nature. Nevertheless, and despite the fact that it is in some respects difficult to square with our own conceptions of judicial activity, voluntary jurisdiction did comport with the Roman conception of jurisdiction as the execution of "a public function upon private juridical interests and relationships." The judge or magistrate was not a "mere automaton," but instead tested the factual basis for the petition, required testimony on the record before granting judicial sanction to the petition, and exercised "control over the legality of the acts of the appearing party or parties."[5]

1.2 The European Reception of Non-Contentious Jurisdiction

Non-contentious jurisdiction retained many of its essential characteristics as Roman law was received into the civil law of continental Europe and Scotland in the Middle Ages. Thomas Wood's influential eighteenth-century treatise *A New Institute of the Imperial or Civil Law*, for example, divides "causes" into "*Jurisdictio Contentiosa*, or Judicial, which is exercised upon Persons whether they consent to it or not," and "*Voluntaria*, which may be used at all times without any manner of contradiction; as Emancipation, Adoption, Manumission; and in several other legal Acts granted by the Judge upon request, and by consent of all Parties." One can see in this description the fundamentally constitutive character of the uncontested decree. In Scotland, where the courts followed the civil law in matters of procedure, instances of voluntary jurisdiction were common, and the distinction between contentious and non-contentious jurisdiction was described in the late eighteenth century by Sir John Erskine, author of a treatise that was well known in Britain and in America.[6]

Non-contentious jurisdiction remains a feature of continental judicial systems today. In France, the civil code extends voluntary jurisdiction, or *juridiction gracieuse*, to encompass both ex parte proceedings and feigned controversies. French law empowers the proper court to assert non-contentious jurisdiction "over all claims not involving an adversary and not contestable by a third party; and . . . over all claims in which the parties, not being in disagreement, are required by their status or the nature of the affair, to obtain a court decision."

The depictions of St. Ives, a French lawyer and jurist and later the patron saint of lawyers (Figure 1.1), nicely capture the dual role of the judge in French civil law adjudication. In the portrait on the left, St. Ives administers equal justice to rich and poor, occupying the traditional role of judge as arbiter between two competing claimants. In the second depiction, St. Ives appears alone, with a scroll in hand, as he might have appeared when presiding over the inquisitorial proceedings necessitated by the exercise of non-contentious jurisdiction.

Drafters of the German civil code in the sixteenth century similarly incorporated elements of non-contentious jurisdiction, although German law did not perfectly map onto ancient forms. Other countries took a less formal approach. Italian courts exercise the functional equivalent of non-contentious jurisdiction (*giurisdizione volontaria*) in the absence of any formal codification in the rulebooks.[7]

Although defining the construct in its modern guise presents conceptual challenges, scholars agree that courts exercising non-contentious jurisdiction perform somewhat the same role as administrative officers or agencies. Thus, after recognizing the distinction between contested and uncontested matters, one scholar characterized non-contentious jurisdiction as a "prudential administration of justice, for the security of private legal interests." Another scholar defined non-contentious jurisdiction as "a form of judicial intervention that borders on the field of tasks falling, as a rule, within the realm of executive power, . . . tasks that could (at least in principle) be performed by administrative bodies as well." As we shall see, Justice Louis Brandeis adopted a similar formulation in upholding naturalization authority in *Tutun v. United States*. Professor Mauro Cappelletti reports that many scholars characterize voluntary jurisdiction as involving the "public administration of private law by judicial organs." Often, non-contentious proceedings seek a form of official recognition viewed as "necessary to create individual rights," comparable in some respects to petitions for the recognition of patents, copyrights, and titles to public land.[8]

Non-contentious procedures vary somewhat from nation to nation. In Italy, non-contentious matters have been handled by a judge "in chambers," rather than during the formal sitting of the court. In Germany, by contrast, much non-contentious jurisdiction was assigned to the local or district courts. Scholars agree that the proceedings have a judicial quality: one treatise on German law explained that although it was non-contentious, "this jurisdiction is in no way 'non-judicial.'" But the character of the proceeding reflects its non-contentious roots. Thus, non-contentious jurisdiction requires the judge to play an active role in developing the factual record; the court cannot rely on an adverse party to help frame the issues. One German scholar thus characterized the judge in non-contentious matters as enjoying "a great deal of freedom" to "take any evidence." An Italian scholar echoed that conclusion: non-contentious proceedings "are marked by the extensive inquisitorial powers bestowed upon the judge in charge of the case" which grant the judge "ample discretion as regards the evidence-taking phase of the procedure."[9]

The frequently ex parte character of non-contentious proceedings has led to predictable concern with the protection of the rights of third parties.

European countries have dealt with third-party rights in a variety of ways. Sometimes, as in Italy, the courts may deny preclusive effect to the decrees of tribunals exercising non-contentious jurisdiction, thereby limiting their preclusive and hence prejudicial effect. In Germany, the constitutional court has found that individuals have a due process right to be informed about and to participate in any non-contentious proceedings that might affect their interests. Such decisions resemble to some extent those in the United States that restrict reliance on in rem forms of jurisdiction. The German constitutional court also has held that the parties to a non-contentious proceeding may seek the recusal of an interested or biased judge. In general, scholars agree that non-contentious jurisdiction can sometimes threaten third-party rights and caution against its unthinking expansion.[10]

A great many matters have been assigned to the courts' non-contentious jurisdiction. Several countries, for example, provide for judicial oversight of probate matters in an effort to ensure proper resolution of potentially fraught issues of inheritance and succession. As we will see, common-form probate proceedings in Anglo-American law resemble these forms of non-contentious jurisdiction. In addition, courts in the European civil law tradition sometimes exercise non-contentious jurisdiction to oversee the appointment and supervision of guardians and the formal registry of interests in real property. Finally, European courts rely on non-contentious proceedings to provide for the formal registration of contracts and to handle certain matters of insolvency and bankruptcy.[11]

1.3 Non-Contentious Jurisdiction in England and Colonial America

The situation in England and America was more complicated, if only because of the somewhat rockier reception the civil law encountered in those countries. The common-law courts of England fought and largely succeeded in preventing Roman and civil law from usurping the central place of the common law as the foundation of the English legal system, and the common law (eventually at least) was adopted as the primary source of law in much of the United States. Nevertheless, many English and American courts adopted civil law practices, including some forms of uncontested adjudication.[12]

Many of those proceedings took place in courts bearing the stamp of civilian influence—such as courts of equity and the ecclesiastical and admiralty courts. But some uncontested proceedings predated the Norman Conquest and (well before the time of Blackstone) grew organically out of the common business of local courts. For example, the courts of Anglo-Saxon England and the county courts of medieval England conducted the voluntary transfer of land and the sanctioning of documents through judicial process. By witnessing these and other formal acts, such as marriages, the courts provided legal recognition and public legitimacy. Similarly, according to Professor William Burdick, the non-contentious Roman procedure *in iure cessio* was "undoubtedly the inspiration of the collusive or fictitious suits in early English law known as fine and common recovery," a cognizable action in English common law courts. Later, British ecclesiastical courts utilized non-contentious jurisdiction in a wide variety of proceedings, including the probate of wills and the issuance of marriage licenses. One of the chief functions of admiralty courts was the condemnation of prizes in what frequently were ex parte proceedings.[13]

The Court of Chancery also possessed a non-contentious jurisdiction, which it exercised in such matters as the appointment of guardians for infants, and in the creation of an equitable receivership. Somewhat similar to the manner in which applications for a receivership often assumed the form of a fictional dispute, however, courts of equity predicated the appointment of a guardian for a minor upon a fictional suit over property held in the district. Notably, Joseph Story reported on this development with some puzzlement, wondering why the fiction of a dispute was necessary to trigger a court's equitable powers of appointment. To summarize, then, many non-contentious proceedings made their way to the American colonies and were deployed in the equity, admiralty, and probate courts of the early United States.[14]

That said, this book makes no specific claim about the process by which non-contentious jurisdiction was transplanted into the legal soil of the New World. In some respects, governmental systems lacking a sophisticated administrative apparatus, such as those of Anglo-Saxon England and the early colonial American settlements, would understandably use courts to exercise jurisdiction over non-contentious business as much out of convenience as out of any desire to replicate the Roman tradition of voluntary jurisdiction. The administration of prize cases by courts of admiralty, for example, reflects more the desire of nations caught up in seagoing warfare to provide conclusive legal title to the captures taken by their licensed privateers than the desire to adopt the forms of Roman law.[15]

Indeed, local colonial courts often exercised jurisdiction over both contested and uncontested matters, and some even acted in a purely executive or legislative function, such as by maintaining county buildings, conducting inquests, raising taxes, and planning highways. Many colonial courts were assigned quintessentially non-contentious tasks such as recording land transfers and other instruments, conducting examinations for the admission of attorneys to the bar, and evaluating petitions for liquor licenses. Colonies and territories established orphans' courts for the protection of the estates and welfare of orphans and invested courts with probate powers to administer estates. Still others were granted wide-ranging and nonspecialized jurisdiction over common-law as well as probate, admiralty, and equity cases, thereby assuming the role played by both the Court of Chancery and the ecclesiastical courts in England.[16]

Regardless of whether the Framers specifically contemplated a link between the judicial power they conferred on federal courts and the voluntary jurisdiction of Roman and civil law, one sees an obvious link between European developments and the practices cataloged in the next part. Members of the founding generation were well versed in Roman political history, and many were close students of Roman and civil law and of the practices of the English admiralty, equity, and ecclesiastical courts. Civil law was in fact central to the education of the more sophisticated American lawyers, including such luminaries as John Marshall, Thomas Jefferson, James Wilson, and John Adams. The courts of the colonies and the early Republic often, implicitly or explicitly, looked to the courts of England in developing processes and procedures, including the procedures employed in local courts, courts of equity, and probate and prize proceedings. Application of the civil law in appropriate cases was assumed at the Constitutional Convention, and the Process Act of 1789 prescribed that the forms and modes of proceedings of civil law would govern in cases of admiralty and equity jurisdiction. The judicial power with which federal courts were invested surely encompassed both the common and civil law traditions. In that cosmopolitan legal world, the decision of Congress to assign uncontested proceedings to federal courts does not present much of a mystery.[17]

Notes

1. On the origins of non-contentious jurisdiction in Roman law, *see* Walter Neitzel, *Non-Contentious Jurisdiction in Germany*, 21 HARV. L. REV. 476, 480–81 (1908) (linking the German practice of non-contentious jurisdiction to precursors in Roman law relating to matters of adoption, guardianship, and registration of land titles); Elisabetta Silvestri, *Jurisdiction Without Conflict? Remarks on Non-adverse Proceedings in Italy*, *in* VOLUNTARY (NON-CONTENTIOUS) JURISDICTION AROUND THE WORLD 133, 133–34 (V.V. Argounov ed., 2017) (collecting authority for the "well established" proposition "that Roman law made a distinction between contentious jurisdiction and *iurisdictio voluntaria*"). The quoted definitions of voluntary and contentious jurisdiction appear in Adolf Berger, *Encyclopedic Dictionary of Roman Law*, *in* 43 TRANSACTIONS OF THE AM. PHIL. SOC'Y 333, 524 (1953); *see also* ANTONIO FERNANDEZ DE BUJAN, JURISDICCION VOLUNTARIA EN DERECHO ROMANO [VOLUNTARY JURISDICTION IN ROMAN LAW] 20–23 (1986). Voluntary jurisdiction defined in Berger at 524. The "voluntary" nature of this form of jurisdiction lay not in any choice on the part of the magistrate on whether to exercise jurisdiction, but rather in the voluntary appearance of the party or parties in the court who were submitting their petition for resolution or ratification. *See* FERNANDEZ DE BUJAN at 23.
2. Berger at 524. *See* FERNANDEZ DE BUJAN at 23.
3. Berger at 524. One comparative scholar expressly drew this connection between non-contentious jurisdiction and naturalization proceedings. *See* MAURO CAPPELLETTI ET AL., THE ITALIAN LEGAL SYSTEM: AN INTRODUCTION 121 (1967) (observing that the "judicial intervention" in non-contentious matters "borders on administration rather than adjudication" and commenting that, in Italy, "citizenship is conferred upon aliens by an administrative act," whereas in America it is conferred "by the courts"). Quoted text on *emancipatio* appears in Berger at 451. *Emancipatio* was a derivative form of *mancipatio*, which in the ancient Roman law was "the only method by which important kinds of property could be legally transferred from the seller to buyer." WILLIAM L. BURDICK, THE PRINCIPLES OF ROMAN LAW AND THEIR RELATION TO MODERN LAW 313 (1938); *see also* Berger at 573 (describing *emancipatio* as a form of *mancipatio*). *Mancipatio* was a ceremony held before witnesses, involving a declaration of title by the purchaser not contradicted by the seller. Berger at 573; *see also* BURDICK at 330–31 (describing *mancipatio* as a "formal legal procedure" for the transfer of ownership, marriage, adoption, emancipation, and testaments).
4. BURDICK at 331. Any description of procedure in "Roman law" is incurably inexact, given that the Roman law evolved over several centuries, such that its early forms might have been unrecognizable to later Roman citizens. *In iure cessio*, for instance, was superseded by *mancipatio*, which itself eventually fell into obsolescence. ("Even in the time of Gaius, *mancipatio*, he says, was generally employed instead of *in jure cessio*, because it was less difficult to transfer property in the presence of one's friends than to go into court before the praetor."). *Id.* at 331–32. On the evolution of non-contentious jurisdiction in Rome, *see* Neitzel at 480 (contrasting "old" Roman law's

refusal to recognize a role for the state in guardianships with the law of the Empire, which assigned the appointment of guardians to judicial officials).

5. Fernandez De Bujan (1986) at 16; *see also id.* at 23–27 (describing various views of the propriety of classifying voluntary jurisdiction as truly jurisdictional or judicial in nature). *Id.* at 16. As de Bujan explains in more detail, "In my view, although there are opinions against the use of the word 'voluntary' as an adjective [qualifying jurisdiction], there is room to argue in favor of such a use: that, from a formal point of view, in these cases the interested parties or petitioners—because we cannot speak of parties in a strict sense—seeking judicial intervention come before the magistrate voluntarily . . . not for the magistrate to protect the exercise of a right or to determine a disputed interest, but for the magistrate to collaborate in the birth of a legal relationship agreed upon by the applicants or appearing parties." *Id.* at 27 (author's translation). For the Romans, jurisdiction (*iurisdictio*, or "the power to speak the law") denoted both the power invested in the magistrate and the fulfillment of the duties for which the power was bestowed. Quoted text on the judicial role appears in *id.* at 23–24 (author's translation).
6. Professor Edwin Borchard has described constitutive judgments as "judgments of forfeiture, partition, dissolution of partnership, divorce, annulment of a voidable marriage; or else they sanction a relation entirely new, such as the admission of a will to probate, the appointment of guardians and receivers. These judgments—whether they require or permit of execution—because they effect a change of status and are primarily a source of new jural relations, may be called constitutive, or, as they are sometimes called, 'investitive.'" Edwin Borchard, Declaratory Judgments 23 (2d ed. 1941). *See* F.H. Lawson, Remedies of English Law 12–13 (2d ed. 1980) for a discussion of constitutive ("creat[ing] a legal situation that did not formerly exist") as opposed to coercive (resulting in a judgment against a litigant) legal remedies. Lawson notes the German term *Gestaltungsurteil*, describing a judgment affecting a legal relationship, which does not have an exact English equivalent. *Id.* at 239. On reception, *see* Franz Wieacker, *The Importance of Roman Law for Western Civilization and Western Legal Thought*, 4 B.C. Int'l & Comp. L. Rev. 257, 258–61 (1981). Thomas Wood, A New Institute of the Imperial or Civil Law 293 (J. & J. Knapton et al. eds., 4th ed. 1730) (emphases in original). 1 John Erskine, An Institute of the Law of Scotland 27–28 (James Badenach Nicolson ed., Edinburgh, Bell & Bradfute 1871) (1773); *see also id.* at 71–72 (discussing the ministerial powers of the Court of Session, Scotland's supreme civil court exercised as part of its *nobile officium*, or equitable powers).
7. Cappelletti at 122 n.52. France distinguishes between *juridiction gracieuse* and *juridiction contentieuse*. On the German civil code, *see* Neitzel at 480–81 (reporting on the inclusion of non-contentious jurisdiction in the German civil code of the sixteenth century). Neitzel suggests that a non-contentious role for the judiciary in appointments of guardians first became a feature of German law as part of the sixteenth-century codification. Contrast the Roman treatment of property as a mere *res* with the German notion of property as a communal matter. German law required greater formalities to secure a transfer of property. *Id.* On Italy, *see* Silvestri at 134–35

(observing that the Italian code of civil procedure "makes no specific reference to non-contentious jurisdiction," but noting the conventional view that such jurisdiction applies to a variety of "special proceedings").

8. *See, e.g.*, PETER L. MURRAY & ROLF STÜRNER, GERMAN CIVIL JUSTICE 443 (2004) (describing the boundary between contentious and non-contentious jurisdiction as "not always very clear"); CAPPELLETTI at 120 ("It is not easy to define 'voluntary jurisdiction.'"). The "prudential administration" definition appears in KARL GAREIS, INTRODUCTION TO THE SCIENCE OF LAW: SYSTEMATIC SURVEY OF THE LAW AND PRINCIPLES OF LEGAL STUDY 261 (Albert Kocourek trans., 1911). The "judicial intervention" definition is found in Silvestri at 134. CAPPELLETTI at 121 (quoting PIERO CALAMANDREI, ISTITUZIONI DI DIRITTO PROCESSUALE CIVILE § 23 (2d ed. 1943)); Cappelletti also notes here that many scholars do not accept the definition. On the creation of rights, Neitzel (1908) at 477; *see also* CAPPELLETTI (1968) at 121 (describing the unifying element in the voluntary jurisdiction cases as the presence of a "private law activity" that "cannot be undertaken without an order, authorization, or some other kind of judicial intervention").

9. On Italian procedure, *see* CAPPELLETTI at 121–22; Silvestri at 136. On assignment to German courts, *see* MURRAY & STÜRNER at 442–43 (local courts); Neitzel at 482–83 (reliance on the district courts in 1908). On German procedure, MURRAY & STÜRNER at 444; Neitzel at 483–84. On Italy, *see* Silvestri at 136–37.

10. *See* CAPPELLETTI at 122 (confirming that decrees in non-contentious proceedings have no res judicata effect); Silvestri at 137 (same). On the German constitutional court, Mauro Capelletti, *Fundamental Guarantees of the Parties in Civil Litigation: Comparative Constitutional, International and Social Trends*, 25 STAN. L. REV. 651, 686 n.198 (1973). On the modern limits on in rem forms of jurisdiction, *see* Shaffer v. Heitner, 433 U.S. 186 (1977) (concluding that all assertions of jurisdiction, including those based on in rem and quasi in rem forms of process, must satisfy the due process standard of *International Shoe v. Washington*, 326 U.S. 310 (1945), by showing parties interested in the disposition of property have the requisite contacts with the forum state). Common form probate proceedings, which proceed on an ex parte basis in the courts of the United States, did not traditionally require notice to all potentially interested parties, thereby raising due process concerns. *See* Sheldon S. Levy, *Probate in the Common Form in the United States: The Problem of Notice in Probate Proceedings*, 1952 WIS. L REV. 420 (1952).

11. On inheritance, *see* GAREIS at 261 (describing the role of non-contentious jurisdiction in matters of German inheritance and succession); MURRAY & STÜRNER at 442–43 (same); Silvestri at 135 (Italian law). On guardians, *see* GAREIS at 261 (German law relating to the appointment of guardians); MURRAY & STÜRNER at 442–43 (same); Silvestri at 137 (noting that Italian law provides for non-contentious proceedings for the appointment of guardians). On title to landed property, *see* MURRAY & STÜRNER at 442 (registration of real estate interests); GAREIS at 262 (registry officers take action to effect the transfer of land). Registry of land titles apparently played a role in the development of non-contentious feigned litigation in Rome as well. On registration of contracts, *see* Neitzel at 494. In nineteenth-century German procedure,

non-contentious forms were used in insolvency and bankruptcy proceedings. Gareis at 263 (describing property concerns in insolvency and bankruptcy proceedings as belonging to the "sphere of non-contentious jurisdiction"); *cf.* Silvestri at 139–41 (noting that the Italian legislature has sometimes assigned matters, such as bankruptcy and the management of companies, to courts for processing in chambers under the forms of non-contentious jurisdiction, but questioning the wisdom of such assignments).

12. On the reception of Roman law in England, *see* Brian P. Levack, The Civil Lawyers in England 1603–1641: A Political Study (1973). On the efforts of common law courts to resist and circumscribe the jurisdiction of civil law–based courts, *see* 5 Holdsworth at 423–30. *See, e.g.*, Pfander & Birk, *Article III and the Scottish Judiciary*, at 1628, 1646 (discussing adoption of common law in America and citing sources). Although the reception of Roman law was nowhere near as complete in England as it was in Scotland or on the Continent, Roman and civil law influenced non–common law courts in England, shaping developments in the law of nations, conflicts of laws, and mercantile law. On the influence of Roman law in England, *see* Thomas Edward Scrutton, *Roman Law Influence in Chancery, Church Courts, Admiralty, and Law Merchant*, *in* 1 Select Essays in Anglo-American Legal History 208, 212–13 (1907) (explaining that the judges of the common law courts did not recognize civil law as authoritative, but that the admiralty, equity, and ecclesiastical courts "were largely influenced by the Civil Law, if their procedure was not entirely derived from it"). On the differences between civil and common law as practiced in English courts, *see* Charles Donahue Jr., *Ius Commune, Canon Law, and Common Law in England*, 66 Tul. L. Rev. 1745 (1992); Peter G. Stein, *Roman Law, Common Law, and Civil Law*, 66 Tul. L. Rev. 1591 (1992).

13. The *witengamote*, or "public moots," of Anglo-Saxon England regularly exercised a voluntary jurisdiction in ceremonial acts that was influenced to varying degrees by custom and the proliferation of "Roman ideas and forms." Paul Vinogradoff, *Transfer of Land in Old English Law*, 20 Harv. L. Rev. 532, 532, 546 (1907). England's Statutes of Merchants called for merchants and their debtors to register their contracts in a non-contentious proceeding before the Mayor's Court; these registered obligations had the status of a matter of record and would trigger the seizure of debtor's goods or the imprisonment of the debtor in cases of default. *See* Statute of Merchants, 11 Edward I (1283); Statute of Merchants, 13 Edward I (1285), both cited in 1 Statute of the Realm 53, 98 (1235–1377), http://aalt.law.uh.edu/AALT1/H6/CP40no677/aCP40no677fronts/IMG_0555.htm [http://perma.cc/DQ4E-4NKQ]. Transfer of land under old English law also was accomplished through judicial process, and the manorial courts of England later used voluntary jurisdiction to effect various transactions related to real property through the practices of surrender and admittance. *See* Vinogradoff at 533–36, 543–47. Burdick at 332. Until most of their powers were abolished or transferred to the Court of Probate and the Divorce Court in the mid-nineteenth century, the ecclesiastical courts in England "exercised a very extended jurisdiction, comprising not only what we should ordinarily call ecclesiastical causes, but matrimonial suits and divorces *a mensa et thoro*, all testamentary

causes and suits, suits for church rates, and suits for defamation." *The English Law Courts VI: The Ecclesiastical Courts*, 8 GREEN BAG 330, 330 (1896). On the reception of civil law in England, *see* David J. Seipp, *The Reception of Canon Law and Civil Law in the Common Law Courts before 1600*, 13 OXFORD J. LEGAL STUD. 388, 408 (1993) (reporting that, circa 1515, all twelve masters in the High Court of Chancery were civilians). For a discussion of admiralty courts, *see* chapter 2.3.

14. *See* JOSEPH STORY, COMMENTARIES ON EQUITY JURISPRUDENCE § 1338, at 927 (photo. reprint 2006) (London, Stevens & Hayes 1884). In the same place, Story explained that when the Court of Chancery appointed a guardian for an infant "where there is none other, or none who will, or can act, at least, where the infant has property." Story described the fictional dispute as follows: "It often occurs, that a bill is filed for the sole purpose of making an infant a ward of chancery; but in such a case the bill always states, however untruly, that the infant has property within the jurisdiction, and the bill is brought against the person in whose supposed custody or power the property is." *Id.* § 1351 n.4. Story continued: "Why such a mere fiction should be resorted to, has never, as it seems to me, been satisfactorily explained; and why the Lord chancellor, exercising the prerogative of the crown as *parens patriae*, might not, in his discretion, appoint a guardian to an infant, having no other guardian, without any bill being filed, seems difficult to understand upon principle." *Id.* § 1351 n.4. Notably, the chancellor's power to appoint conservators of the estates of "idiots and lunatics" derived from the Crown's prerogative and authorized appointment without any need to invoke a fictional dispute. *See* A. HIGHMORE, A TREATISE ON THE LAW OF IDIOCY AND LUNACY 11–15 (Exeter, N.H., G. Lamson 1822) (describing the Crown's prerogative power to act as "trustee of the persons and fortunes of ideots [*sic*] and lunatics" but distinguishing the Crown's power over infants as "by no means similar").
15. This book addresses these matters in chapter 2.3.1 (Prize and Salvage Cases), chapter 7.7 (Trademark Seizure Orders), and chapter 5 (Administrative Subpoenas). On prize litigation, *see* R.G. Marsden, *Early Prize Jurisdiction and Prize Law in England*, 26 ENG. HIST. REV. 34 (1911).
16. *See, e.g.*, Warren M. Billings, *Pleading, Procedure, and Practice: The Meaning of Due Process of Law in Seventeenth-Century Virginia*, 47 J.S. HIST. 569, 578 (1981). Despite their ability to exercise such powers, the county sessions courts of colonial Massachusetts were subject to the traditional limitation on courts that they could only act when others brought public business before it. Hendrik Hartog, *The Public Law of a County Court: Judicial Government in Eighteenth Century Massachusetts*, 20 AM. J. LEGAL HIST. 282, 284 (1976). *See* George B. Haskins, *The Beginnings of the Recording System in Massachusetts*, 21 B.U. L. REV. 281 (1941) (land transfers); Benjamin R. Curtis, *The Colonial County Court, Social Forum and Legislative Precedent: Accomack County, Virginia, 1633–1639*, 85 VA. MAG. HIST. & BIOGRAPHY 274, 275, 282 (1977) (registration of certificates of sale, payment or acknowledgment of debt, wagers, and indenture agreements); Alan F. Day, *Lawyers in Colonial Maryland, 1660–1715*, 17 AM. J. LEGAL HIST. 145, 146–47 (1973) (bar admissions); Hartog at 288–91 (liquor licenses). On orphans' courts, *see* Erwin C. Surrency, *The Evolution of an Urban Judicial System: The Philadelphia Story, 1683 to 1968*, 18 AM. J. LEGAL HIST. 95, 97, 119 (1974). For a description of the "simplified system of inferior

and appellate courts" in colonial Virginia "that combined the jurisdictions of such English courts as the leet, quarter sessions, the assizes, king's bench, common pleas, chancery, and the admiralty, as well as that of the church courts," *see, e.g.*, Billings at 572; Spencer R. Liverant & Walter H. Hitchler, *A History of Equity in Pennsylvania*, 37 DICK. L. REV. 156, 165–67 (1933) (equitable powers conferred on Pennsylvania general common-law courts).

17. *See* DAVID J. BEDERMAN, THE CLASSICAL FOUNDATIONS OF THE AMERICAN CONSTITUTION 17–26 (2008); FORREST McDONALD, NOVO ORDUS SECLORUM: THE INTELLECTUAL ORIGINS OF THE AMERICAN CONSTITUTION 67–69 (1985). The deep familiarity of many Americans in the founding generation with Roman and civil law has been canvassed exhaustively elsewhere. *See* Pfander & Birk, *Article III and the Scottish Judiciary*, at 1629–31, for a summary. *See generally* M.H. HOEFLICH, ROMAN AND CIVIL LAW AND THE DEVELOPMENT OF ANGLO-AMERICAN JURISPRUDENCE IN THE NINETEENTH CENTURY (1997); Daniel R. Coquillette, *Justinian in Braintree: John Adams, Civilian Learning, and Legal Elitism, 1758–1775*, *in* 62 PUBL'NS OF THE COLONIAL SOC'Y OF MASS., LAW IN COLONIAL MASSACHUSETTS 1630–1800, at 359 (Daniel R. Coquillette et al. eds., 1984). One also can glean the importance of civil law sources to American legal practice by viewing Alexander Hamilton's application of such sources in his law practice. *See* 4 THE LAW PRACTICE OF ALEXANDER HAMILTON: DOCUMENTS AND COMMENTARY 627–35 (Julius Goebel Jr. & Joseph H. Smith eds., 1980). For a time, the civil law possessed a surprising amount of traction in the United States, particularly among those quarters that disdained the English legal tradition and hoped for the emergence of a distinctively American jurisprudence based on internationalist sources. *See generally* Peter Stein, *The Attraction of the Civil Law in Post-Revolutionary America*, 52 VA. L. REV. 403 (1966). On civil law at the Constitutional Convention, *see* 2 MAX FARRAND, THE RECORDS OF THE FEDERAL CONVENTION OF 1787, at 431 (1911) ("Mr. Govr. Morris wished to know what was meant by the words 'In all the cases before mentioned it (jurisdiction) shall be appellate with such exceptions &c,' whether it extended to matters of fact as well as law—and to cases of Common law as well as Civil law. Mr. Wilson. The Committee he believed meant facts as well as law & Common as well as Civil law. The jurisdiction of the federal Court of Appeals had he said been so construed."). For the Process Act, *see* Act of Sept. 29, 1789, ch. 21, 1 Stat. 93. The court to which Wilson referred, the Court of Appeals in Cases of Prize and Capture, was the only federal court under the Articles of Confederation, which served as the nation's governing document before the Constitution's ratification in 1788.

2

Uncontested Proceedings on Federal Dockets in the Early Republic

Adapting the forms with which they were familiar, members of the First Congress of the United States promptly assigned the adjudication of uncontested matters to the federal courts. This chapter explores four such original forms of adjudication: naturalization proceedings; warrant proceedings; various non-contentious forms of adjudication that were to appear on the admiralty dockets of the district courts; and veterans' pension claims. The chapter shows that Congress conferred and the federal courts willingly exercised jurisdiction over matters that were understood to proceed on an ex parte basis without the joinder of adverse parties. (Even the judiciary's storied refusal to hear veterans' claims was based, as we shall see, on the lack of judicial finality.) Although the forms varied, these uncontested proceedings resulted in *constitutive* decrees that established new rights in individuals or new legal relationships, all in accordance with federal law.

2.1 The Antebellum Naturalization Proceeding

Looking back to legislation adopted in the early years of the Republic, perhaps nothing will strike the modern reader as more curious than the manner in which the First Congress (1789–90) implemented its power to establish a "uniform rule of naturalization." The power conferred in Article I reflected dissatisfaction with the manner in which the states were handling applications for citizenship. Some states had been requiring the adoption of legislative acts to confer rights of citizenship on foreign nationals; others provided more streamlined proceedings. Some states demanded long waiting periods; others admitted foreigners to citizenship with greater dispatch. These variations were proving disruptive. For foreign nationals contemplating a move to the United States, citizenship was an essential element in securing and inheriting good title to real property. To attract new immigrants

Cases Without Controversies. James E. Pfander, Oxford University Press. © James E. Pfander 2021.
DOI: 10.1093/oso/9780197571408.003.0003

and settle a seemingly boundless national domain, the United States promised both land and the citizenship on which land ownership depended. In one of its least controversial grants of power, Article I, Section 8 wards off state-to-state variation by empowering Congress to establish a "uniform rule."[1]

In implementing the naturalization power, Congress assigned the responsibility for the determination of naturalization claims to any "common law court of record," state or federal. In the Act of 1790, Congress limited citizenship to persons who had resided in the United States for at least two years, were of good character, and were willing to take an oath of allegiance to the United States (and to abjure allegiance to their country of origin). To make out a case for naturalized citizenship, the Act required foreign nationals to file an ex parte petition with the court along with supporting materials and affidavits. The Act then called upon the judge of the court to conduct an inquiry into the fact of the matter, to ascertain if the applicant had satisfied all of the requirements for citizenship, to administer the oath, and to enter a decree formalizing the grant of citizenship. While the decree was to be entered as part of the court's official record, the Act made no provision for notice to any opposing party and did not contemplate any contestation or disputation. Nor, in keeping with its departure from common law forms, did it provide for trial by jury.[2]

The decision of Congress to bring the judicial power to bear on naturalization petitions by assigning them to "courts of record" made a good deal of functional sense at the close of the eighteenth century. Open proceedings in courts of record would ensure a searching judicial inquiry into the status of the applicant and could help to prevent the naturalization of those with suspiciously limited ties to the community. Judicial involvement would also ensure a degree of uniformity and the creation of a permanent and conclusive record of the alien's admission to citizenship. Such a permanent record was of central importance in a world in which only citizens enjoyed the right to own land. In addition, the conclusive quality of judgments "of record" would protect citizenship decisions from attack in subsequent disputes over title to property.[3]

The archives of the federal district court in New York City offer some insight into the manner in which one federal judge, James Duane, handled applications for naturalized citizenship. Duane served as the judge of New York's federal district court from 1789 to 1794. Petitioners seeking naturalization would file a petition and supporting affidavits, all of which were copied into the record. These affidavits sought to establish that the petitioner had resided in the United States for the then-requisite two-year period and satisfied the good character requirement. Then, at a date specified, the petitioner would appear in court to take the statutorily required oath of allegiance. On occasion, Duane refused to grant naturalized citizenship after finding some discrepancy in the submission. But on most occasions, Duane would administer the oath and enter the requested decree. The fact of citizenship thus became a part of the official record of the court. In the typical case, the court would also issue a certificate of naturalized citizenship as evidence of the petitioner's new status.[4]

Much as did Judge Duane in federal proceedings, state courts understood that naturalization petitions called upon judges to play an inquisitorial role in evaluating the proffered evidence. One New York court explained the need for a more active judicial role by distinguishing uncontested matters from adversarial proceedings:

> As between parties litigant, their admissions and agreement may satisfy a court of the existence or non-existence of material facts: but in applications for naturalization there are no hostile parties who can adjust or establish anything by way of stipulation. The court cannot take the mere statement of any person unsupported by an oath. Such a course would be unprecedented in a court of justice; and beyond all question, upon the terms of this act alone, the court would be bound to require legal evidence to establish all the facts upon which the judgment is finally to be rendered.

While the court obviously regarded the naturalization process as an exercise of judicial power culminating in a judgment, uncontested matters were understood to demand that judge play a more active, inquisitorial role in assessing the evidentiary submissions of the petitioner.[5]

Reports published by William Cranch offer further insight into how federal courts conducted these inquisitions. Known for his reports of Supreme Court decisions, Cranch also served as a judge of the U.S. Circuit Court for the District of Columbia and published reports of that court's decisions as well. One finds in those reports a collection of ex parte naturalization cases from the early years of the nineteenth century that display a judicious concern with factual sufficiency. The naturalization statute had been amended to require a five-year period of continuous residence; Cranch's court rejected petitions from individuals who could not make the showing of continuity.

One applicant in particular had filed an earlier affidavit in which his account of his absences from the country contradicted his statements in a subsequent petition, a discrepancy on which the court relied in denying the later request. One applicant sought to take advantage of a provision that offered naturalized citizenship based on two years of residence before 1795. But the court found that the conclusory statements in the supporting affidavit were insufficient to establish residency; at most they demonstrated mere presence.[6]

Although the mine-run of proceedings would turn on the sufficiency of the petitioner's factual showing, courts often confronted questions of law in the course of uncontested naturalization adjudication. Cranch reported that the federal circuit court had granted naturalized citizenship to a married woman, a notable conclusion at a time when the law often assigned married women the domicile and citizenship of their husbands. Cranch also reported that, despite his court's strict application of the statutory requirement of continuous residence, some relaxation was permitted in appropriate cases. Thus, the court granted the naturalization petition of a blue-water sailor who was living in Alexandria, Virginia; apparently time away at sea in the pursuit of one's trade did not violate the rule of continuous residence. Justice Story, riding circuit in Massachusetts during the War of 1812, rejected the naturalization petition of a British national. Story found that the petitioner, as an alien enemy, had no legal standing to pursue his claim in the courts of the United States under the terms of the applicable law.[7]

Naturalization judgments were subject to review in the ordinary course of judicial proceedings. Thus, a court might order the cancellation of a decree of naturalization on a finding that the applicant had lied in the petition or supporting materials. But in the absence of any such irregularity, naturalization decrees became a part of the court's record as final judgments. Like other final judgments, moreover, naturalization decrees were largely immune from collateral attack. Thus, in *Campbell v. Gordon*, an 1810 case in which title to real property turned on whether one claimant's father had been duly naturalized in a state court proceeding, the Supreme Court applied a deferential standard of review. Speaking for a unanimous bench, Justice Bushrod Washington explained that "if the oath be administered, and nothing appears to the contrary, it must be presumed that the court, before whom the oath was taken, was satisfied as to the character of the applicant. The oath, when taken, confers upon him the rights of a citizen, and amounts to a judgment of the court for his admission to those rights."[8]

The Supreme Court applied similarly deferential review in *Spratt v. Spratt*, a case from 1830 in which title to land turned on citizenship. In arguing against the validity of the naturalization decree, one party urged that the process was merely ministerial and thus did not produce a judgment of record. In an opinion by Chief Justice Marshall, the Court squarely rejected that claim:

> [Judges in naturalization proceedings] are to receive testimony, to compare it with the law, and to judge on both law and fact. This judgment is entered on record as the judgment of the court. It seems to us, if it be in legal form, to close all inquiry; and, like every other judgment, to be complete evidence of its own validity.[9]

Viewing naturalization decrees as judgments worthy of respect, other courts were also quite reluctant to look beneath the surface of an apparently valid record when considering collateral attacks on such decrees.

The absence of party contestation may appear to complicate the process of securing appellate oversight. But early courts took the position that uncontested matters, such as naturalization proceedings, were subject to ex parte appellate review through mandamus petitions to a superior court. Building on earlier cases, the Supreme Court pioneered this approach to appellate oversight of naturalization practice in *Ex parte Fitzbonne*, an unreported decision from 1800. At issue in *Fitzbonne* was legislation, adopted alongside the Alien and Sedition Acts of 1798, in which Congress lengthened the residency requirement and prohibited the naturalization of citizens or subjects of a country at war with the United States. The district court in Philadelphia had declined to naturalize applicants from France, taking the position that the two countries were effectively at war. Alexander Dallas, the Court's reporter and Fitzbonne's attorney, sought review. The Supreme Court issued a mandamus directing the district court to proceed with the matter, concluding that the undeclared war with France did not trigger the statutory bar to naturalization of enemy aliens.[10]

As the caption in *Ex parte Fitzbonne* suggests, the mandamus proceeding was not contested. The petitioner sought relief by way of an "original" mandamus petition in the Supreme Court. While such petitions seek mandatory relief against the judge of an inferior court, the judge does not necessarily appear as a party in the appellate court, much less submit an argument on the merits. As a practical matter, then, the Court will often resolve such matters in the absence of adverse-party contestation. In other words, the mandamus proceeding itself can often best be characterized as a non-contentious proceeding: the disappointed petitioner seeks the recognition and enforcement of a claimed right that was denied by a lower court. Just as the naturalization petitioner had no obligation to join an opposing party in the first instance, a disappointed petitioner could seek appellate oversight without formally joining an adverse party.[11]

We can say somewhat more about the practice of naturalization than about its scope and impact: no one has combed through judicial archives to determine how many foreign nationals gained naturalized citizenship in the antebellum period. The Department of State did not begin collecting information on the arrival of new immigrants in the ports of the United States until 1820. Even then, only those arriving at eastern ports were counted as immigrants. Immigrants arriving by land from the north or the south and from the inland waterways bordering Canada did not appear in the tabulation until much later. Naturalizations occurred in individual state and federal courtrooms around the country; there was no Administrative Office of the U.S. Courts to compile statistics. Indeed, no national data on naturalizations were collected until the early twentieth century. One thus struggles to find solid information as to the number of naturalization petitions on the dockets of the federal courts or as to the manner in which those courts managed the petitions that did arrive as time wore on and the flow of immigrants grew.[12]

Nonetheless, an investigatory document prepared at the instance of the Senate Judiciary Committee in 1845 provides some insight into the day-to-day practice of naturalization in the courts of three important port cities: New York, Philadelphia, and Baltimore. From a collection of depositions reproduced in the Senate document, we learn that, at least by the 1840s, the political parties had come to play an outsized role in naturalization proceedings, especially as election days drew near. In New York, for example, a committee on naturalization at Tammany Hall solicited and paid the cost of naturalization proceedings for individual petitioners well disposed to Tammany's candidates and then promptly sent these newly naturalized citizens (and their certificates) to the polls. Much of this electoral naturalization business flowed to state courts; judges of the New York Marine Court, for example, reported that they devoted much of their dockets in the period surrounding election days to the adjudication of naturalization petitions. Meanwhile, naturalization business in the federal courts proceeded at a much more sedate rate. The flood of state petitions reflected both the clerks' desire to earn the fee-based income such petitions would bring to them personally and the perception that friendly clerks would ease the path to citizenship for dubious applicants.[13]

One can see the impact of machine politics on the naturalization process as reported in the Senate document. Sheer numbers tell part of the story. Over a *twenty-year* period from 1823 to 1845, the U.S. District Court for the Southern District of New York conferred naturalized citizenship on 171 applicants. Meanwhile, the New York state Court of Common Pleas naturalized some 495 applicants on a *single election day in 1842.* All told, the New York state Court of Common Pleas naturalized well over 5,000 applicants over a four-year period from 1841 to 1844; the New York state Marine Court naturalized several thousand more over the same period. Similar disparities emerged in Philadelphia, where the federal court naturalized 82 applicants over a seven-year period, as compared with the 4,811 applicants that gained citizenship through proceedings in the Pennsylvania state court of quarter sessions.[14]

With the mass of petitions to process, state courts inevitably cut corners. The Senate document collects reports of fraudulent and procedurally suspect naturalizations, mostly in the state courts. Many applicants had arrived in the United States too recently to meet the five-year residency rule or had failed to make the required declaration of intent to naturalize three years in advance of their application. Evidence emerged of a lively traffic in forged declarations, aimed at working around that requirement. Similarly, many citizens requested duplicate copies of their naturalization certificates, prompting suspicions that certificates were being subjected to the antebellum equivalent of Photoshopping for use by other voters. Some witnesses and many candidates for naturalization could not speak English; interpreters stepped in to translate. Evidence collected in Baltimore was said to show that certain countries encouraged their "paupers and vagabonds" to immigrate to America. Ready access to citizenship for such immigrants predictably raised concerns. Intriguingly, though, the solution proposed at the time was not to build a wall but to improve the process by which foreign nationals were admitted to citizenship. Rather than curtail immigration, the Senate bill drafted to address these concerns (proposed but never enacted) included provisions that would have assigned naturalization proceedings to the exclusive jurisdiction of the federal courts. The process would have remained inquisitorial, rather than adversarial, and the Senate drafters would ensure greater probity by relying on the inquisitorial powers of the federal judiciary.

Uncontested proceedings on this view posed a problem only when the courts in question failed to conduct them with the necessary attention to factual detail.[15]

Despite evidence of slipshod practices, no substantial reform of the naturalization process was to occur until the early years of the twentieth century. In legislation that sought to limit the flow of new immigrants to the United States, and to restrict access to citizenship, Congress empowered a newly created agency to oversee the naturalization process. In addition, while Congress preserved a role for the federal courts in reviewing and adjudicating petitions for naturalized citizenship, Congress assigned a large and growing role to the agency. By the 1920s, when the Court was called upon in *Tutun v. United States* to assess the legality of naturalization practice, Congress had given the U.S. government a more substantial role in reviewing and contesting problematic naturalization claims. The era of the uncontested adjudication of naturalization petitions was quickly coming to an end.[16]

2.2 Antebellum Warrant Proceedings

The Fourth Amendment assumes that courts and magistrates will conduct ex parte proceedings in the course of evaluating arrest and search warrants. The well-thumbed terms of the Amendment prohibit "unreasonable" searches and seizures and further declare that "no Warrants shall issue, but upon probable cause, supported by Oath or affirmation." Although scholars debate the meaning of the Warrant Clause and its connection to the ban on unreasonable searches, and although the Court has tugged and pulled at the Clause over time, key features seem relatively clear for our purposes. First, the Warrant Clause follows the course of the common law in contemplating the submission of an application to a "neutral and detached magistrate," typically in an ex parte proceeding in which a government officer gives sworn testimony in support of the proposed warrant. Second, the issuance of a warrant had genuine legal consequences at common law, in that a lawful warrant immunized an officer who stayed within its bounds from subsequent civil liability.[17]

During the early Republic, representatives of all three branches of government presumed that ex parte warrant applications were proper in Article III courts. Congress authorized "any court of the United States" to hear warrant applications aimed at enforcing Alexander Hamilton's 1791 federal excise tax on distilled spirits. The law declared that any distilled spirits "fraudulently deposited, hid or concealed" with the intent to evade the payment of tax were subject to forfeiture.

> And for the better discovery of any such spirits . . . , it shall be lawful for any judge of any court of the United States, or either of them, or for any justice of the peace, upon reasonable cause of suspicion, to be made out to the satisfaction of such judge or justice, by the oath or affirmation of any person or persons, by special warrant or warrants by their respective hands and seals, to authorize any of the officers of inspection, by day, in the presence of a constable or other officer of the judge or justice of the peace, to enter into all and every such place or places in which any of the said spirits shall be suspected to be so fraudulently deposited, hid or concealed, and to seize and carry away any of the said spirits.

For obvious reasons, the statute did not require advance notice to the warrant's target and did not condition the issuance of the warrant on the target's participation in the judicial proceeding.[18]

Consider also the affair of Captain Barré, a French sailor who apparently found life in the United States preferable to the vagaries of the French Revolution. Under a treaty with France, the United States had agreed to arrest deserters from French vessels and deliver them to the French consul for return to their country. The French consul filed papers before Judge Richard Laurance in New York federal district court, seeking a warrant for Barré's arrest following his alleged desertion from a French ship. Although Barré did not appear in the proceeding, the evidence tended to establish that he had in fact deserted. Nonetheless, Judge Laurance refused to issue an arrest warrant until the French consul produced evidence of Barré's enlistment on the ship's register or roll (as apparently contemplated in the language of the treaty). When the consul failed to produce the specific proof demanded, Laurance declined to issue the warrant.[19]

The French, not surprisingly, viewed the somewhat formalistic basis on which Laurance denied the arrest warrant as an affront to their rights under the treaty. Pressed by the French envoy, the Washington administration filed a petition for a writ of mandamus in the Supreme Court to compel Judge Laurance to issue the warrant. In a unanimous decision, the Supreme Court declined to intervene. Reasoning that Judge Laurance had acted in a "judicial capacity," the Court said that it lacked power by way of mandamus to compel the judge to decide "according to the dictates of any judgment but his own." *L'Affaire Barré* thus confirms two important truths about arrest warrant proceedings. First, both the district court and the Supreme Court resolved the case on an ex parte basis; Barré did not appear. No one involved in the affair seems to have doubted the power of the federal courts to conduct uncontested proceedings. Second, its evaluation of the mandamus petition confirms that the Supreme Court regarded Judge Laurance as having acted in a judicial, rather than ministerial, capacity and thus as immune from mandamus review as to discretionary factual determinations made within the scope of his judicial authority. Like naturalization proceedings, warrant proceedings were viewed as a proper exercise of the judicial power.[20]

2.3 In Rem Proceedings in Admiralty

The federal courts also exercised jurisdiction over ex parte and uncontested transfers of maritime property. In the eighteenth and nineteenth centuries, before the advent of contemporary due process protections, in rem proceedings in admiralty were commonly brought in English and American courts to secure a transfer of title to property that was regarded, in the parlance of the day, as binding on "all the world." Often, these in rem proceedings began and proceeded to judgment on an ex parte basis. Captors of a vessel claimed as prize would initiate proceedings with the ex parte submission of a petition (or "libel") to the proper court, seeking an order that would arrest the captured vessel and institute the condemnation process. While admiralty courts welcomed the appearance of adverse parties, the court's power to transfer title in the captured property did not depend on their participation. It was possible, therefore, that an ex parte disposition could foreclose the rights of interested parties who had not appeared in the proceeding. Yet the courts nonetheless took the position that such dispositions were conclusive judgments, binding in the absence of fraud.[21]

2.3.1 Prize and Salvage Cases

Antebellum federal courts sitting in admiralty presided over a considerable docket of prize and salvage claims to seagoing property captured from an enemy or protected from loss. Prize claims were a commonplace of eighteenth- and early nineteenth-century seagoing warfare; governments authorized both the officers of their navies and certain duly licensed privateers to intercept and claim as prize the merchant ships and naval vessels of opposing nations. The administration of prize claims occupied the lion's share of the dockets of the colonial vice-admiralty courts and of the state admiralty courts under the Articles of Confederation. Salvage was awarded to the crew that helped, without any prior legal obligation, to save a stranded or damaged vessel or retook a friendly ship that the enemy had captured as prize.[22]

Under the Judiciary Act of 1789, federal courts were assigned exclusive jurisdiction over cases of prize and capture. Rules promulgated by the First Congress declared that "civil law" process was to govern proceedings in federal courts of admiralty (as well as in suits brought in equity). Federal courts accordingly used an inquisitorial model to adjudicate prize claims, collecting and assessing evidence, issuing decrees, and ordering the sale of captured vessels without insisting on adversary representation. Given the widespread view that such matters of prize and capture were proper subjects of federal adjudication, no one appears to have raised doubts about the power of the federal courts to adopt an inquisitorial model or to entertain the proceedings on an ex parte basis. The role of the district court in administering prize cases was not always or even primarily to adjudicate disputes. Indeed, the issuance of dispositive decrees upholding the legality of naval captures played a crucial role in national defense and international relations in the early Republic. That this task was assigned to federal district courts sitting in admiralty (as it was assigned to the admiralty courts in England) suggests that lawmakers expected the federal courts to play a role in the administration of law beyond mere dispute resolution.[23]

A quick look at the practice and procedure of early prize cases confirms their inquisitorial quality. Commissioners appointed by the federal district court, sitting in admiralty, would themselves collect the captured ship's papers. Commissioners would also take the depositions, on written questions, of the master or principal officers and crew of the captured vessel. Similar depositions were taken of the captors who were mounting the prize claim. Notably, as Justice Story explained in his note on practice in prize cases, the witnesses in such cases were to be examined solely by commissioners and were not allowed to have "communication with, or to be instructed by, counsel." Inquisitorial practice thus foreclosed a key feature of modern adversarial procedure in which attorneys "woodshed" their witnesses by carefully preparing them to present their recollection of events in the light best calculated to serve the client's interest.[24]

In addition to depositions, the commissioners would place the ship's papers in the custody of the district court, thereby creating the record on which the district court was to decide the case. Story described the court's reliance on this documentary record as the very "essence" of the administration of prize law. It was a mistake, he held, to allow "common law notions, in respect to evidence" to inform such inquisitorial proceedings, which "have no analogy to those at common law." Thus the practice strongly disfavored oral testimony from witnesses, particularly those who might shape their testimony to take account of what others had said. Story recognized that such witnesses might attempt to defeat the just rights of the captors with "contrivances, explanations, and frauds." Rather than allowing witnesses to tailor their testimony to the facts revealed in the documents, it was better to rely in good inquisitorial fashion on the documents themselves.

Other aspects of prize litigation conformed to the inquisitorial model. Thus, upon the filing of the libel, the district court was to issue a "monition," or a form of notice to the world at large "citing all persons" to appear and show cause why the property in question should not be "condemned as prize." Story explained that this monition proceeding was borrowed from Roman law to address situations in which it was "impracticable to serve the party with a personal citation." Depending on the inclination of the district judge, monitions might be nailed to the mast of the vessel in question or published in a local newspaper or both. The monition announced a return day, perhaps twenty days after the notice was published, on which any persons with claims adverse to the captors were expected to appear and state their claim. While adverse parties could appear, in many cases the captured vessel was so obviously a good prize that no one showed up to contest the fact. On such occasions, the prize court would note the default in the record.

Rather than treat the default as conclusive, however, the prize court in such cases was expected to conduct an inquisitorial proceeding to determine the validity of the prize claim. On Story's account, after entering the default, the court "will then proceed to examine the evidence; and if proof of enemy's property clearly appear, it will immediately decree condemnation." Prize claims were not adversarial; they were inquisitorial. That meant that (as with the naturalization practice described in section 2.1) the court could not rely on the silence of potential adversaries to establish the truth of the prize claim. Instead, the court was obliged to consult the evidence and satisfy itself that the elements of the prize claim had been established. As Justice Story explained, this meant that the prize court played a much more active role than was customary in the adversary proceedings before common law courts. Instead of relying on the formal joinder of adverse parties, the prize court itself acted as the "general guardian" of all of the interests that might appear in the litigation. Given this perception of the court's role, the legal effect of prize decrees did not depend on the appearance of any opposing party; indeed Section 30 of the Judiciary Act of 1789 confirmed that no adverse party might even be named. Still, the absence of adverse parties did not deprive the court of power to decree in such a case.[25]

One can also see the impact of inquisitorial practice on the way admiralty courts handled salvage claims. Maritime law recognized the viability of salvage claims as a reward to those who undertook perilous service to preserve or save maritime property. The legal procedure was similar to that in prize litigation in that the petitioner filed a libel against identified property. But salvage claims differed in that they entitled the claimant only to a share of the property's value. To make out a good case, according to one treatise, salvage claimants must prevail on three elements: they must show that the property in question was exposed to marine peril; they must demonstrate that the salvage efforts were voluntary (rather than the result of an existing duty); and they must show that the salvage efforts were successful in saving property, at least in part. A variety of factors might inform the measure of the salvage award, including the risk incurred in saving the property and the skill and energy the salvors devoted to the task.[26]

Salvage litigation in the early federal courts reveals something about the way jurists of that day regarded the duties of inquisitorial judging. Thomas Bee, judge of the district court of South Carolina, often sat in admiralty cases and published a collection of his admiralty decisions. Bee's reports include two revealing cases from the 1790s: *Wilkie v. 205 Boxes of Sugar*, a claim to certain articles of commerce that were saved from a floating derelict known as the *San Pedro*; and *Hindry v. Schooner Priscilla*, a libel against a derelict vessel brought to shore. Judge Bee rejected the argument that derelict vessels were abandoned property whose ownership would pass to the first party to lay claim to them. Instead, they remained the property of their original owners, subject to claims of salvage. Accordingly, the court fixed the salvage fee at one-half the value of the libeled property and directed sale of the property and delivery of that share to the libellants. What became of the other half? The judge ordered the marshal to deposit that share in a local bank for a period of twelve months, to await the eventual appearance of any owner who could make an authoritative claim to the property. Even where the owners did not appear to contest the libel, in short, the admiralty judge served (as Justice Story would confirm) as the "general guardian" of all interests in the litigation. That meant Judge Bee conducted his own research into the maritime law of title to derelicts and acted to protect the absentee property owner's share.[27]

While prize and salvage claims in admiralty might well provoke adverse-party disputation, in many cases the claims went forward without the slightest contestation whatsoever. As we have seen, commissioners took written statements from all of the witnesses and delivered to the prize court any manifests, ownership documents, or other relevant papers located on board the captured vessel. On the date set for the hearing, the court unveiled all of this material: the depositions were opened and read for the first time and the relevant documents evaluated. Such suits might mimic the form of an adversary proceeding through the fiction of the ship as defendant, but they often lacked the "concrete adversity" and the vigorous opposing submissions that provide the rationale for an adverseness requirement.[28]

Records of the relative number of disputed and undisputed claims have proven elusive. But the magnitude, and value, of prize and capture litigation was substantial. During the Quasi-War with France in the late 1790s, French spoliation of U.S. ships was valued at $20 million. During the War of 1812 with Great Britain, U.S. crews mounted prize claims in the amount of $45 million. One American privateer, sailing the *Snapdragon*, captured forty-three British vessels along the coast of North Carolina, valued at $4 million.[29]

2.3.2 Maritime Finds and Treasure Claims

Inquisitorial proceedings also took place in connection with claims to maritime property that was found on, or under, navigable waters. According to ancient maritime law, "[p]roperty found in the sea, 'in floods or in rivers, if it be precious stones, fishes or any treasure of the sea, which never belonged to any man in point of property,' was adjudged to the first finder." Admiralty courts might decree a good find, thereby establishing title to the property in question, without contestation, and indeed, without the appearance of any adverse interest. The salvage of sunken treasure could present similar issues, but these proceedings have grown ever more contentious with the advent of new salvage technology. Treasure hunters might claim the property found in and around a sunken vessel on the theory that the property had been permanently abandoned and was owned by the first finder. In other contexts, however, the property might not be regarded as abandoned and maritime law would allow the salvor to claim only a share of the property's value as salvage.[30]

Even today, the practice in such treasure/salvage cases reflects the fact that they do not depend on the joinder of an adverse party. To institute a proceeding, the salvor must bring up a concrete artifact from the wreck site and use that item as the predicate for an assertion of in rem maritime jurisdiction over the wreck. The salvor must also show present ability to salvage the property. Once the federal admiralty court obtains jurisdiction over the salvage claim, it has the authority to adjudicate any adverse party claims that may arise as others seek to stake a claim to the wreck. The salvage proceeding thus begins as an in rem action against the property but may (as in Roman law or in a common-form probate proceeding) evolve into a contested matter if adverse claimants appear.[31]

2.4 Veterans' Pension Claims

This oft-told story began in 1792, when Congress assigned the federal circuit courts responsibility for reviewing the pension applications of disabled war veterans. The statute called for the claimant to file a petition with the court, along with supporting evidence of military service, rank, and related information. The statute did not, however, require the veterans to join the government as an opposing party. In passing on these petitions, the circuit courts were to conduct a physical examination of the veteran, assess the extent of the injuries, and prepare an opinion as to the degree of disability and the proper compensation. The court's decision, together with the veteran's supporting evidence, were to be forwarded to the Secretary of War for review. Assuming that the Secretary found that the court's decision revealed no sign of "imposition or mistake," the petitioner would be added to the pension list for submission to Congress. Three federal circuit courts refused to exercise the judicial power conferred upon them by the pension scheme, in part because the Secretary's revision power rendered the courts' decisions nonfinal, and in part for reasons that have been the cause of frequent speculation. As we shall see, scholars have long argued that the objection to the adjudication of pension claims was rooted in their non-adversary character, but chapter 9 rejects that claim. Properly understood, the episode that legal historians have come to know as *Hayburn's Case* offers further support for the proposition that early Republic legislators and jurists viewed the federal courts as a proper forum for non-adversarial adjudication.[32]

2.5 Uncontested Proceedings Ancillary to Dispute Resolution

Apart from original petitions for the issuance of constitutive decrees in uncontested proceedings, litigants in the nineteenth century frequently invoked the power of the federal courts to enter judgments in nominally contested adjudicative settings. One can usefully distinguish these ancillary proceedings from original petitions (like those seeking naturalization or pension benefits) on the basis that they occur in shadow of adverse-party disputation.

2.5.1 Default Judgments

In perhaps the most familiar example of the exercise of judicial power in uncontested ancillary proceedings, federal courts have the power to enter default judgments on an ex parte basis. Modern process, based on longstanding practice in courts of law and equity, calls on the court to ensure that the defendant has been duly served with process and that the plaintiff has a prima facie right to recover. As embodied in the Federal Rules of Civil Procedure, federal practice under Rule 55 establishes some procedural safeguards, requires the district court to exercise broad inquisitorial powers to investigate the facts that bear on the proposed judgment, and prohibits the court from entering the judgment unless the claim has been established through the submission of "evidence satisfactory to the court." But Rule 55 does not condition the court's power to issue a judgment on party opposition.[33]

2.5.2 Uncontested Equity Receiverships

In the latter part of the nineteenth century, with no federal bankruptcy law in place until 1898, railroads and their creditors often turned to the equity receivership to restructure their affairs. In theory, the receivership was designed to protect the interests of creditors who could not otherwise enforce and collect their debts. In practice, the railroads themselves often welcomed the initiation of a receivership to secure the stay of litigation triggered by such a proceeding and to secure an orderly administration and restructuring of their debts.[34]

In one such proceeding, intervening parties contested the power of the federal court to entertain "friendly" receiverships. The Supreme Court found no violation of the adverse-party requirement and upheld the friendly receivership, because the party initiating the receivership had an unsatisfied demand against the railroad that was neither denied nor paid. That failure to pay was sufficient to ground the federal trial court's jurisdiction. In this sense, then, one can view the friendly receivership as the product of an agreed-upon resolution of the potentially adverse interests of those with a claim on the assets of the railroad in question.[35]

2.5.3 Guilty Pleas

Government enforcement proceedings often involve federal courts in the approval of a negotiated settlement between the government and the target of the enforcement action. As one example, plea agreements arose some 150 years ago as a capitulation to the demands placed on criminal dockets by mass society. Consent decrees are another. Critics identify flaws with the plea-bargaining system, but most doubt that the criminal justice system can function in its absence. Plea bargaining represents, in the words of federal Judge Gerard Lynch, an "informal, administrative, inquisitorial process of adjudication." In the typical case, the prosecutor and the defendant have agreed in advance on the sentence or its parameters in exchange for the defendant's agreement to plead guilty to a particular offense. Needless to say, most guilty pleas do not occasion any adversary presentation to the court; both the prosecutor and defense seek substantially the same disposition. But the agreement alone does not suffice to ensure the legal effectiveness of the plea bargain; the court must go along. Thus, the district court must conduct a colloquy with the defendant to ensure that the plea and associated waiver of constitutional rights was knowing and voluntary; the courts must enter a judgment of conviction on the basis of the plea; and the court must sentence the defendant to a term consistent with the plea agreement and the sentencing guidelines. In these respects, the court plays a non-contentious role, evaluating the parties' agreed disposition to ensure that it comports with federal criminal and sentencing norms.[36]

2.5.4 Letters Rogatory

Federal courts often play an ex parte role when parties to a foreign proceeding seek discovery of facts in the United States. Under longstanding international practice, parties to litigation in one country can apply through diplomatic channels for "letters rogatory" to facilitate the collection of evidence in another country. Today, many such evidentiary requests are handled through the 1972 Hague Evidence Convention, which the United States joined as an original signatory. The convention directs such requests to a country's designated "Central Authority" for submission to the proper court. The application to a court of the United States typically proceeds on an ex parte basis and may or may not lead to litigation, depending on the target's response to the discovery request. If the district court agrees with the evidentiary request, it will typically appoint a commissioner to take the deposition or collect the evidence and will certify the result to the requesting tribunal. While the target's opposition to the discovery in any particular case can certainly create a measure of adverseness, ex parte applications for letters rogatory can proceed on an uncontested basis. The district court's role – to authorize the taking of discovery and to certify the result – does not serve to resolve any dispute in the federal system. But the ancillary role in overseeing discovery in support of foreign litigation has been one the federal courts have long played.[37]

In this representative, but hardly exhaustive, catalog, one encounters a nineteenth-century world of uncontested adjudication that poses an important challenge to some sweeping modern statements of the nation's traditional devotion to an adversarial ideal. Notably, though, as the next chapter explains, the federal courts were somewhat selective in accepting assignments of uncontested adjudication and focused their attention on matters governed by federal law.

Notes

1. U.S. CONST., art. I, § 8 (specifying Congress's power to enact a uniform rule of naturalization). On the inability of foreign nationals to take title to land in the United States, *see* Dawson's Lessee v. Godfrey, 8 U.S. 321 (1808) (British national with no physical ties to the United States could not inherit land in Maryland owned by a citizen of the United States).
2. An Act to Establish an Uniform Rule of Naturalization, ch. 3, 1 Stat. 103 (1790) [hereinafter Act of 1790]. On the framing of the Constitution's Naturalization Clause and the drafting of the 1790 Act generally, *see* James E. Pfander & Theresa R. Wardon, *Reclaiming the Immigration Constitution of the Early Republic: Prospectivity, Uniformity, and Transparency*, 96 VA. L. REV. 359 (2010).
3. Early legislation frequently relied on the people as a check on official action. The first census law directed the marshal of the district courts to conduct an enumeration and to place the results before the grand jury for an assessment of the quality of the returns. *See* Act of 1790, ch. 2, 1 Stat. 101 (1790). On the nature of the inquiry required in naturalization proceedings, *see In re* an Alien, 7 Hill 137 (N.Y. 1845) (viewing the statute as requiring the court to satisfy itself through some form of inquiry that the applicant for citizenship had made out an appropriate case). On the connection between naturalized citizenship and the ownership of land, *see* Pfander & Wardon at 366–68. In a variety of early Republic disputes over property ownership, the official record was introduced to resolve questions about an alien's admission to citizenship. *See, e.g.*, Spratt v. Spratt, 29 U.S. (4 Pet.) 393, 408 (1830) (expressing reluctance to look behind the record as "productive of great mischief, if, after the acquisition of property . . . an individual might be exposed to the disabilities of an alien on account of an error in the court"); Stark v. Chesapeake Ins. Co., 11 U.S. (7 Cranch) 420 (1813).
4. The minute book of the federal district court in New York, for example, includes naturalization entries that date from shortly after the 1790 Act took effect. For a typical example of Judge Duane's work, *see* Minutes and Rolls of Attorneys of the U.S. District Court for the Southern District of New York, 1789–1841, Roll 1, Target 1, Slide 36 (Nov. 2, 1790), *microformed on* Nat'l Archives of the United States, M886 (Nat'l Archives Microfilm Publ'n) (recording Duane's conclusion that one Philip Dubey had resided in the United States for two years and in New York City for at least one year and was "a person of good character" and was entitled to take the oath for admission to citizenship, which "was administered to the said Philip Dubey accordingly").
5. *In re* an Alien, 7 Hill 137, 138 (N.Y. 1845).
6. *See Ex parte* Saunderson, 21 F. Cas. 540 (C.C.D.D.C. 1804) (No. 12,378) (refusing to naturalize an applicant whose period of residence in the United States was interrupted by trips back to England); *Ex parte* Walton, 29 F. Cas. 125 (C.C.D.C. 1804) (No. 17,127) (denying naturalization to an applicant who had been abroad for a lengthy period and previously filed a conflicting affidavit); *see also* Anonymous, 1 F. Cas. 1023 (C.C.D. Pa. 1817) (No. 468) (refusing to accept parol evidence, offered by the petitioner, as to the length of his residency).

7. *See Ex parte* Pic, 19 F. Cas. 580 (C.C.D.C. 1808) (No. 11,118) (naturalizing a married woman); *Ex parte* Pasqualt, 18 F. Cas. 1283 (C.C.D.C. 1805) (No. 10,788) (granting naturalization to a sailor, resident in Alexandria, who was often away from home on voyages). *Ex parte* Newman, 18 F. Cas. 96 (C.C.D. Ma. 1814) (No. 10,174) (Story, J.).
8. Campbell v. Gordon, 10 U.S. 176, 182 (1810) (Washington, J.).
9. Spratt v. Spratt, 29 U.S. (4 Pet.) 393, 408 (1830).
10. *Ex parte* Fitzbonne (1800) (unreported). For an account, *see* 8 THE DOCUMENTARY HISTORY OF THE SUPREME COURT: 1789–1800, at 389–90 (Maeva Marcus ed., 2007), which describes the litigation and the import of the Court's decision to issue the writ directing the naturalization to proceed. For the prohibition against naturalization of alien enemies, *see* Act of June 18, 1798, ch. 54, § 1, 1 Stat. 556, 567. During the Quasi-War between the United States and France (1797–1801), Federalists opposed easy terms of naturalization out of a fear that French citizens displaced by the French Revolution could too readily vote in the United States.
11. In *Hayburn's Case*, 2 U.S. (2 Dall.) 411 (1792), the Court similarly entertained an ex parte petition for mandamus that sought to compel the lower federal courts to proceed with the adjudication of pension claims and did so without raising any doubts about its appellate authority. The veterans' pension program that gave rise to the litigation, further discussed in chapter 9, plays an important and misunderstood role in debates over uncontested adjudication.
12. On antebellum naturalization, *see generally* FRANK G. FRANKLIN, THE LEGISLATIVE HISTORY OF NATURALIZATION IN THE UNITED STATES FROM THE REVOLUTION WAR TO 1861 (1906); JAMES H. KETTNER, THE DEVELOPMENT OF AMERICAN CITIZENSHIP, 1607–1870 (1978). Franklin notes that "[t]here are no reliable statistics" for immigration before 1820 but concludes that we can infer that immigrants were "chiefly English and French" and wealthy (given the high cost of transportation and limited number of passengers carried across the Atlantic). FRANKLIN at 184. Even so, this data collection focused on immigrants arriving by sea on the East Coast. *Id.* at 184–87. The federal government began to collect national immigration statistics in 1907. Louis DeSipio & Harry P. Pachon, *Making Americans: Administrative Discretion and Americanization*, 12 CHICANO-LATINO L. REV. 52, 54 (1992) (collecting data from 1907 to 1988).
13. Report Submitted by the Senate Committee on the Judiciary, to whom were referred sundry memorials and resolutions relative to the naturalization laws of the United States, S. REP. No. 28-173 (1845).
14. S. REP. No. 28-173, 24 (testimony of George Morton) (S.D.N.Y.); *id.* at 60 (naturalizations in New York state court on election day); *id.* at 58–59 (testimony of Andrew Warner, Exhibit B) (state court naturalizations 1841–44); *id.* at 66–69 (testimony of Abraham Assten) (marine court); *id.* at 106 (testimony of Archibald Randall) (Philadelphia federal court); *id.* at 103 (testimony of Thomas Doyle) (quarter sessions).
15. For an example of procedural issues with naturalization applications at the New York Marine Court, *see* former Judge Hammond's deposition in S. REP. No. 28-173, at 6 ("I remember to have dismissed eight applications in the course of about one week, for want of this qualification of continued residence."). For instances of potential abuse

of duplicate certificates, *see id.* at 4–5 (N.Y. Marine Court); *id.* at 111 (Pa. Court of Common Pleas); *id.* at 15 (depo. Judge Randell, N.Y. Marine Court) ("I would further state, that about the times of election there are numerous applications for duplicate certificates . . . ; sometimes fifty in a day. This opens a wide door for fraud, in enabling applicants to personate others, and obtain a naturalization under a fraudulent use of papers, and by assuming the name of the person mentioned in such declaration."). *See, e.g., id.* at 5, 13, 28 (reliance on interpreters). *Id.* at 109, 123–44 (Baltimore evidence on "bad character" of immigrants). S. 99, 28th Cong. § 3 (1845) (proposing to allow an alien meeting the requirements for citizenship "to appear before any circuit or district court of the United States, and, upon presenting a petition . . . he or she may be admitted by the court").

16. For example, the federal Office of Superintendent of Immigration was created within the Treasury Department in 1891. Immigration Act of 1891, ch. 551 § 7, 26 Stat. 1084, 1085 (1891). A few years earlier, Congress called upon state and federal authorities to collect head taxes on new immigrants and exclude many Chinese immigrants from the country. Immigration Act of 1882, ch. 376, §§ 1–2, 22 Stat. 214, 214–15 (1882); Chinese Exclusion Act, ch. 126, 22 Stat. 58 (1882). The Naturalization Act of 1906 re-formed the existing Bureau of Immigration into the "Bureau of Immigration and Naturalization," giving it authority over "all matters concerning the naturalization of aliens." Naturalization Act of 1906, ch. 3592, § 1, 34 Stat. 596, 596 (1906). On the transition to an administrative model of naturalization, *see* Nancy Morawetz, *Citizenship and the Courts*, 2007 U. Chi. Legal F. 447, 450–54 (2007); DeSipio & Pachon at 55–56 (noting that the administrative model arose in part to meet the influx of immigrants at the turn of the century). Chapter 7.1 discusses *Tutun v. United States* in more detail.

17. U.S. Const., amend. IV. Much has been written about the warrant requirement and the scope of Fourth Amendment protections from unreasonable searches and seizures. *See* Gerstein v. Pugh, 420 U.S. 103, 117 (1975) (emphasizing the importance of transferring the judgment from the prosecutor to "a neutral and detached magistrate"); Johnson v. United States, 333 U.S. 10, 14 (1948) (holding that probable cause must be determined by a "neutral and detached magistrate"). *See generally* Nelson B. Lasson, The History and Development of the Fourth Amendment to the United States Constitution 120 (1937) (distinguishing between the "sober" judgment of a judicial official in issuing a warrant with the perhaps ill-informed judgment of the "ministerial" officer who executes the warrant, subject to the possibility of "civil and criminal liability" if he exceeds the authority conferred). In general, scholars agree that warrants in the eighteenth century, when valid, conferred immunity from civil liability. *See* Akhil Reed Amar, *Fourth Amendment First Principles*, 107 Harv. L. Rev. 757, 778 (1994). For an account of a successful legal challenge to a search pursuant to a general warrant that resulted in a substantial award of damages against a high government official, *see* Thomas Y. Davies, *Recovering the Original Fourth Amendment*, 98 Mich. L. Rev 547, 562–63 n.21 (1999). Professor Davies shows that Americans likely learned of these developments through newspaper accounts and pamphlets. *Id.* at 563–65.

18. *See* Act of March 3, 1791, ch. 15, § 32, 1 Stat. 199, 207 (1791). Congress's first customs tax, adopted in 1789, did not rely on the federal courts to issue search warrants, but provided instead for applications to any "justice of the peace." An Act to Regulate the Collection of the Duties Imposed by Law on the Tonnage of Ships or Vessels, and on Goods, Wares and Merchandise Imported into the United States, 1 Stat. 29, ch. 5, § 24 (1789). By choosing to assign the warrant-issuing authority to state officials, the 1789 legislation does not imply that Article III courts lacked power to conduct such proceedings. Rather, it may simply reflect the lack of an existing federal option. Congress did not adopt its system of lower federal courts and judges until September 1789, and President Washington made his first appointments to those courts in early 1790, several months after the customs law took effect. For an account of the First Judiciary Act, *see* 4 Documentary History of the Supreme Court, at 22–35.
19. For an account of Barré, *see* Susan Low Bloch, *The Early Role of the Attorney General in Our Constitutional Scheme: In the Beginning There Was Pragmatism*, 1989 Duke L.J. 561, 613–16 (1989). *See* Convention Between His Most Christian Majesty and the United States of America, for the Purpose of Defining and Establishing the Functions and Privileges of Their Respective Consuls and Vice-Consuls, U.S.-Fr., art. IX, Nov. 14, 1788, 8 Stat. 106, 112; *see also* 6 Documentary History of the Supreme Court at 522, 524–25 (specifying that proof was to be by "an exhibition of the register of the vessel or ship's roll"). The desertion likely had something to do with the changing politics of the French Revolution. When the famed Citizen Genet fell from grace in February 1794, he left his position as minister and retired to a farm in New York rather than return to France to face the guillotine. *See* William Casto, *America's First Independent Counsel: The Planned Criminal Prosecution of Chief Justice John Jay*, 1 Green Bag (n.s.) 353, 357 (1998).
20. *See* United States v. Laurance, 3 U.S. (3 Dall.) 42, 53 (1795). (The judge's name is styled Lawrence in the opinion but is typically spelled Laurance.) For an account of the French consul's efforts to secure the support of the executive, *see* Bloch at 613–15. Notably, Justice James Wilson participated in the mandamus case, posing a question about the state of the factual record below. His failure to raise doubts about the ex parte character of the proceeding may lend a measure of support to the conclusion that such doubts did not underlie his concern with the "judicial nature" of invalid pension claims in *Hayburn's Case*. Nor did the Court question the Attorney General's authority to seek a writ on behalf of the French consul's application for the warrant. *See* Bloch at 613–17 (contrasting the Court's willingness to entertain the *Laurance* mandamus petition with its refusal to hear Randolph's ex officio application in *Hayburn's Case*). Chapter 9 discusses the implications of *Hayburn's Case*.
21. The Due Process Clause of the Fourteenth Amendment has been interpreted to impose an obligation on fiduciaries to give notice "reasonably calculated" to inform the beneficiaries of events pertaining to the administration of a trust. *See, e.g.*, Mullane v. Cent. Hanover Bank & Trust Co., 339 U.S. 306, 318 (1950). Quoted language appears in Grignon's Lessee v. Astor, 43 U.S. (2 How.) 319, 342 (1844). As recently as 1945, Lewis Simes, a law professor and the reporter of the Uniform Probate Code, published a spirited defense of the traditional conception of probate as an in rem proceeding.

See Lewis M. Simes, *The Administration of a Decedent's Estate as a Proceeding In Rem*, 43 MICH. L. REV. 675 (1945). Two cases from the nineteenth century illustrate the conclusive quality of proceedings in the probate courts. In *Grignon's Lessee*, arising in the Wisconsin territory, the administrator of the decedent's estate filed an ex parte petition with the local court, requesting the court to approve the proposed sale of the decedent's land to satisfy the estate's debts. The court duly granted its approval in an ex parte proceeding and issued what the Supreme Court described as a "license to sell." Heirs of the decedent later moved to unwind the sale and to reclaim the land. But the Court concluded that the license to sell qualified as the judgment of a court of record that immunized the sale from subsequent challenge. A similar result obtained in a case arising in Pennsylvania. An ex parte decree of the orphan's court, authorizing the sale of a decedent's land to support his children, was viewed as conclusive. McPherson v. Cunliff, 11 Serg. & Rawle 422 (Pa. 1824). Conclusive quality also was ascribed to proceedings in admiralty over title to vessels captured or salvaged at sea and claimed as lawful prize. *See id.* at 430; *Grignon's Lessee* at 338 (noting that probate sales "are analogous to proceedings in admiralty").

22. William R. Casto, *The Origins of Federal Admiralty Jurisdiction in an Age of Privateers, Smugglers, and Pirates*, 37 AM. J. LEGAL HIST. 123–29, 149–53 (1993). *See also* Frederick Bernays Wiener, *Notes on the Rhode Island Admiralty, 1727-1790*, HARV. L. REV. 44, 47 (1932) (describing heavy prize business in the Rhode Island colonial court of admiralty during King George's War with France). STEVEN L. SNELL, COURTS OF ADMIRALTY AND THE COMMON LAW: ORIGINS OF THE AMERICAN EXPERIMENT IN CONCURRENT JURISDICTION 160–61, n.128 (2007); CHARLES ANDREWS, 4 THE COLONIAL PERIOD OF AMERICAN HISTORY 253 (1938).
23. Casto, *Origins of Federal Admiralty Jurisdiction*, at 140. The frustrating experience of the Federal Court of Appeals in Cases of Capture, which heard appeals from state courts adjudicating prize cases under the Articles of Confederation, may have motivated Congress's decision to assign such cases to the exclusive jurisdiction of the federal courts. An Act to Regulate Processes in the Courts of the United States, ch. 21, § 2, 1 Stat. 93-94 (1789). For an example of inquisitorial practices, the admiralty court in Boston promptly adopted the civil law practice on letters rogatory in the course of seeking to procure relevant evidence in other countries. *See* ANDREW DUNLAP, A TREATISE ON THE PRACTICE OF THE COURTS OF ADMIRALTY IN CIVIL CAUSES OF MARITIME JURISDICTION; WITH AN APPENDIX CONTAINING RULES IN THE ADMIRALTY COURTS OF THE UNITED STATES, AND A FULL COLLECTION OF PRACTICAL FORMS 200-02 (2d ed. 1850). Early admiralty courts adopted rules of procedure designed to facilitate an inquisition into prize and capture claims. *See id.* at 368–82 (setting forth rules of the Federal District Court for the Southern District of New York that required early notice to the court in cases of prize and capture, judicial collection of relevant papers, and an inspection of the vessel, all before any libel had been filed). On the role of naval capture in international relations, *see* Casto, *Origins of Federal Admiralty Jurisdiction*, at 133–34.
24. On the practice of woodshedding and its rejection in inquisitorial systems, *see* John H. Langbein, *The German Advantage in Civil Procedure*, 52 U. CHI. L. REV. 823, 833–34

(1985) (contrasting the partisan preparation of witnesses in the adversary system with the German model of judicial control in which ethical rules prohibit attorneys from discussing the case with witnesses). For Story's account of prize practice, *see On the Practice in Prize Cases*, *in* HENRY WHEATON, REPORTS OF CASES ARGUED AND ADJUDGED IN THE SUPREME COURT OF THE UNITED STATES app. at 494 (Frederick C. Blightly ed., 4th ed. 1883). For the attribution of the note to Story, *see* Kevin Arlyck, *Forged by War: The Federal Courts and Foreign Affairs in the Age of Revolution* 234 (Sept. 2014) (unpublished Ph.D. dissertation, New York University) (on file with author) (noting the reliance of the United States on privateers during the War of 1812).

25. An Act to Establish the Judicial Courts of the United States, ch. 20, § 30, 1 Stat. 73, 89 (1789). For descriptions of prize condemnation proceedings in England and the United States, *see* Matthew P. Harrington, *The Legacy of the Colonial Vice-Admiralty Courts (Part II)*, 27 J. MAR. L. & COM. 323, 329 (1996); L. Kinvin Wroth, *The Massachusetts Vice Admiralty Court and the Federal Admiralty Jurisdiction*, 6 AM. J. LEGAL HIST. 250 (1962).
26. 1 ROBERT FORCE, ADMIRALTY AND MARITIME LAW 163–68 (2d ed. 2013).
27. 1 THOMAS BEE, REPORTS OF CASES ADJUDGED IN THE DISTRICT COURT OF SOUTH CAROLINA 82–85 (1810) (reporting Wilkie v. 205 Boxes of Sugar, 29 F. Cas. 1247 (D.S.C. 1796) (No. 17,662); *id.* at 1–2 (reporting Hindry v. The Priscilla, 12 F. Cas. 201 (D.S.C. 1792) (No. 6,515)).
28. *See* Pfander & Birk, *Article III Judicial Power*, at 1420 n.349 (quoting Justice Story's recognition that adverse parties need not appear to ground Article III jurisdiction because the court acts as the "general guardian" of all interests brought to its attention); Arlyck at 264–65. *See* CHARLES ALAN WRIGHT & MARY KAY KANE, LAW OF FEDERAL COURTS, § 12, at 60 (8th ed. 2017) (noting the "risk that comes from passing on abstract questions rather than limiting decisions to concrete cases in which a question is precisely framed by a clash of genuine adversary argument exploring every aspect of the issue" (citing United States v. Fruehauf, 365 U.S. 146 (1961), and Golden v. Zwickler, 394 U.S. 103 (1969)) in that order).
29. *See* I ENCYCLOPEDIA OF THE WAR OF 1812: A POLITICAL, SOCIAL AND MILITARY HISTORY 90 (Spencer C. Tucker ed. 2012) (recounting the story of Otway Burns, prize master of the *Snapdragon*). *Id.* at 609 (during negotiation of the treaty between France and the United States, "it was agreed in 1801 . . . that the U.S. government would assume claims against France up to $20 million"). *Id.* at 599 (during the War of 1812, "[t]he economic impact of American high-tonnage prize captures and other naval actions amounted to more than $45 million in vessel and cargo losses for the British during the war as well as skyrocketing insurance rates for British shipping").
30. Quoted language appears in Lawrence J. Lipka, Note, *Abandoned Property at Sea: Who Owns the Salvage "Finds"?*, 12 WM. & MARY L. REV. 97, 98 (1970) (quoting The Laws of Oleron, Art. XXXIV (Eng.), *reprinted in* 30 F. Cas. 1171, 1184 (1897)). Admiralty courts might decree a good find without contestation, and indeed, without any adverse interest.
31. FORCE at 166–67 (distinguishing finds from salvage).
32. Disabled veterans began filing legislative petitions as soon as Congress convened in 1789, seeking benefits they had been promised by the old Congress under the

Articles of Confederation. *See* William C. diGiacomantonio, *Petitioners and Their Grievances: A View from the First Federal Congress*, *in* THE HOUSE AND SENATE IN THE 1790S, at 29, 47–56 (Kenneth R. Bowling & Donald R. Kennon eds., 2002) (describing the petitions of invalid veterans). For an account of the legislation, *see* James E. Pfander, *Judicial Compensation and the Definition of Judicial Power in the Early Republic*, 107 MICH. L. REV. 1, 34–40 (2008), which sketches the 1792 controversy over the assignment of pension claims to the federal circuit courts. *See* Hayburn's Case, 2 U.S. (2 Dall.) at 414 (quoting letters from the judges of circuit courts). We consider the mystery of *Hayburn's Case* in more detail in chapters 7 and 9. Two other grants of non-contentious jurisdiction appeared in the 1790s. *See* Act for Relief of Refugees, ch. 26, §3, 1 Stat. 547, 548 (April 7, 1798) (providing for the judges of the district and supreme courts of the United States to take "proof of the several circumstances" entitling refugees from Canada to pursue land claims under the Act); An Act for the Government and Regulation of Seamen in the Merchants Service ch. 29, § 3, 1 Stat. 131, 132 (authorizing crew to contest a vessel's seaworthiness by petition to the district judge of the district and directing the district judge to commission a report by knowledgeable citizens and, after receiving the report, to "adjudge and determine . . . whether the said ship or vessel is fit to proceed on the intended voyage"). This grant of authority appears to have derived from the practice by which the colonial vice-admiralty courts, following the "custom of all trading nations," ordered surveys to ascertain the condition of vessels. *See* 4 CHARLES ANDREWS, THE COLONIAL PERIOD OF AMERICAN HISTORY 253 & n.1 (1938) (describing colonial practice in which the captain, whose ship that had grown unseaworthy, would submit a "public instrument of protest" against the ship in the vice-admiralty courts, asking for a warrant of survey that could result in sale of the ship and its cargo by court order).

33. Rule 55 was first adopted as a blend of default procedures then available in actions in law and equity. *See* FED. R. CIV. P. advisory committee's note (1937). In proceedings at common law, failure to respond resulted in the entry of a default judgment; courts of equity entered what were called decrees *pro confesso*. *See* Thomson v. Wooster, 114 U.S. 104 (1885) (describing the origin and evolution of practice on the decree *pro confesso* and likening it to the common law practice of default); CHARLES ALAN WRIGHT ET AL., FEDERAL PRACTICE AND PROCEDURE § 2681, at 7 (3d ed. 2008) [hereinafter WRIGHT & MILLER]. In both instances, traditional practice called for the court to investigate the amount of damages if the figure was not liquidated. *Id.* at 400. Today, under Rule 55(c), a court may conduct a hearing to determine whether to enter a default judgment. A leading treatise explains, "The hearing is not considered a trial, but is in the nature of an inquiry before the judge." 10A WRIGHT & MILLER § 2688, at 58. Rule 55(b)(2) provides, "The court may conduct hearings or make referrals—preserving any federal statutory right to a jury trial—when, to enter or effectuate judgment, it needs to . . . establish the truth of any allegation by evidence; or . . . investigate any other matter." Fed. R. Civ. P. 55(b)(2)(C)–(D). In cases of default at common law, the court would issue a writ of inquiry to convene a special jury to fix the amount of damages. *See* JAMES OLDHAM, THE SEVENTH AMENDMENT: TRIAL BY JURY AND ANGLO-AMERICAN SPECIAL JURIES 45–79 (2006); *cf.* Chisholm v. Georgia, 2 U.S.

(2 Dall.) 419, 452–53 (1793) (noting the availability in cases of default of a "writ of inquiry" into damages). Quoted language is found in Fed. R. Civ. P. 55(d). *See* 10A Wright & Miller, § 2702, at 184 (reading Rule 55 to preclude procedural defaults and to require "in all cases" that the claims must be proven on a prima facie basis). Courts sometimes refer to the assessment of damages in a default case as an "inquisition of damages" to capture this investigative role. *See* Paul H. Aloe, *Civil Practice*, 60 Syr. L. Rev. 717, 730–31 (2010) (noting the use of an "inquest of damages" following entry of default).

34. On stays in equitable receiverships as ancillary proceedings that do not offend the anti-injunction act, *see* James E. Pfander & Nassim Nazemi, *The Anti-Injunction Act and the Problem of Federal-State Jurisdictional Overlap*, 92 Tex. L. Rev. 1 (2013).
35. As the Court explained, "[I]t is insisted now that there was no dispute or controversy in that case within the meaning of the [diversity] statute, because the defendant admitted the indebtedness and the other allegations of the bill of complaint, and consented to and united in the application for the appointment of receivers." *In re* Metro. Ry. Receivership, 208 U.S. 90, 107 (1908). *Id.* at 108; *see also* Pope v. United States, 323 U.S. 1, 11 (1944) ("When a plaintiff brings suit to enforce a legal obligation it is not any the less a case or controversy upon which a court possessing the federal judicial power may rightly give judgment because the plaintiff's claim is uncontested or incontestable."); Pac. R.R. v. Ketchum, 101 U.S. 289 (1880) (approving the defendant's confession of judgment and the entry of judgment on the basis of stipulated facts).
36. *See* Albert W. Alschuler, *Plea Bargaining and Its History*, 13 Law & Soc'y Rev. 11 (1979) (arguing that pleas became the primary method of disposing of criminal cases after the Civil War); George Fisher, *Plea Bargaining's Triumph*, 109 Yale L.J. 857, 859–61 (2000). The Court has expressed a growing willingness to police the fairness of plea bargaining by insisting on effective assistance of counsel at that stage of the process. *See, e.g.*, Missouri v. Frye, 566 U.S. 134 (2012). *See* Padilla v. Kentucky, 559 U.S. 356, 372–73 (2010) (noting that plea bargaining accounts for some 95 percent of the criminal matters closed in U.S. courts). Lynch, *Screening Versus Plea Bargaining* at 1404; *see also* Gerald E. Lynch, *Our Administrative System of Criminal Justice*, 66 Fordham L. Rev., 2117, 2118 (1998) (arguing that, because of plea bargaining, "the American system as it actually operates in most cases looks much more like what common lawyers would describe as a non-adversarial, administrative system of justice than like the adversarial model they idealize").
37. Letters rogatory, or letters of request, have deep roots in civil law practice. For an account of current practice concerning letters rogatory, *see* Walter B. Stahr, *Discovery Under 28 U.S.C. § 1782 for Foreign and International Proceedings*, 30 Va. J. Int'l L. 597 (1990). *See* Hague Convention on the Taking of Evidence Abroad in Civil or Commercial Matters, March 1–July 27, 1970, 23 U.S.T. 2555, 847 U.N.T.S. 231; *cf.* Société Nationale Industrielle Aérospatiale v. U.S. Dist. Court, 482 U.S. 522, 530 (1987) (holding that the Hague Evidence Convention does not provide the exclusive means of discovery, leaving open the possibility that courts in the United States can compel discovery by a foreign party over which they have obtained personal jurisdiction). Consider the process of responding to discovery in one apparently representative

case. A criminal investigation in London of corporate misconduct had targeted an individual living in the United States. Scotland Yard initiated a request for letters rogatory, which worked its way through diplomatic channels to the Department of Justice. There, an attorney applied to federal court in the District of Columbia on an ex parte basis for an order authorizing discovery from a witness. The district court's order, in turn, named a Justice Department attorney as commissioner to take the evidence. The target objected, moving to quash the application on various statutory grounds. *See In re* Letter of Request from the Crown Prosecution Serv., 870 F.2d 686 (D.C. Cir. 1989).

3

Probate and Domestic Relations Proceedings

Despite the willingness of antebellum federal courts, in general, to adjudicate uncontested claims, they sometimes declined to handle such matters. Among other prominent examples, federal courts refused to hear petitions for the probate of decedents' estates and for the issuance of constitutive orders and decrees in connection with the supervision of domestic relations. Scholars have offered a range of explanations for federal judicial diffidence in such matters, including the idea that family law matters were viewed as beneath the dignity of the federal courts. One might add that the federal courts were reluctant to administer the law in uncontested proceedings unless the law in question was federal. This chapter sketches the history of probate and domestic relations litigation in England and the way judicial work was allocated between the ecclesiastical courts and those of common law and equity. Then it describes the Supreme Court's skeptical reaction to efforts by nineteenth-century litigants to steer some aspects of those proceedings to the federal judiciary.

3.1 Probate Proceedings in English Law

By the latter half of the eighteenth century, English ecclesiastical courts conducted two kinds of probate proceedings: probate in the common form and probate in the solemn form. Probate in the common form was an ex parte proceeding that the executor generally initiated upon production of the decedent's will. The ecclesiastical court would grant probate upon the oath of the executor as to the validity of the will or, in the event of some irregularity, its proof by affidavit. These proceedings were not contested and, because no notice was given to the next of kin, those with an adverse interest were neither necessarily present nor formally joined as parties. This process established prima facie validity by simply confirming that the will met with canon

Cases Without Controversies. James E. Pfander, Oxford University Press. © James E. Pfander 2021.
DOI: 10.1093/oso/9780197571408.003.0004

law requirements. Probate in the common form was relatively quick and inexpensive, but it was not binding on future proceedings to probate the will in solemn form. Probate in the common form was not a prerequisite for the initiation of a solemn form proceeding, and parties foreseeing disputes over the validity of the will might pursue the solemn form in the first instance.[1]

Probate in the solemn form established the final, rather than the prima facie, validity of the will. In contrast to common form, solemn form proceedings provided formal notice to all interested parties and invited them to participate and be heard. Executors could initiate this process themselves, though the process was also triggered if any interested party disputed the validity of the will, even if it had already been proved in a prior common form proceeding. Solemn form probate generally followed canon law rules of procedure used by the ecclesiastical courts, distinct from the adversarial procedures used in English courts of common law or equity. At the conclusion of the proceeding, the court would either grant probate to the will or, if the will was invalid, appoint a representative to administer the decedent's estate under the rules of intestate succession.[2]

Apart from initial matters of probate and administration, ecclesiastical courts could handle a number of disputes related to the estate. Parties named in the will could bring *inter partes* suits in ecclesiastical court against the executor to collect debts from the decedent's estate, at least where the will mentioned payment of just debts. However, limitations on the jurisdiction of the ecclesiastical courts meant that some parties could satisfy their interests in the decedent's estate only by pursuing separate actions in England's secular courts. Common law courts handled various debts claims and disputes over the inheritance of land, while the courts of equity oversaw the administration and enforcement of trusts and acted as courts of last resort when remedies were unavailable in other tribunals.[3]

The division of judicial labor in England helped to shape the understandings of those who, in drafting the Judiciary Act of 1789, extended the federal judicial role to suits in law and equity. Common law courts did not assert jurisdiction over probate. Indeed, the validity of a will was, at least in England, a matter for ecclesiastical authority alone. Still, common law courts were the primary venue for resolving disputes over the inheritance of freehold property. Under feudal assumptions, ownership of land was thought to pass immediately to one's legal heirs. Common law courts exercised jurisdiction over title to land through the all-purpose action in ejectment and retained that jurisdiction in the sixteenth century when restrictions on the decedent's ability to transfer freehold property by will and devise were loosened. Common law courts thus came to deal with wills indirectly, as evidence for use in the course of otherwise proper proceedings.[4]

The role of the courts of equity was to provide relief where no adequate remedy was available in another forum. As remedial gaps appeared during the tug-of-war between the ecclesiastical and common law courts over the remedies they could provide, courts of equity stepped in. Creditors who sought to collect debts from the lands of the deceased found their remedies at law inadequate and turned to equity. Having authority to enforce trusts on freehold property, equity came to agree that it had the power to impose and oversee a constructive trust on inherited lands. Chancery also agreed to require detailed accounts from the personal representatives of decedents' estates, after concluding that the alternatives were too highly technical and narrow in scope to provide effective relief. Over time, these roles grew; once an ecclesiastical court had passed on the probate of a will and appointed a personal representative, courts of equity could exercise comprehensive power over many disputes touching the decedent's estate. There was, in short, nothing inherent in matters of probate or inheritance that blocked courts of law and equity from adjudicating.[5]

3.2 Probate Proceedings in Federal Court

While Article III and the Judiciary Act of 1789 extended federal judicial power to law, equity, and admiralty, no jurisdiction over probate and other ecclesiastical matters was conferred. Nor can one readily see how the federal courts might have been invested with such jurisdiction. As their name suggests, ecclesiastical courts in England were responsible for adjudicating claims relating to the obligations owed by members of the established church. These obligations extended quite broadly, including duties to refrain from blasphemy and defamation, from loaning money on usurious terms, and from engaging in such religious improprieties as drunkenness, fornication, and adultery. The Church of England had acceded to power over domestic relations by virtue of its authority over marriage, birth, bastardy, and the like. Its power over probate matters grew out of end-of-life confession of sins, deathbed bequests, and a perception that most individuals who died intestate would want their assets, if any, used for religious purposes. In any case, the remedy for an individual's refusal to comply with the order of an ecclesiastical court was excommunication—exclusion from the established church.[6]

When one recognizes that the mind of the eighteenth-century lawyer tended to categorize law by linking writs and remedies, it quickly becomes clear that no one involved in drafting Article III could have seriously entertained the possibility of adding ecclesiastical jurisdiction to the federal jurisdictional menu. While some of the states had church establishments at the time of the framing, the United States as a whole had no established church. Even though the First Amendment's ban on laws respecting church establishments would not take effect until 1791, the Constitution contemplated a secular rather than a religious government. The document itself refrains from any invocation of the deity and explicitly forbids any religious test for office.[7]

It would have been incongruous in the extreme for the Framers of such a secular government to have invested the federal judiciary with the powers of ecclesiastical courts. The federal government had no business issuing judicial decrees of excommunication to any parishioner, no matter how far she had lapsed from some conception of the true faith. As a consequence, one searches the records of the federal convention in vain for any proposal to include in Article III a provision for federal courts to exercise ecclesiastical jurisdiction. Similarly, no one in Congress appears to have urged the assignment of ecclesiastical or probate jurisdiction to the new federal courts in 1789. These matters were understood to have been left to the state courts.[8]

How then were the federal courts to exercise their jurisdiction over disputes between citizens of different states while still preserving the primacy of state courts in the probate of wills and administration of decedents' estates? By following the English model. There, as we have seen, superior courts of law and equity enjoyed concurrent jurisdiction over disputes that arose in the course of administering decedents' estates, but initial probate court decisions in the common or solemn form about the validity of a will did not necessarily provide an occasion for the adjudication of a dispute in law or equity. In 1827, the Supreme Court declared in *Armstrong v. Lear* that state courts exercising ecclesiastical jurisdiction had the exclusive right to probate a will of personal property. In dismissing a federal bill in equity based on a testamentary document that had not yet been probated, Justice Story offered this explanation:

> By the common law, the exclusive right to entertain jurisdiction over wills of personal estate, belongs to the ecclesiastical Courts, and before any testamentary paper of personalty can be admitted in evidence, it must receive probate in those Courts. . . . [T]he probate of wills of personalty belong exclusively to the proper [probate] Court here, exercising ecclesiastical jurisdiction.

Some years later, the Court in *Fouvergne v. City of New Orleans* reiterated that the "courts of the United States have no probate jurisdiction," holding that state probate court decisions on the validity of a will are conclusive and that challenges to such findings must be brought in state, not federal, court.[9]

In highlighting the federal courts' inability to exercise probate jurisdiction, the Court's antebellum decisions do not rule out federal adjudication of all disputes that have some connection to wills and estates or would have been grist for ecclesiastical adjudication in England. Many disputes over freehold property doubtless turned on the meaning of wills and a range of ecclesiastical matters (like defamation claims) have migrated to the secular courts of the United States. Rather, the Court sought to ensure the primacy of state probate and orphans' courts in making decisions about a will's validity. As we have seen, at least some such decisions were made on an uncontested basis, as the executor sought probate in the common form. Lacking probate jurisdiction, federal courts clearly lacked the authority to make such an uncontested state law determination. Even in situations where a dispute had arisen, moreover, Justice Story's account of the exclusive jurisdiction of state probate courts meant that such disputes (at least over the validity of wills) were for the state courts to handle. Probate jurisdiction in the state courts thus resembled admiralty jurisdiction over prize and salvage claims in the federal courts: it provided for one court to exercise exclusive authority over property that was understood to be *in custodia legis* in the custody and control of the court. Perceptions of the degree to which that initial exclusivity barred all such related litigation would change a bit over time, but probate in the common form had no place on federal dockets.

With one important exception: when Congress created non-Article III courts in the territories, they could exercise jurisdiction over matters of local law that lay beyond the reach of the typical federal court. Among other powers, territorial courts were charged with handling the probate of wills and the administration of decedents' estates. Such matters of local law were nonetheless thought proper for adjudication by the territorial federal courts in the first instance and, on occasion, by way of appeal to the Supreme Court. In cases where federal law conferred a constitutionally permissible form of probate jurisdiction, in short, the uncontested quality of a probate proceeding posed no barrier to its resolution by a federal tribunal.[10]

3.3 Domestic Relations Proceedings in Federal Court

As with the common form admission of wills to probate, the antebellum federal courts were not viewed as a proper forum in which to address the varied relationships that define the family. Here again, we must distinguish what we might call family law's constitutive rulings from the disputes over existing status that crop up from time to time in the domestic relations context. Constitutive rulings consist of those that change the legal status of the parties, either by investing them in a new status (married) or divesting them of that status (divorced). Apart from marriage and divorce, examples of constitutive decrees include an order to pay alimony, the establishment of a guardianship, and a decree awarding child custody. Such constitutive rulings differ from the stuff of ordinary litigation, where the parties disagree about the way settled law applies to their factual situation or about the content of unsettled law. In resolving such ordinary disputes, courts may create or better define current legal reality, but do not typically set out to bring a new legal status quo into being. While the antebellum federal courts viewed themselves as competent to hear the unusual disputes between family members that happened to satisfy the requirements of diversity, they disclaimed any role in performing constitutive work in the family law arena.

We can better understand the limited role of the federal courts after reviewing the rules of family law, which define both the *substantive* legal rights and obligations of those who enter into family life and the *process* by which changes in legal status occur. As for the rules of family life, the law prescribed the power of a married couple to own, acquire, and dispose of property; the obligations that a married woman owed to her husband; and the duties of support that her husband owed her in return. The children of the marriage similarly entered a web of correlative rights and obligations, enjoying (at least in theory) a right to financial support and owing services to their parents until they reached majority. Law answered a range of related questions: it defined the (limited) rights of illegitimate children, specified how the couple's property was to be distributed on the occasion of their death, and called for the appointment of guardians to manage the property of children who lacked any other legal representative.[11]

The *process* by which members of families changed their status was also regulated by law. Entry into the marital estate was relatively straightforward: it was accomplished through the voluntary, formal, and public exchanges of vows. But the alteration or termination of one's marital status was a much more complicated business; early nineteenth-century law took seriously the admonition that marriage contracts were meant to last a lifetime. As a result, simple legal forms of divorce did not become widely available until the twentieth century. True, the English ecclesiastical courts had the power to grant a limited form of divorce, known as separation from bed and board, but the marriage continued in force and duties of support and dower rights survived such decrees. In addition, certain marriages were terminated as nullities, either because the parties were too closely related or because they could not consummate the marriage. Such absolute divorces dissolved the marriage and left the parties free to remarry. Outside these circumstances, only the legislature had the power to grant an absolute divorce. Yet securing a private legislative divorce bill was a time-consuming and expensive endeavor practically unavailable to those with modest means.[12]

Questions concerning the status of children arose as incidents to marriage, divorce, and death. The parents of a child were considered lawful guardians, but the parents' death (or incompetence) would necessitate the appointment of a substitute. The task of appointing guardians in England fell to the High Court of Chancery, exercising the prerogative powers of the Crown. Custody was a different matter. English law naturally assigned custody to the child's parents; custody or wardship would arise as an issue in ecclesiastical courts when the minor asserted rights, or potential rights, to part of a decedent's estate. Courts would fix support obligations to take account of the cost of raising children; property settlements, alimony, and other support obligations were adjusted to take account of such costs. Absolute divorce was thought to terminate the marital estate and had far-reaching consequences in redefining the status of the children of the nullified union. The common law treated such children as illegitimate and deemed them incapable of inheriting the landed property of their parents.[13]

Nineteenth-century federal courts were willing to adjudicate disputes in the family law arena but shied away from making the constitutive rulings that would alter the status of family members. One finds this distinction between dispute-resolution and constitutive rulings reflected in the leading nineteenth-century case on the role of federal courts in adjudicating matters of family law. In *Barber v. Barber*, the New York state courts granted the wife a divorce and imposed an alimony duty on the husband, who later headed west to establish a new home in Wisconsin. When he failed to pay, the wife brought suit in Wisconsin federal circuit court on the basis of diversity of citizenship, seeking to enforce the alimony obligation. After reviewing the authorities, the Supreme Court allowed the action to proceed on the basis that the former husband and wife, with newly separate domiciles and states of citizenship, could satisfy the requirements of diversity.[14]

Accepting that some family law matters like an alimony-enforcement action might satisfy the requirements of diversity, the Court cautioned that the jurisdiction of the lower federal courts did not extend to such constitutive or status-related matters as the divorce proceeding itself, or the order granting alimony. Pressed by a dissenting opinion that urged the exclusion of all family law matters from federal dockets, the Court explained the limits of its ruling:

> We disclaim altogether any jurisdiction in the courts of the United States upon the subject of divorce, or for the allowance of alimony, either as an original proceeding in chancery or as an incident to divorce *a vincula*, or to one from bed and board.

One can certainly interpret this language as identifying situations in which the requisite elements of diversity of citizenship were often unavailable. Most couples, seeking a divorce, share a common domicile; many alimony payments would fall below the amount-in-controversy threshold for diversity jurisdiction. But one can also see a distinction between orders that change the legal status of the parties (from married to divorced and obligated to pay alimony) and those that resolve disputes about the parties' existing status. At least where the parties sought status-altering decrees in the context of uncontested proceedings, nineteenth-century federal courts viewed themselves as lacking authority to adjudicate.[15]

Federal practice thus distinguished between naturalization and admiralty matters on the one hand and probate and domestic relations matters on the other hand. The next chapter suggests that this differential approach reflected Article III's distinction between cases and controversies: uncontested matters of federal law, such as naturalization and admiralty, were thought to qualify as "cases," but uncontested matters of state law did not present "controversies" within the meaning of Article III.

Notes

1. ALISON REPPY & LESLIE J. TOMPKINS, HISTORICAL AND STATUTORY BACKGROUND OF THE LAW OF WILLS: DESCENT AND DISTRIBUTION, PROBATE AND ADMINISTRATION 112 (1928). *See also* LLOYD BONFIELD, DEVISING, DYING AND DISPUTE: PROBATE LITIGATION IN EARLY MODERN ENGLAND 250–51 (2012) (discussing uncontested English ecclesiastical court probate proceedings). *See* John F. Winkler, *The Probate Jurisdiction of the Federal Courts*, 14 PROB. L.J. 77, 84 n.34 (1997) (explaining ecclesiastical courts would use canon law to establish prima facie validity of will). BONFIELD at 251 (contrasting common form and solemn form).
2. Winkler at 85. REPPY & TOMPKINS at 112. The plaintiff (usually the will's advocate) would first make their case and call witnesses, after which the adverse parties would make their allegations and call their witnesses, until finally the judge made a determination. *Id.* at 112–13.
3. *Id.* at 132. Ecclesiastical courts could also demand an inventory of the decedent's estate and an accounting of the administration. *Id.* at 118. Winkler at 85.
4. *See, e.g.*, The King v. Inhabitants of Netherseal, (1742) 100 Eng. Rep. 1006, 1007 (K.B.) ("[N]othing but the probate, or letters of administration with the will annexed, are legal evidence of the will in all questions respecting personality."); *see also* Winkler at 84 n.32 (explaining that common law courts could not raise issue of will validity not previously established). *Id.* at 82–83. Statute of Wills, 1540, 32 Hen. 8, c. 1 (Eng.). *See* Winkler at 83 n.25 (citing Eccleston v. Petty, (1689) 90 Eng. Rep. 650 (K.B.)) (noting that common law courts only determined will validity indirectly and dealt with it similar to validity of a deed).
5. *See* REPPY & TOMPKINS at 148–49 (describing the role of Chancery in bringing estate administrators to account). To be sure, some cases suggest that courts of equity had no power to set aside a will once it had been established in ecclesiastical court because parties could always obtain adequate relief in another forum. *See, e.g.*, Kerrich v. Bransby, (1727) 3 Eng. Rep. 284, 286 (H.L.) (casting doubt on Chancery's power to entertain a will contest).
6. *See generally* 3 BLACKSTONE at *62, *422–33 (Chapter 15). On the jurisdiction of the ecclesiastical courts, *see* 1 HOLDSWORTH at 619; THE SPECIAL AND GENERAL REPORTS MADE TO HIS MAJESTY BY THE COMMISSIONERS APPOINTED TO INQUIRE INTO THE PRACTICE AND JURISDICTION OF THE ECCLESIASTICAL COURTS OF ENGLAND AND WALES 112–70 (London et al. eds., 1832) (describing ecclesiastical court jurisdiction over such matters as marriage, adultery, church seats, dilapidations, tithes, sequestrations, brawling, and defamation). Unlike chancery, which had "considerable powers of enforcement," the remedies of the church courts were limited to

"excommunication." HELMHOLZ at 97. But that remedy threatened the target with the following serious consequences:

> He was excluded from pleading in secular courts. His company was to be shunned by all Christians. In England he could be arrested and imprisoned if the bishop "signified" to the King that he had remained unrepentantly excommunicate for 40 days or more. Excommunication was, in short, an unhappy position from which an ordinary man would seek to be released.

Id.

7. For a persuasive argument that eighteenth-century thinking about the use of judicial power tended to revolve around remedies, *see* Anthony J. Bellia Jr., *Article III and the Cause of Action*, 89 IOWA L. REV. 777, 784–92 (2004). For an account of the Framers' experience with established churches, both in England and in the several states, *see* Michael W. McConnell, *Establishment and Disestablishment at the Founding, Part I: Establishment of Religion*, 44 WM. & MARY L. REV. 2105, 2110–11, 2126 (2003) (reporting that five southern colonies and four counties of Metropolitan New York had established religions at the time of the Revolution, that three colonies were created as havens for dissenters, and that the Puritan establishment lasted in Massachusetts until 1833). The United States, in keeping with the First Amendment, has never created an established church at the national level. *See generally* ALVIN W. JOHNSON & FRANK H. YOST, SEPARATION OF CHURCH AND STATE IN THE UNITED STATES 4–16 (2d ed. 1948) (tracing the idea that church and state should be separated to a Declaration of Rights adopted by the Virginia House of Burgesses in 1776, before the adoption of the Declaration of Independence). U.S. CONST. art. VI, cl. 3 ("[N]o religious Test shall ever be required as Qualification to any Office or public Trust under the United States."). Religious tests were an element of religious establishment. *See* McConnell at 2113.
8. *See* 4 FARRAND at 125 (omitting any reference to ecclesiastical courts from the index to debates at the constitutional convention).
9. Armstrong v. Lear, 25 U.S. 169 (1827). *Id.* at 175–76. Fouvergne v. City of New Orleans, 59 U.S. 470, 473 (1855) (citing Tarver v. Tarver, 34 U.S. 174, 179–80 (1835), which earlier had supported the same proposition by reference to *Armstrong v. Lear*). Later still, a decedent's next of kin challenged the issuance of letters of administration by a state probate court in a federal equity proceeding. *See* Caujolle v. Ferrié, 80 U.S. 465, 465 (1871). The Court dismissed the challenge, holding that federal courts sitting in equity were bound by the determinations of a state probate court on the matter of who should administer an estate, resting the decision on the fact that such actions by an ecclesiastical court in England would be binding on English chancery courts. *See id.* at 473–74.
10. As early as the Northwest Ordinance (1787), Congress provided for the operation of territorial courts vested with the power to oversee the probate of decedents' estates. Ordinance of 1787, 1 U.S.C. (2018). The U.S. code places the Northwest Ordinance together with the Declaration of Independence and the Constitution in its Front Matter. Decisions from the nineteenth century upheld the Supreme Court's power to review probate decisions of the territorial courts, thus posing questions about the breadth of the Article III probate exception. *See* James E. Pfander & Emily Damrau,

A Non-Contentious Account of Article III's Domestic Relations Exception, 92 NOTRE DAME L. REV. 117 (2016). Notably, the territorial statutes provide a federal law predicate for the assertion of judicial power and arguably transform all territorial probate proceedings into cases arising under federal law for purposes of Article III. Federal courts can exercise broader authority over federal law probate matters than over matters based on state law.

11. For recognition of the estate-like quality of domestic relations, *see* Jones v. Brennan, 465 F.3d 304, 307 (7th Cir. 2006) (Posner, J.) (likening disputes over the marital estate to an in rem proceeding). 1 JOEL PRENTISS BISHOP, NEW COMMENTARIES ON MARRIAGE, DIVORCE, AND SEPARATION AS TO THE LAW, EVIDENCE, PLEADING, PRACTICE, FORMS AND THE EVIDENCE OF MARRIAGE IN ALL ISSUES ON A NEW SYSTEM OF LEGAL EXPOSITION §§ 15, 16 (Chi., T.H. Flood & Co. 1891) (discussing the effect of marital status on property rights); *id.* at §§ 1184, 1195 (by the rules of common law, marriage confers on the husband "the right to the companionship and services of his wife, and compels him to protect and support her"; describing the husband as "the head of the family"). *See also* NANCY F. COTT, PUBLIC VOWS: A HISTORY OF MARRIAGE AND THE NATION 11 (2000) (the obligations owed to each spouse were set by the common law); HENDRIK HARTOG, MAN AND WIFE IN AMERICA: A HISTORY 136 (2000) ("Being a husband meant that one possessed, one represented, one governed, one cared for."). BISHOP at § 39 ("The husband is under obligation to support his wife; so is he to support his children."). *See* MICHAEL GROSSBERG, GOVERNING THE HEARTH: LAW AND THE FAMILY IN NINETEENTH-CENTURY AMERICA 234 (1985) (discussing the role of a parent to control the minor in the child custody context); *id.* at 197–201 (noting the evolution of bastard rights through post-Revolutionary America). BISHOP at § 16 (property distribution after death). On the appointment of guardians, *see* R.H. HELMHOLZ, CANON LAW AND THE LAW OF ENGLAND 243 (1987).

12. *See, e.g.*, BISHOP at § 40 (describing marriage under common law as a union for life). The ecclesiastical courts' jurisdiction allowed them to proclaim a marriage void *ab initio* and to grant a divorce *a mensa et thoro* (from bed and board). *See* HOLDSWORTH at 622–23. Alimony awarded by ecclesiastical courts after a divorce from bed and board "merely constituted a recognition and enforcement of the husband's duty to support the wife which continued after the judicial separation." HOMER H. CLARK JR., THE LAW OF DOMESTIC RELATIONS IN THE UNITED STATES 619 (2d ed. 1987). BISHOP at §§ 472, 473 (defining nullity of a marriage). *See* LAWRENCE STONE, ROAD TO DIVORCE: ENGLAND 1530–1987, at 141 (1990) (describing two roads to divorce, the first by suing for separation in ecclesiastical court and the second by act of Parliament); HOLDSWORTH at 623 (discussing the introduction of divorce by private act of Parliament arising at the end of the seventeenth century and the steps necessary to obtain such a divorce). *See also* LAWSON at 240–41 (distinguishing legally "void" marriages from "voidable" ones, which a court must dissolve by legal act, i.e., a divorce decree).

13. In England, the father was considered the common law guardian of his minor children. The mother obtained guardianship only upon the father's death and did so "not to its full extent." BISHOP at §§ 1152–53. The King, in his position as *parens*

patriae, was the legal guardian of his people. His power over infants was delegated to the Lord Chancellor, who then was able to appoint guardians through exercising the prerogatives of the King. JOSEPH CHITTY JR., A TREATISE ON THE LAW OF THE PREROGATIVES OF THE CROWN; AND THE RELATIVE DUTIES AND RIGHTS OF THE SUBJECT 155–56 (London, Joseph Butterworth & Son, 1820). Custody was historically granted first to the father then to the mother. In either instance, parents could not "by any contract not expressly authorized by law cast off permanently, whatever temporary arrangements they may make, the personal duty and correlative right of [the child's] custody and support." BISHOP at § 1169 (footnote omitted). *See* HELMHOLZ, CANON LAW, at 243. Although ecclesiastical courts were without jurisdiction to determine custody in divorce suits, they were able to adjust alimony awards with the custody of the child in mind. BISHOP at § 1185. An absolute divorce makes both spouses "single, freeing them as effectually form the marriage bond as does the sentence of nullity." *Id.* at § 1623. *See id.* at §§ 1601, 1602 (naming as legitimate only those children born in wedlock, including those begotten prior to wedlock and born after the marriage is dissolved but stating that no others are legitimate; children of a marriage decreed null are "conclusively illegitimate").

14. Barber v. Barber, 62 U.S. 582 (1858). *Id.* at 584, 597–98 (stating that sufficient authority had been cited to show "that a wife under a judicial sentence of separation from bed and board is entitled to make a domicil for herself, different from that of her husband").
15. *Barber*, 62 U.S. at 584. The Court was careful to note at the outset of its opinion that the suit before it was not asking for the allowance of alimony but the enforcement of an alimony decree granted by a court of competent jurisdiction, a state court in New York. *Id.* For the cogent suggestion that *Barber* represents a canonical example of family law localism, primarily explicable through the logic of coverture, *see* JILL ELAINE HASDAY, FAMILY LAW REIMAGINED 24–26 (2014).

4

The Nineteenth-Century Perspective on Federal Judicial Power

Scholars today often deem nineteenth-century practice hopelessly complex, confused, and unprincipled. On occasion, as with naturalization petitions and prize claims in admiralty, the federal courts would entertain uncontested proceedings in apparent defiance of any adverse-party requirement; on other occasions, as with suits to establish the validity of a will, the same jurists would disclaim any federal judicial role. Some courts would welcome collusive or feigned proceedings; others would look askance. No wonder scholars, looking backward, view the nineteenth-century conception of judicial power to have been something of a mishmash. One scholar captured modern sentiments, explaining that, in the beginning, there was pragmatism.[1]

Instead of looking backward with eyes informed by modern conceptions of judicial power, this chapter seeks to understand federal judicial practice in nineteenth-century terms by focusing on the way jurists at the time explained their practices to the legal world. We find them drawing a distinction between judicial power in cases from that in controversies. As for "cases," which included both federal law claims for naturalization and prize claims in admiralty, the Supreme Court required only a claim of right in the form prescribed by law. As for "controversies," the Court insisted upon the presence of parties aligned in opposition as specified in Article III. This chapter seeks to reclaim the nineteenth-century case–controversy distinction as the basis for an explanation of the scope and limits of judicial power that reflects at least as much principle as pragmatics.

4.1 The Marshall Court's Distinction Between Cases and Controversies

In a series of iconic decisions, *Martin v. Hunter's Lessee*, *Cohens v. Virginia*, and *Osborn v. Bank of the United States*, the Marshall Court defined Article

Cases Without Controversies. James E. Pfander, Oxford University Press. © James E. Pfander 2021.
DOI: 10.1093/oso/9780197571408.003.0005

III's reference to cases and controversies. But instead of conflating the two terms in an across-the-board case-or-controversy requirement, the Marshall Court drew a sharp line between them. Perhaps the best-known account appears in *Cohens*, where the Chief Justice differentiated between the federal subject matter of cases and the party-based focus of controversies:

> Jurisdiction is given to the Courts of the Union in two classes of cases. In the first, their jurisdiction depends on the character of the cause, whoever may be the parties. This class comprehends "all cases in law and equity arising under this constitution, the laws of the United States, and treaties made, or which shall be made, under their authority." This clause extends the jurisdiction of the Court to all the cases described, without making in its terms any exception whatever, and without any regard to the condition of the party. . . . In the second class, the jurisdiction depends entirely on the character of the parties. In this are comprehended "controversies between two or more States, between a State and citizens of another State," "and between a State and foreign States, citizens or subjects." If these be the parties, it is entirely unimportant what may be the subject of controversy.

Here, Chief Justice Marshall followed Justice Story in treating "cases" as matters that implicate federal law and qualify for federal adjudication on the basis of their subject matter "without regard to the condition of the party." Marshall treated "controversies," by contrast, as controlled for jurisdictional purposes by the presence of specified opposing parties. If the proper parties were aligned in opposition to one another, jurisdiction attached even as to subjects that did not implicate federal law.[2]

In his opinion for the Court in *Martin v. Hunter's Lessee*, Justice Story explained why Article III distinguishes between the federal subject matter of cases and the party-alignment focus of controversies. As Story explained, "cases arising under the constitution, laws, and treaties of the United States; cases affecting ambassadors, other public ministers and consuls, and cases of admiralty and maritime jurisdiction" were thought to implicate "the safety, peace, and sovereignty of the nation." Article III's provision for jurisdiction over controversies was thought to serve a different purpose: the Constitution "enables the parties, under the authority of congress, to have the controversies heard, tried, and determined before the national tribunals." It did so on the basis of a presumption "(whether rightly or wrongly we do not inquire) that state attachments, state prejudices, state jealousies, and state interests, might sometimes obstruct, or control, or be supposed to obstruct or control, the regular administration of justice." In short, jurisdiction in controversies reflects the assumption that, in disputes between specified opposing parties, the lack of state court impartiality might necessitate the provision of a neutral federal forum.[3]

In accounting for the Constitution's provision for jurisdiction over controversies, Justice Story's neutral forum account presumes the existence of an actual dispute between specified parties. He described the jurisdiction as enabling multiple "parties" to have their controversies "heard, tried, and determined." Story plainly had in mind contested matters between adversaries, or what the civilians referred to as contentious jurisdiction. That conclusion follows both from Article III's textual reference to controversies, or contested matters, and from the structural logic of the provision. Only when the specified parties appear as opponents does Story's concern arise as to possible state court attachments, prejudices, and jealousies. For Justice Story, then, Article III extends the judicial power to controversies to enable Congress to afford a neutral forum for disputes in which the alignment of opposing parties may raise doubts about state court impartiality.

In contrast to those defined as controversies, matters brought within the federal judicial power as "cases" arising under federal law did not include a requirement of contestation between adversaries. As both Marshall and Story explained, jurisdiction over "cases" turned on the fact that the claim implicated certain federal subjects: the Constitution, laws, and treaties of the United States, ambassadors, public ministers, and consuls, and admiralty and maritime law. Chief Justice Marshall put the idea this way in *Osborn*:

> This clause [extending jurisdiction to federal question "cases"] enables the judicial department to receive jurisdiction to the full extent of the constitution, laws, and treaties of the United States, when any question respecting them shall assume such a form that the judicial power is capable of acting on it. That power is capable of acting only when the subject is submitted to it by a party who asserts his rights in the form prescribed by law. It then becomes a case, and the constitution declares that the judicial power shall extend to all cases arising under the constitution, laws, and treaties of the United States.

Marshall thus broadly defined jurisdiction over cases without suggesting that the term applies only to contested matters. Story's *Commentaries on the*

Constitution adopts the same formulation: "A case, then, in the sense of this clause of the constitution, arises when some subject touching constitution, laws, or treaties of the United States is submitted to the courts by a party who asserts his rights in the form prescribed by law." Thus, a case arises when "any question" respecting the specified federal subjects assumes a form on which the judicial power can operate. Jurisdiction over cases did not depend on the necessity of resolving a dispute between opposing parties.[4]

Indeed, far from suggesting or implying a requirement of adverse-party contestation, Marshall's definition plainly contemplates that cases under Article III can arise upon the submission of an uncontested application to claim a right under federal law. Consider first that, in speaking about what creates a case for purposes of Article III, Marshall emphasized the claim of a single "party." Use of the singular term differs sharply from the consistent references to multiple opposing "parties" that we find in Justice Story's account of controversies. Moreover, Marshall explains that a "case" arises when a matter of federal law has been submitted to the federal courts by a "party who asserts his rights in the form prescribed by law." Here, Marshall emphasizes the federal law subject matter of the claim of right, and says nothing to indicate that the claimant must join an opposing party. Marshall's emphasis on the subject, rather than the parties, maps nicely onto the subject-matter/party-alignment distinction between cases and controversies that Marshall articulated in *Cohens*. Finally, in suggesting that the party must proceed "in the form prescribed by law," Marshall's definition seems ideally formulated to encompass uncontested applications such as naturalization petitions. Such petitions set up a claim of right to a federal subject, naturalized citizenship, in the form prescribed by law.

To be sure, Marshall's iconic definitions of the term "case" were not formulated in litigation directly challenging the power of the federal courts, say, to process naturalization petitions. But knowledge of the naturalization process was widespread among federal judges and formed the backdrop for Marshall's discussion of the nature of judicial power over cases. Thus, in *Osborn v. Bank of the United States*, where Marshall defined the term "case" as a federal claim of right by a party in the form prescribed by law, the example of naturalization was squarely before the Court. Dissenting, Justice William Johnson argued that Marshall's theory of subject-matter jurisdiction, allowing the Bank to sue on nonfederal claims, would logically enable Congress to authorize any naturalized citizen to litigate nonfederal claims in federal courts; the status of both parties was the product of a congressional act. Earlier, in *Cohens v. Virginia*, federal practice on naturalization petitions was offered to the Court as an example of a case that clearly arose under the laws of the United States for purposes of Article III. Marshall acknowledged that naturalization proceedings were in fact "cases" under federal law, but rejected Virginia's argument that federal question jurisdiction extended only to similar situations where a "party comes into Court to demand something conferred on him by the constitution or a law." Rather, a federal question case was said to encompass both the federal rights of claimants (such as petitioners in naturalization proceedings) and defendants (such as the Cohens) who sought to resist enforcement of state law on federal grounds. Leading jurists in the *Cohens* litigation, in short, agreed that naturalization petitions were obviously cases under Article III and the question was how much more broadly the category extended.[5]

If something short of a clear holding, Marshall's opinion in *Cohens v. Virginia* nonetheless acknowledged a fundamental truth about antebellum legal practice: ex parte naturalization petitions were cases arising under the laws of the United States, suitable for conclusive federal adjudication. Marshall confirmed the judicial quality of such proceedings some years later, squarely holding that ex parte applications for naturalization were matters suitable for judicial decision and, when granted, gave rise to judgments that were binding in later disputes. In *Spratt v. Spratt*, attorneys in a dispute over inheritance sought to mount a collateral attack on the legality of one party's naturalization, arguing that ex parte proceedings to naturalize were merely ministerial and did not enjoy the conclusive quality of matters of record. Marshall flatly rejected the argument that ex parte proceedings were nonjudicial and thus nonbinding:

> It seems to us, if [the record of naturalization] be in legal form, to close all inquiry; and, like every other judgment, to be complete evidence of its own validity. . . . It might be productive of great mischief, if, after the acquisition of property on the faith of his certificate, an individual might be exposed to the disabilities of an alien on account of an error in the court, not apparent on the record of his admission.

Marshall's opinion in *Spratt* thus confirmed the judicial character of ex parte adjudication and ensures that such adjudications enjoy the finality necessary for an exercise of the judicial power.[6]

4.2 Applying the Case–Controversy Distinction

During the latter half of the nineteenth century, the Court applied the Marshall Court's distinction between cases and controversies in explaining the scope of federal authority over matters relating to the probate of wills. Recognizing that issues of probate were governed by state law, the Court sharply distinguished between the "controversies" or *inter partes* disputes that were proper for federal adjudication and the sort of ex parte administrative work that federal courts could not undertake in probate matters. While an uncontested application to claim a federal right (like citizenship) might qualify as a case within the meaning of Article III, it would not so qualify where the subject matter of the right in question (like probate) had its roots in state law. Thus, the Court consistently denied that the federal judiciary could take up the ex parte (that is, the constitutive) aspects of probate, but repeatedly reaffirmed federal judicial power over controversies between properly aligned opponents.

Consider *Gaines v. Fuentes*, which arose from the attempted removal to federal court of a state suit concerning the validity of a Louisiana landowner's will. In explaining why removal was proper, the Court explained:

> The Constitution imposes no limitation upon the class of cases involving controversies between citizens of different States, to which the judicial power of the United States may be extended; and Congress may, therefore, lawfully provide for bringing, at the option of either of the parties, all such controversies within the jurisdiction of the Federal judiciary.
>
> . . .
>
> There are, it is true, in several decisions of this court, expressions of opinion that the Federal courts have no probate jurisdiction, referring particularly to the establishment of wills; and such is undoubtedly the case under the existing legislation of Congress. The reason lies in the nature of the proceeding to probate a will as one *in rem*, which does not necessarily involve any controversy between parties: indeed, in the majority of instances, no such controversy exists. . . . [B]ut whenever a controversy in a suit between such parties arises respecting the validity or construction of a will, or the enforcement of a decree admitting it to probate, there is no more reason why the Federal courts should not take jurisdiction of the case than there is that they should not take jurisdiction of any other controversy between the parties.

These passages convey two important ideas: that federal court power extends to any controversy or dispute between diverse parties, even where it happens to involve the validity of a will, and that the proceedings at the core of the probate exception were those of an uncontested or non-adversarial character.[7]

Subsequent decisions echo the idea that federal judicial power under Article III does not extend to in rem, ex parte probate proceedings. Consider the account in *Ellis v. Davis*:

> Jurisdiction as to wills, and their probate as such, is neither included in nor excepted out of the grant of judicial power to the courts of the United States. So far as it is *ex parte* and merely administrative, it is not conferred and cannot be exercised by them at all until, in a case at law or in equity, its exercise becomes necessary to settle a controversy of which a court of the United States may take cognizance by reason of the citizenship of the parties.

The *Ellis* Court thus confirmed that the federal judiciary could hear any *inter partes* dispute, so long as the diversity requirements were met. At the same time, the Court specified that the ex parte or constitutive probate decision must occur in a state court because controversies could arise only over rights flowing from a will, rights that did not exist until created by a grant of probate in state court that often, and perhaps typically, resulted from an ex parte proceeding.[8]

One final articulation of the distinction between ex parte proceedings and controversies over matters of state law appears in *Byers v. McAuley*, a decision in which the Court overturned a lower federal court's decision to impose equitable administration on the estate of a decedent. The Court recognized that federal courts have power to perform comparable administrative chores when they oversee equitable receiverships to restructure the affairs of a corporation for the benefit of creditors. Such receiverships, though predicated on a diverse-party dispute, were understood as empowering the court to take control of the property of the debtor corporation as a *res* and to exercise ancillary jurisdiction over the claims of nondiverse parties. But, as the Court explained, such an expansive view of federal equity did not extend to decedent's estates, since in an equity receivership

> [p]ossession of the res draws to the court having possession all controversies concerning the res. If original jurisdiction of the estates of deceased persons were in the federal court, it might, by instituting such an administration, and taking possession of the estate through an administrator appointed by it, draw to itself all controversies affecting that estate. . . . But it has no original jurisdiction in respect to the administration of a deceased person. It did not, in this case, assume to take possession of the estate in the first instance; and it cannot, by entertaining jurisdiction of a suit against the administrator, draw to itself the full possession of the estate, or the power of determining all claims against it.

For the *Byers* Court, the power to administer decedents' estates was thought to derive from the power to appoint the administrator in the initial, often ex parte, constitutive proceeding to admit the will to probate. If, hypothetically, the federal courts were given original jurisdiction over the initial probate application, the Court suggests that they could probate the will and oversee the estate's administration. But lacking the power to hear the initial petition under jurisdictional grants that encompass only state-law controversies and confer no original federal probate jurisdiction, federal courts cannot take on the constitutive and administrative duties of the state courts.[9]

Once probate proceedings get underway in state court, moreover, rules of equitable priority may require a measure of federal deference. Just as an admiralty court proceeds in rem and brings the property in question within the custody of the court, so too do probate proceedings entail an assumption of in rem jurisdiction that brings the decedent's estate *in custodia legis*. Equitable priority protects the authority of the state court to administer such property, free from federal judicial interference. Thus, while federal courts were authorized to hear disputes between properly aligned parties as in *Gaines v. Fuentes*, *Byers* would block them from taking control over the administration of the probate estate.[10]

To summarize, one finds in nineteenth-century practice the outlines of an important and apparently coherent distinction in the work of the federal judiciary. Of course, one must always proceed cautiously when claiming to find coherence in the past; sometimes, historians furnish a clarity that would have been anything but obvious to those living through the period in question. Still, in word and deed, federal courts in the nineteenth century viewed themselves as empowered to adjudicate both the contested and uncontested matters of federal law that Congress assigned them. In contrast, as to matters of state law, the federal courts viewed their authority as more circumscribed, extending only to the resolution of disputes between properly aligned opponents. This broad distinction in the scope of judicial power seems to follow from the textual distinction between "cases" and "controversies" and explains the federal courts' willingness to accept naturalization work and their reluctance to admit wills to probate. The next part explains the transition from the settled views of nineteenth-century jurists to a twentieth-century world in which the Supreme Court chose to link the two broad sources of judicial power in a conjoined case-or-controversy requirement.

Notes

1. Susan Low Bloch, *The Early Role of the Attorney General in Our Constitutional Scheme*, 1989 Duke L.J. 561.
2. *See* Martin v. Hunter's Lessee, 14 U.S. 304 (1816). Cohens v. Virginia, 19 U.S. 264 (1821). Osborn v. Bank of the United States, 22 U.S. 738 (1824). For the quote, *see Cohens*, at 378.
3. *Martin*, 14 U.S. 304, 334, 347. *Id.*
4. *Osborn*, 22 U.S. 738 at 819. Marshall said much the same thing in *Marbury v. Madison*, 5 U.S. 137, 173–74 (1803), explaining that the judicial power "is expressly extended to all cases arising under the laws of the United States; and consequently, in some form, may be exercised over the present case; because the right claimed is given by a law of the United States." Here again, Marshall defines Article III "cases" as the assertion in "some form" of a "right claimed" under a "law of the United States." *See also* Weston v. City Council of Charleston, 27 U.S. (2 Pet.) 449, 464 (1829) (explaining that the term "suit" encompasses "any proceeding in a court of justice, by which an individual pursues that remedy . . . which the law affords him"); *Cohens*, at 408 (1821) (defining the term "suits" to include "all cases where the party suing claims to obtain something to which he has a right." Story, Commentaries on the Constitution, at 485. For both Marshall and Story, then, the key to a "case" was the assertion of a federal question claim of right in the form prescribed by law. *Id.*
5. Counsel for Virginia distinguished between self-executing constitutional provisions, such as the bill of attainder clause, and executory provisions, such as the provision for the adoption of uniform laws of naturalization. For counsel, then, cases "arising under the constitution, are those which arise under its self-executing provisions; and those arising under the laws of the United States, are those which occur under some law, passed in virtue of the executory provisions of the constitution." *Cohens*, at 292. For Marshall's rejection of the argument, *see id.* at 379 ("If [the Commonwealth's invocation of the naturalization example] be to maintain that a case arising under the

constitution, or a law, must be one in which a party comes into Court to demand something conferred on him by the constitution or a law, we think the construction too narrow. A case in law or equity consists of the right of the one party, as well as of the other.").

6. Chief Justice Marshall flatly rejected the argument that ex parte judicial proceedings to naturalize were merely ministerial and did not enjoy the conclusive quality of matters of record. *See* Spratt v. Spratt, 29 U.S. (4 Pet.) 393, 402 (1830) (argument of counsel) (contending that naturalization proceedings were not judicial but merely "ministerial"; that there were no parties to the proceeding but that instead "[a]ll is ex parte"). For the rejection of that argument, quoted in the text, *see id.* at 408. *See also* McCarthy v. Marsh, 5 N.Y. 263 (1851) (viewing the judgment of naturalization by the court of record as conclusive); Campbell v. Gordon, 10 U.S. (6 Cranch) 176 (1810) (same).
7. Gaines v. Fuentes, 92 U.S. 10, 18, 21–22 (1875). The majority in *Gaines* implied that any exception to federal jurisdiction in matters of probate was statutory, but Justice Joseph Bradley in dissent was far more specific, declaring that the statutory grant of federal diversity jurisdiction extended only to suits in law and equity, and that probate matters were not included in this grant because they were resolved in ecclesiastical courts, not those of law or equity:

   Now, the phrase, "suits at common law and in equity," . . . must be construed to embrace all litigations between party and party which in the English system of jurisprudence, under the light of which the Judiciary Act, as well as the Constitution, was framed, were embraced in all the various forms of procedure carried on in the ordinary law and equity courts, as distinguished from the ecclesiastical, admiralty, and military courts of the realm. . . . This court has in repeated instances expressly said that the probate of wills and the administration of estates do not belong to the jurisdiction of the Federal courts under the grant of jurisdiction contained in the Judiciary Act; and it may, without qualification, be stated, that no respectable authority, in the profession or on the bench, has ever contended for any such jurisdiction. . . . The controversy is not of that sort or nature which belongs to the category of a suit at law or in equity, as those terms were used in the Judiciary Act.

   Id. at 24–25 (Bradley, J., dissenting). Justice Bradley was careful to say that contested probate proceedings could constitutionally be removed to federal court should Congress pass a new statute conferring diversity jurisdiction over controversies without the law and equity restriction. *Id.*
8. Ellis v. Davis, 109 U.S. 485, 497 (1883). "The original probate, of course, is mere matter of state regulation, and depends entirely upon the local law; for it is that law which confers the power of making wills, and prescribes the conditions upon which alone they may take effect." *Id. See also* O'Callaghan v. O'Brien, 199 U.S. 89, 110 (1905) (distinguishing pure probate from *inter partes* proceedings).
9. Byers v. McAuley, 149 U.S. 608 (1893). *Id.* at 619.

10. On the rules of equitable priority as they developed in the context of federal-state concurrent jurisdiction, *see* Pfander & Nazemi, *The Anti-Injunction Act and the Problem of Federal-State Jurisdictional Overlap*. On the power of the federal courts to hear friendly equitable receivership petitions, *see In re* Metro. Ry. Receivership, 208 U.S. at 90, 107 (1908). *See generally* Pfander & Birk, *Article III Judicial Power*. Later decisions acknowledge that federal power to adjudicate controversies relating to probate may exhaust the assets in the decedent's estate and, as a practical matter, displace much of the state court's administrative role. *See* Markham v. Allen, 326 U.S. 490 (1946).

PART II

ANTITHESIS: THE PROGRESSIVE RESTATEMENT OF AN EMERGING CASE-OR-CONTROVERSY REQUIREMENT

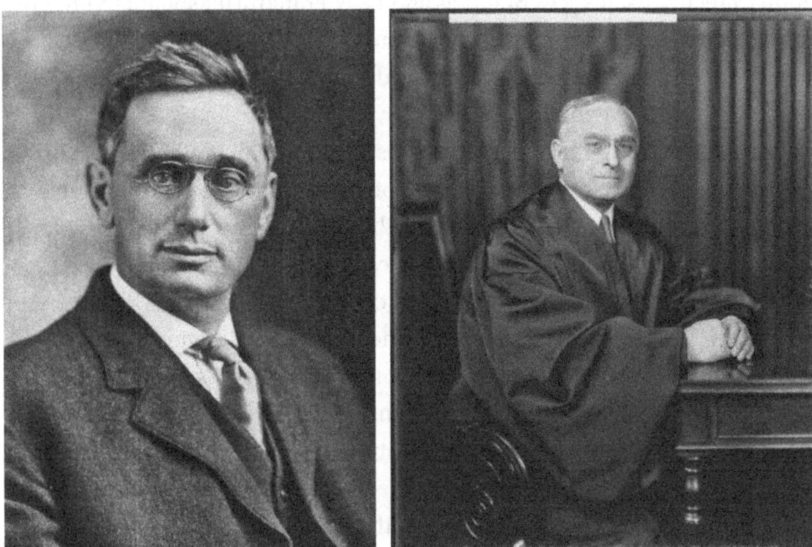

Image: Brandeis and Frankfurter: The Progressive Justices
Associate Justices Louis Brandeis (1916–39) and Felix Frankfurter (1939–62) worked together on many law reform projects. By 1940, they had largely succeeded in their efforts to restrict the exercise of judicial power. But by linking Article III's distinct provisions into an all-purpose "case-or-controversy" requirement, the reformers created a framework that many now see as incompatible with uncontested adjudication.
Photo credit-Brandeis: Harris & Ewing.
Photo credit-Frankfurter: Harris & Ewing.

To help illuminate the way progressives reworked justiciability doctrine into today's case-or-controversy requirement, this part begins by describing the law they inherited: a new body of jurisdictional law that emerged during the *Lochner* era. In seeking to avoid judicial entanglements in administrative work, the *Lochner* Court applied jurisdictional restrictions rooted in the case-or-controversy language of Article III in an effort to forestall some forms of direct judicial review. By thus awaiting completion of the administrative process, *Lochner*-era jurists hoped to preserve a post-hoc de novo model of judicial review. At the same time, the *Lochner* Court considerably broadened the power of federal courts sitting in equity to oversee the constitutionality of state and federal government activity.

Progressives redefined the case-or-controversy requirement to restrict access to *Lochner*-style constitutional adjudication. Building on turn-of-the-century precursors, Justices Brandeis and Felix Frankfurter sought to limit the law-saying capacity of the federal courts and the expansive potential of *Ex parte Young*—the 1908 decision that broadened the power of federal courts to enjoin pending or threatened constitutional violations. By the 1940s, the modern case-or-controversy requirement was an established feature of American law.

Although the progressive makeover of justiciability seems inexorable in retrospect, one can sense its novelty in the brilliant and learned dissents of Professor Edwin Borchard. Borchard argued passionately in favor of the declaratory judgment as a tool state and federal courts could use to clarify uncertain legal rights. In the course of defending the declaratory judgment as a proper exercise of judicial power, he noted with some dismay the way an evolving conception of the case-or-controversy rule in the hands of the progressives had undermined recognized forms of adjudication. His work helps us better see the way progressive and New Deal jurists redefined the scope of judicial power to correspond with their evolving notions of the proper limits of the judicial role.

Following the consolidation of the progressive restatement, traditional uncontested adjudicatory practices of the federal judiciary have frequently collided with the new case-or-controversy learning of the early twentieth century. Indeed, federal judicial power over a surprisingly large range of proceedings—including naturalization petitions, habeas applications, bankruptcy petitions, and warrant proceedings—has been challenged on the theory that the petitions in question do not qualify as cases. That tension persists to this day. Federal appellate courts occasionally deny review of uncontested matters in the district courts on the basis that they do not qualify as cases or controversies, but the Supreme Court has so far yet to embrace so restrictive a view of the judicial role.

5

The Judicial Response to the Administrative State

The seeds of the modern case-or-controversy requirement were sown in the latter half of the nineteenth century in a decision by Justice Stephen Field, resisting a judicial role in enforcing the subpoenas of a federal commission charged with investigating Leland Stanford and the Pacific Railroad. Over time, as the demand for contestation took hold, the Supreme Court limited the adjudication of feigned or collusive cases and refused to oversee some forms of administrative activity. The Court also developed a body of standing law, in part to cabin the potentially transformative implications of the *Lochner*-era decision in *Ex parte Young*. Together, these doctrinal innovations ripened into modern restrictions that we know today as the case-or-controversy requirement of Article III.

5.1 The Field Theory of Contestation

Justice Field was no stranger to innovation and no friend to government regulation. His brother, David Dudley Field, had pioneered the codification of the Field code, merging law and equity into a single cause of action and anticipating the "one civil action" that would later emerge in the 1938 adoption of the federal procedural rules. Justice Field himself was a leading architect of the doctrine of substantive due process, urging use of the Fourteenth Amendment as a shield against excessive government regulation of private enterprise. Although Field left the Court nearly a decade before *Lochner* came down in 1905, he was quite sympathetic to the impulse behind that decision. Indeed, worried that a federal commission would invade the privacy interests of railroads, Field introduced the idea of contestation to the definition of "cases" under federal law as a way to block federal courts from enforcing the commission's subpoenas.[1]

Cases Without Controversies. James E. Pfander, Oxford University Press. © James E. Pfander 2021.
DOI: 10.1093/oso/9780197571408.003.0006

Justice Field rose to political and judicial prominence in California, where he served on the state supreme court before his appointment to the Supreme Court in 1863. Notable for his dissent in the *Slaughterhouse Cases*, which urged judicial invalidation of economic regulation of New Orleans meat processors, Field also wrote a number of opinions for the Supreme Court that helped to define the scope of federal judicial power. But one might argue that Field made his most lasting contribution to modern understandings of the meaning of Article III in his capacity as the Circuit Justice for California. In 1887, the U.S. attorney for San Francisco sought the enforcement of a subpoena that proposed to compel the Pacific Railway and its president, Leland Stanford, to answer questions about the disbursement of certain railroad funds. The subpoena had been issued by the Pacific Railway Commission, a board created by an Act of Congress to investigate railroad activities. Although Congress had empowered the commission to invoke the subpoena power of the federal courts to compel the production of evidence and testimony by the parties in question, Circuit Justice Field held in *In re Pacific Railway Commission* that federal courts had no power to play this role. For Justice Field, the business of issuing a subpoena was a distinctly judicial function to be undertaken by the federal courts only in the resolution of cases and controversies that were before the courts themselves. Administrative and legislative investigations were to be handled by and through the established officers and procedures of those bodies. Only when the executive branch was ready to initiate claims against the railroad, through some sort of enforcement proceeding, would the federal courts have authority to issue subpoenas and compel testimony.[2]

Justice Field's account of the connection between "cases" and "controversies" reads as follows:

> The judicial article of the [C]onstitution mentions cases and controversies. The term "controversies," if distinguishable at all from "cases," is so in that it is less comprehensive than the latter, and includes only suits of a civil nature. By cases and controversies are intended the claims of litigants brought before the courts for determination by such regular proceedings as are established by law or custom for the protection or enforcement of rights, or the prevention, redress, or punishment of wrongs. Whenever the claim of a party under the constitution, laws, or treaties of the United States takes such a form that the judicial power is capable of acting upon it, then it has

become a case. *The term implies the existence of present or possible adverse parties whose contentions are submitted to the court for adjudication.*

Note the move here. Justice Field first suggested the broad similarity of the terms "cases" and "controversies." Then, after restating and expanding the nineteenth-century Marshall-Story definition, Field argued that the term "case" must imply the existence of present or possible adverse parties, whose contentions are submitted to the court for adjudication.[3]

Having restated the definition of a "case" to require present or possible adversaries, Field came to the nub of his opinion. Railroads and their presidents were said to have a privacy interest in their books and papers that Congress had no power to invade through compelled production. How, then, could Congress secure those books and papers through reliance on the federal judiciary? Field explained that "the court, when its aid is invoked, should examine the subject of the inquiries to see their character, so as to be able to determine the propriety and pertinency of the questions, and the propriety and necessity of producing the books, papers, and documents asked for before the commission." But the court could play such an oversight role only in one of two capacities: in the exercise of "advisory functions in an administrative or political proceeding" or in the "exercise [of] judicial power." Field argued that advisory functions could not be assigned to the federal courts. Hence, "the power can only be exercised in the cases or controversies enumerated in the constitution, or in cases of habeas corpus." But no such case or controversy was present before the court. Thus, the "provision of the act authorizing the courts to aid in the investigation in the manner indicated must therefore be adjudged void."[4]

To see the novelty of this claim, compare Field's account with that articulated a few years earlier in lectures on federal jurisdiction that the former Supreme Court Justice, Benjamin Curtis, delivered at Harvard. Published in 1880, and soon a leading treatment of federal jurisdictional law, Curtis's lectures essentially restated the Marshall-Story conception of cases and controversies. Curtis explained in his first lecture that when the Constitution speaks of "cases," it refers to "a subject on which the judicial power is capable of acting, and which has been submitted to it by a party—that is, one who is interested in the subject—in the forms required by law." In discussing jurisdiction over controversies on the basis of party alignment in a later lecture, Curtis asked "to what parties, then, by reason of their character, does the jurisdiction of the Circuit Courts extend?" Both formulations track the

Marshall-Story account and their separate treatment belies any sense that the terms were thought to form a single case-or-controversy requirement. The Curtis lectures appear to confirm that, writing seven years later, Justice Field broke new ground.[5]

One can also see a reflection of the novelty of Field's case-or-controversy requirement in his attempt to distinguish other recognized proceedings from the railroad subpoenas under consideration. He first considered letters rogatory, which call upon the courts of one country to "furnish assistance" to the courts of another country "by taking the testimony of witnesses to be used in the foreign country." Such proceedings bear an obvious resemblance to those in support of investigations. But Justice Field found that letters rogatory were effectively issued at the behest of foreign nations who were invoking rights of comity in the courts of another sovereign; he found that a "mere investigating commission" cannot call comity to its aid. Justice Field also rejected as unpersuasive a proposed analogy to the power of the federal courts to aid in the proceedings of grand juries. He acknowledged that, in support of such proceedings, federal courts can issue process, compel the attendance of witnesses, and hold those who refuse to cooperate in contempt. But Field viewed these proceedings as part of the broader role of federal courts in resolving cases that arise from the prosecution or indictment of individuals before a grand jury; federal jurisdiction "necessarily covers all proceedings taken from the formal commencement of such cases and controversies to the execution of the judgments rendered therein."[6]

One might fairly question the cogency of Field's distinctions. Whether acting to support a federal investigation of a railroad or a foreign tribunal's proceeding through letters rogatory, the federal courts would play a role limited to overseeing the collection of evidence; they would not bear responsibility for resolving the dispute to which the evidence has been deemed relevant. One can, of course, see differences between the investigative goals of federal commissioners and the courts of foreign nations, but those differences do not affect the nature of the judicial function in collecting evidence. In both instances, the courts have been called upon to support an inquiry unfolding before another forum rather than to conduct the proceeding themselves. Field would allow the federal judiciary to play this role for a foreign court, but not for a domestic commission. As for grand jury proceedings, Field correctly identified the traditional willingness of the federal courts to play a supporting role. But while the Fifth Amendment requires that grand jury indictments precede any federal prosecution for serious crime, grand jury investigations need not lead to indictments and prosecutions. One can easily imagine federal judicial enforcement of grand jury subpoenas that do not produce any subsequent case or controversy. The judicial role thus occurs in the shadow of potential, rather than actual, contestation.[7]

Justice Field's opposition to a federal judicial role in administrative subpoena enforcement did not take hold. The Court later ruled that applications for such subpoenas were proper subjects of judicial cognizance, and the federal courts today oversee the enforcement of administrative subpoenas without raising Article III doubts. Yet Justice Field's reformulation of the Marshall-Story definition of a "case," shifting from one that contemplates ex parte applications to one that requires "present or possible adverse parties," has had greater influence. When the Court later rejected Field's view of administrative subpoenas, three Justices dissented substantially on the grounds stated in his circuit court opinion. Later, Justice Field introduced the case-controversy conjunction into Supreme Court jurisprudence in *Smith v. Adams* in 1889, restating his own words from *Pacific Railway*: "By those terms are intended the claims or contentions of litigants brought before the courts for adjudication by regular proceedings established for the protection or enforcement of rights, or the prevention, redress, or punishment of wrongs." Although one can certainly read Field's restatement to preserve the core distinction between claims and disputes, he had permanently introduced the idea of contestation into Article III's definition of "cases."[8]

Twenty years later, in *Muskrat v. United States*, the Court recited the "present or possible adverse parties" idea from *Pacific Railway* in the course of refusing to issue what it perceived as a congressional request for an improper advisory opinion on an issue of constitutional law. The case arose after Congress enlarged the number of tribal members who were to participate in a land allotment, and thereby reduced the size of the stake of the original members of the group. When litigation was later filed seeking to enjoin the Interior Department from enforcing the later legislation, Congress authorized certain tribal members to challenge their reduced allotment by suing the United States in the Court of Claims. When that suit was dismissed, the tribal members sought review under a provision of the law authorizing direct appeal to the Supreme Court. The Court held that the matter lay beyond the power of the Article III judiciary. In the Court's view, Congress was simply seeking an advisory opinion as to the constitutionality of the subsequent legislation, whereas the resolution of constitutional questions was limited to disputes between adverse parties. Notably, one year later, the Court addressed the constitutional issue in the more familiar context of adversary litigation between tribal members and the Interior Department.[9]

5.2 The Rise of *Lochner*-Style Adjudication

Having taken root, the case-or-controversy requirement has displayed remarkable tenacity as a limit on federal adjudication. On occasion, the Supreme Court has deployed case-or-controversy limits to narrow access to equitable relief from unlawful government activity, access that the Court had considerably expanded in *Ex parte Young*. (Announced just three years after the 1905 decision in *Lochner*, *Ex parte Young* authorizes a federal district court to enjoin state actors from the threatened or continued enforcement of an unconstitutional state law.) On other occasions, the Court's justiciability limits were designed to preserve a certain judicial distance from direct oversight of the work of the burgeoning administrative state. Justiciability was thus a tool the Court used to preserve a measure of continuity with the nineteenth-century private-rights model of litigation. That was, after all, the functional effect of the insistence on adverse parties in *Pacific Railway* and *Muskrat*. Those decisions did not foreclose judicial involvement but insisted that it occur within the context of more conventional judicial proceedings.[10]

One can see the commitment to the conventional private-rights model of litigation in the *Lochner* Court's approach to the judicial review of administrative action. *Ex parte Young* opened up a potentially broad scope of judicial activity, enabling the federal district courts to entertain suits to enjoin state (and federal) government activity that exceeded constitutional limits. The implied right of action, a creature of federal equity, was made available to litigants, even where the government did not threaten to invade core common law property or liberty rights. Individuals who questioned the legality of government programs could, at least in theory, mount suits to enjoin their operation. The development of standing law reflects a desire to moderate the disruptive force of so potent a judicial tool. Thus, in *Frothingham v. Mellon*, the Court unanimously refused to allow a plaintiff to bring suit, as a taxpayer, to block a federal spending program that was alleged to have exceeded congressional power. Unlike the railroad in *Ex parte Young*, the Court viewed the taxpayer in *Frothingham* as less the particular target of the government's regulatory efforts than as an interested bystander.[11]

Apart from standing limits, the Court for a time refused to allow Article III courts to play a role in the direct review of administrative activity. Consider, for example, the Court's decision in a 1927 trademark dispute over the names of competing breakfast cereals. The owner of the "Grape Nuts" trademark petitioned a federal agency to block a competitor from securing a mark in the term "Fig Nuts." After unsuccessfully challenging the agency's rejection of its claim in the District of Columbia courts, the petitioner sought review in the Supreme Court. The Court refused to exercise appellate jurisdiction on the ground that the D.C. court, a non–Article III tribunal, was overseeing the administrative process, and was not engaged in the judicial task of resolving cases and controversies. Once the administrative process had run its course, the Grape Nuts owner could bring suit seeking de novo review of the agency decision. Other cases from the same period took a similarly restrictive view of the propriety of direct judicial review of administrative proceedings.[12]

In an article that discusses the eventual twentieth-century rise of an appellate review model of judicial oversight of the administrative state, Professor Thomas Merrill usefully characterizes these early decisions as seeking to ward off the contamination of the judicial power. On Merrill's account, the Supreme Court during this period was worried that direct oversight of agency action might draw the federal courts too deeply into making the policy and other decisions that lie at the heart of agency processes. To prevent the courts from being contaminated by close association, the Court preferred judicial review through de novo applications to set aside the results of the agency process. Such de novo review, often through suits for injunctive relief comparable to that in *Ex parte Young*, would preserve the power of federal courts to make the factual record on which the constitutional validity of economic regulation was thought to depend. Only later, according to Merrill, would the Court deploy Article III as a way to restrict agency adjudication and preserve the oversight role of federal judiciary.[13]

One can see some continuing commitment to de novo review of agency action reflected as late as 1932 in *Crowell v. Benson*, where the Court was at pains to preserve the right of a regulated party to bring suit to enjoin the enforcement of an agency's decision at least as to certain issues of law and fact. But as Merrill shows, the Court had largely made its peace with direct review of agency action a few years earlier, in *Old Colony Trust*. There, the Court upheld the power of a federal court to review an administrative decision by the board of tax appeals. The statute in question authorized the board to make an initial decision about disputed tax liability, subject to the right of either party to petition the federal court to review and overturn the decision. The Court held that such petitions properly invoke the judicial power, inasmuch as they presented a case between adverse parties within the meaning of the case-or-controversy requirement. So long as the requirements of finality and party adversity have been met, the Court deemed it unnecessary "that the proceeding[,] to be judicial[,] must be entirely de novo."[14]

Despite its growing devotion to the requirement of party-contestation as a measure of judicial cognizability, the Court continued to entertain a collection of friendly suits that seem hard to square with a thoroughgoing adverse-party requirement. Lawyers for regulated firms displayed customary creativity in fashioning forms of litigation designed to frame constitutional challenges to state or federal laws. In *Smith v. Kansas City Title & Trust*, for example, lawyers brought suit on behalf of a shareholder to restrain the trust company defendant from investing its funds in federal farm loan bonds, a tax-exempt security. The point of the enterprise was to set up a test of the constitutionality of farm credit legislation, which effectively created a new federal bank to make loans to farmers.[15]

Similar forms of friendly "private" litigation were a commonplace of the *Lochner* era, and a frequent source of concern for progressive lawyers and jurists. Progressives worried in particular that such suits allowed private parties to challenge the constitutionality of state and federal laws without naming and joining the governments that had enacted the laws and had a logical interest in defending their legality. As the next chapter explains, the progressive distaste for *Lochner* helped to animate a progressive distrust of friendly or collusive suits and to consolidate the adverse-party requirement as a tool with which to resist such litigation.[16]

Notes

1. On the merger of law and equity in the Field code and the Federal Rules of Civil Procedure, *see* Kellen Funk, *The Union of Law and Equity: The United States, 1800–1938*, *in* LAW AND EQUITY: FUSION AND FISSION 46–69 (John C.P. Goldberg et al. eds., 2019). According to Robert A. Mikos, "Congress has enacted more than 300 administrative subpoena statutes, grant[ing] some form of administrative subpoena authority to most federal agencies." Robert A. Mikos, *Can the States Keep Secrets from the Federal Government?*, 161 U. PA. L. REV. 103, 117 (2012) (alteration in original) (internal quotation marks omitted). For a sample of such laws, *see* 29 U.S.C. §§ 161(1)–(2) (2012) (conferring subpoena power on the National Labor Relations Board to

compel testimony and the production of documentary evidence and authorizing NLRB to seek judicial enforcement in case of a refusal to comply with the subpoena).

2. Field's dissent in the *Slaughterhouse Cases*, 83 U.S. 36, 83–111 (1872) (Field, J., dissenting), foreshadowed the Court's later approach to substantive due process in the *Lochner* era: "The question presented is . . . nothing less than the question whether the recent amendments to the Federal Constitution protect the citizens of the United States against the deprivation of their common rights by State legislation. In my judgment the fourteenth amendment does afford such protection." *Id.* at 90. For the administrative subpoena case, *see In re* Pac. Ry. Comm'n, 32 F. 241 (C.C.N.D. Cal. 1887). Field thus distinguished the supervision of grand jury proceedings, which often lead to the issuance of issuance of investigative subpoenas, on the basis that those proceedings were an inherent part of the process of adjudicating criminal charges against a certain class of offenders and necessitated judicial support and oversight. *Id.* at 257 n.2. For years, Congress enforced its own subpoenas by arresting those who refused to appear as witnesses. *See, e.g.*, Kilbourn v. Thompson, 103 U.S. 168, 205 (1880) (recognizing that while the legislative body enjoys immunity for the wrongful arrest of a prospective witness, the executive officer of the body or sergeant-at-arms would face personal liability for wrongful imprisonment). Justice Field drew this conclusion from the Court's handling of veterans' disability claims, from the decision denying the legality of their work as commissioners, and from Chief Justice Taney's interpretation of these events as foreclosing nonfinal judicial administration in *United States v. Ferreira*, 54 U.S. (13 How.) 40, 52–53 (1851).
3. *In re* Pac. Ry. Comm'n, 32 F. 241 at 255 (emphasis added) (citations omitted).
4. *Id.* at 258. Invoking the "administrative" character of the proceeding, Justice Field may be read as criticizing the non-finality of a judicial decree that would produce evidence for use by Congress. Such non-finality might trigger concerns comparable to those that troubled the Justices in *Hayburn's Case*, as discussed more fully in Sections 9.2 and 11.1.2. Yet the judicial decision would have operated as a conclusive determination of the government's right to the evidence in question and thus satisfy finality. What came later, in Congress or elsewhere, would not undermine finality.
5. Benjamin R. Curtis, Jurisdiction, Practice, and Peculiar Jurisprudence of the Courts of the United States (2d ed. 1896). For Curtis's definition of "cases," *see id.* at 11–12. For his treatment of controversies, *see id.* at 14–15.
6. Justice Field distinguished the subpoena enforcement surrounding grand jury proceedings from the administrative subpoenas at issue on the ground that grand juries were required by the Fifth Amendment. *In re* Pac. Ry. Comm'n, 32 F. 241 at 257 n.2. He distinguished letters rogatory on the ground that a controversy was pending on the docket of a foreign tribunal; and he distinguished petitions for habeas corpus relief, treating them as an exception to the Article III adverse-party requirement. *See id.* at 255 & n.1, 256–57 & n.2. Field's approach may have been driven by an antipathy to the regulatory power of the commission and a desire to protect federal dockets from administrative-agency support functions.
7. On the role of federal grand juries in the early Republic, *see* Renee B. Lettow, Note, *Reviving Federal Grand Jury Presentments*, 103 Yale L.J. 1333 (1994). The author

reports that grand juries returned both indictments (signed, and perhaps initiated, by the prosecutor) and presentments. *Id.* at 1337–40. Presentments could include general statements of grievances against officials of the federal government, some of which might never become indictments and never lead to any criminal case in federal court. *Id.* at 1338–39 (reporting on presentments in the nature of grievances against federal officials). Early federal courts took the position that they lacked jurisdiction over criminal matters except as properly founded on a grand jury indictment. *See* Roger A. Fairfax Jr., *The Jurisdictional Heritage of the Grand Jury Clause*, 91 MINN. L. REV. 398, 413 (2006). Although Justice Field made no mention of the fact, federal courts during the early Republic were sometimes called upon to play a supportive role in gathering evidence for the use of Congress. In a law enacted in 1798, Congress authorized Canadian refugees, displaced by their support for American forces during the Revolutionary War, to perfect their claims to the land bounties promised them by the Continental Congress. *See* Act for the Relief of Refugees, April 7, 1798, ch. XXVI, 1 Stat. 547. The statute provided for the refugees to present their claims to the war office, but to support their claims by having their proof "taken" by judges of the federal or state courts. *See id.* at §§ 2, 3. For an account of the eventual distribution of lands in Ohio to the refugees, *see* C.M. Layton, *Canadian Refugee Lands in Ohio*, 24 CAN. HIST. REV. 377 (1943).

8. *See* Interstate Commerce Comm'n v. Brimson, 154 U.S. 447 (1894) (upholding power of Article III court to issue subpoena to enforce obligation of a regulated railroad to comply with agency's request for information). Smith v. Adams, 130 U.S. 167, 173 (1889). The conjunction gained wider currency thereafter, appearing in *Tregea v. Modesto Irrigation District*, 164 U.S. 179, 185 (1896), and *La Abra Silver Mining Co. v. United States*, 175 U.S. 423, 456 (1899), before taking hold completely in twentieth-century doctrine. *In re* Pac. Ry. Comm'n, 32 F. 241.
9. Muskrat v. United States, 219 U.S. 346, 357 (1911). *Id.* at 361–62 (refusing, despite express congressional authority, to address the constitutionality of a statute that reallocated land rights conferred in earlier law). *Id.* at 348–50. That the case lay beyond the power of Article III courts would not necessarily defeat the jurisdiction of the court of claims, a legislative court. But the Court viewed the case as one entirely unsuited for resolution by the court of claims because it did not seek an award of damages for a taking of property or any other form of relief cognizable in the court of claims. Rather, it simply sought a decision as to constitutionality, as a prelude to further review in the Supreme Court under a statute that conferred as-of-right appellate review. *See id.* at 350 (conferring a "right of appeal" on either party to obtain final decision in the Supreme Court). Because the Court viewed the preliminary action in the court of claims as inseparable from Congress's desire to procure a determination by the Court, it chose to invalidate the statute in its entirety and directed the court of claims (which had reached the merits) to dismiss for want of jurisdiction. *Id.* at 363.
10. *Ex parte* Young, 209 U.S. 123 (1908). The decision has been conventionally understood to establish two principles, that the railroad has a right to sue to enjoin the state attorney general in his official capacity from enforcing unconstitutional rates and that

such an officer suit does not violate the Eleventh Amendment as one against the state. *See* HART & WECHSLER 7TH at 927–35.

11. Frothingham v. Mellon, 262 U.S. 447 (1923). Other scholars have recognized *Frothingham*'s contribution to the development of a body of standing law. For accounts, *see* EVAN TSEN LEE, JUDICIAL RESTRAINT IN AMERICA: HOW THE AGELESS WISDOM OF THE FEDERAL COURTS WAS INVENTED (2011).
12. Postum Cereal Co. v. Cal. Fig Nut Co., 272 U.S. 693 (1927). *See* Keller v. Potomac Elec. Power Co., 261 U.S. 428 (1923); Fed. Radio Comm'n v. Gen. Elec. Co., 281 U.S. 461 (1930).
13. *See* Thomas W. Merrill, *Article III, Agency Adjudication, and the Origins of the Appellate Review Model of Administrative Law*, 111 COLUM. L. REV. 939 (2011).
14. Crowell v. Benson, 285 U.S. 22 (1932). Old Colony Trust Co. v. Comm'r of Internal Revenue, 279 U.S. 716 (1929).
15. Smith v. Kansas City Title & Trust Co., 255 U.S. 180 (1921).
16. Justice Brandeis identified a surprisingly large collection of similar suits in *Ashwander v. Tennessee Valley Authority*, 297 U.S. 288, 346 (1936) (Brandeis, J., concurring). *See, e.g.*, Chicago & Grand Trunk Ry. Co. v. Wellman, 143 U.S. 339, 345 (1892) ("It never was the thought that, by means of a friendly suit, a party beaten in the legislature could transfer to the courts an inquiry as to the constitutionality of the legislative act.").

6

The Progressive Response to *Lochner*: Limiting Justiciability

Justice Louis Brandeis and Professor Felix Frankfurter were not alone in theorizing the progressive response to these developments, but they were particularly influential. Appointed to the Supreme Court by President Woodrow Wilson, Brandeis had come to be known as the people's lawyer after a brilliant student career at Harvard and a successful legal practice in Boston. Frankfurter, a generation younger, had returned to Harvard to teach law, after his student days there and a stint in the Wilson administration. A public intellectual before that term had gained its modern currency, Frankfurter championed a broad array of progressive causes, including labor law reform and the innocence of Sacco and Vanzetti. Apart from his academic writing, Frankfurter wrote essays for the *New Republic* that commented, often critically, on Supreme Court decisions. His efforts to end conservative judicial activism included both substantive law reform and jurisdictional restriction. To end the labor injunction as a strike-breaking tool, Frankfurter drafted and urged the adoption of what became the Norris-LaGuardia Act. The Act banned the enforcement of yellow dog contracts and the issuance of labor injunctions and then, for good measure, deprived the federal courts of jurisdiction to entertain such claims.[1]

As Frankfurter understood the challenges of his day, federal jurisdiction conferred power on conservative courts: the power to declare the law and bring it to bear on social problems. If progressives had no authority by ordinary legislation to overturn Supreme Court decisions rooted in the Constitution, then perhaps they could achieve something similar by narrowing federal court power to adjudicate. By leaving matters to state courts or by transferring the front-line regulation of social issues to sympathetic experts in federal agencies, progressives might further blunt the impact of the Court's *Lochner*-izing. Progressives thus proposed jurisdictional solutions for a surprisingly broad slice of the problems they confronted. Judicial hostility to worker injury claims led progressives to support the

Cases Without Controversies. James E. Pfander, Oxford University Press. © James E. Pfander 2021.
DOI: 10.1093/oso/9780197571408.003.0007

creation of compensation boards and agencies; judicial hostility to union organizing led the progressives to propose new federal agencies and legislation depriving courts of their power to adjudicate; and judicial creation of general law to govern the commercial life of the nation eventually led to the decision in *Erie v. Tompkins*, compelling federal judicial deference to state law. This chapter sketches the progressive critique of judicial power, focusing on the way Justice Brandeis, and later Justice Frankfurter, restated a set of ideas aimed at restricting or channeling the process of constitutional adjudication.[2]

6.1 The Brandeis Critique

Justice Brandeis worked along several fronts to narrow the law-saying power of conservative federal courts. The *Erie* decision, needless to say, operated to deny the federal courts any authority to fashion general common law principles to govern matters that Brandeis and others viewed as the rightful province of the state courts. A second target was the Court's insistence on de novo review of agency decisions, a form of review from which Brandeis dissented in *Crowell* on the ground that it threatened to interfere with the policymaking authority Congress had vested in those staffing the agencies. A third target was the collusive action, contrived by private parties to set up a test of constitutionality that refrained from naming the governments themselves as parties.

An influential summary of these emerging doctrines, many of them rooted in claims about the nature of the judicial power, appears in Brandeis's well-known opinion in *Ashwander v. Tennessee Valley Authority*. Brandeis included on his list of concerns both the standing doctrine and the prohibition against the adjudication of collusive suits:

> The Court will not pass upon the constitutionality of legislation in a friendly, non-adversary, proceeding, declining because to decide such questions 'is legitimate only in the last resort, and as a necessity in the determination of real, earnest, and vital controversy between individuals. It never was the thought that, by means of a friendly suit, a party beaten in the legislature could transfer to the courts an inquiry as to the constitutionality of the legislative act.

Here, then, Brandeis gave voice to doctrines of judicial restraint, associated with Article III's "case-or-controversy" requirement. But notably, Brandeis did not regard these doctrines as constitutionally compelled by the terms of Article III. He explained that the rules in question were ones the Court had "developed, for its own governance in the cases confessedly within its jurisdiction." These were rules, in short, that the Court deployed to "avoid[] passing upon a large part of all the constitutional questions pressed upon it for decision."[3]

6.2 The Frankfurter Consolidation

Where Justice Brandeis gave voice to prudential limits on judicial power for the purpose of self-governance, Justice Frankfurter would later consolidate those restrictions and furnish a textual and historical predicate for their application. Thus, in 1930, Brandeis would question the power of the federal courts to issue declaratory judgments, worrying that such an authority could lead to the sort of feigned or collusive litigation he had hoped to quell. Although the Court would uphold the Declaratory Judgment Act of 1934, Justice Frankfurter would later impose a gloss on the statute that sharply restricted its potential to broaden the jurisdiction (and law-saying capacity) of the federal courts. Frankfurter also supplied an intellectual justification for judicial diffidence, portraying the doctrines of restraint as the well-accepted practices of the English courts at Westminster that were naturally incorporated into common law notions of justiciability in the United States and were reflected in the case-or-controversy provisions of Article III.[4]

The new progressive framework quickly took hold, gaining ground in Supreme Court decisions and finding a home in leading casebooks and treatises of the day, including (then-Professor) Frankfurter's own 1938 casebook on the law of federal jurisdiction. By 1941, the attorney general of the United States would explain matter-of-factly, in a report to Congress on judicial review of administrative action, that "judicial power" was to be exercised only in "cases and controversies." Drawn from "the text of article III," these words were said to imply the requirements "of parties in an adversary position who have 'legal standing' to maintain their positions and [of] 'justiciable' issues in such form that the judicial power is 'capable of acting on them.'" When the Hart and Wechsler casebook on the law of the federal courts appeared in 1953, the authors collected materials on standing, mootness, ripeness, adverse parties, political questions, and related matters in a chapter entitled "The Nature of the Judicial Function: Cases and Controversies." Future law professors and Supreme Court Justices would cut their teeth on Hart and Wechsler.[5]

One such professor and future Justice, Antonin Scalia, gave voice to the progressive consensus at the same time he highlighted the choice of language on which the Court had pegged its restrictions. Writing in a candid moment as a judge on the D.C. Circuit, Scalia identified an element of opportunism underlying the Court's use of the case-and-controversy requirement as a tool of restraint. He explained that Article III's standing requirement had been based upon the "case-or-controversy" formulation "for want of a better vehicle." It was "surely not a linguistically inevitable conclusion," but it was one that Judge Scalia nonetheless defended as "an accurate description of the sort of business courts had traditionally entertained." Judge Scalia thus followed the progressives in treating "cases" and "controversies" as a kind of textual hook or placeholder on which the Court has hung a considerable body of justiciability doctrine. He also embraced Frankfurter's claim that the doctrine legitimately limits federal courts to the forms of judicial work that Anglo-American courts traditionally performed.[6]

A few years later, Scalia would join the Court and play a central role in urging that the case-or-controversy rules of Article III should operate as constitutional constraints on the power of the federal courts. His 1992 decision in *Lujan v. Defenders of Wildlife* applied the case-or-controversy rules to invalidate a statutory grant of citizen standing to challenge government activity. In later cases, Justice Scalia consistently viewed the case-or-controversy limits as rooted in the Constitution. Thus, in *United States v. Windsor*, Scalia would describe the adverse-party requirement as a hard constitutional limit on the judicial power, rather than a prudential doctrine that the courts had simply invented. The Court had come a long way since *Ashwander* and the Brandeis depiction of the rules of justiciability as matters of judicial self-government rather than constitutional compulsion.[7]

6.3 The Borchard Dissent

Edwin Borchard, a professor at Yale Law School and a prolific and learned scholar, was well known for his work on declaratory judgments, wrongful incarceration, government liability in tort, and his "lifelong speciality," international law. He saw both the importance of federal judicial engagement with the problems of modern life and the way progressives had narrowed the potential scope of judicial authority with their adherence to the case-or-controversy dogma. In a strikingly prescient 1936 article, published in the same year as Brandeis's concurring opinion in *Ashwander*, Borchard described what the Court had done in the name of the *Muskrat* decision:

> This unfortunate case started a train of thought in the court directed toward great conservatism in adjudicating cases, and resulted in a narrow construction of the terms "cases" or "controversies." This was an incident of the increasing reluctance of the court to pass on constitutional questions. . . . The strict rules evolved in the court for the adjudication of constitutional questions were imperceptibly deemed to apply to all legal issues and have been so applied by state courts, thus narrowing unduly the judicial function as compared with the practice in other countries. Moreover, the various objections to adjudication, such as prematurity or mootness, inadequacy of party interest or inconclusiveness of the judgment were all read into the words "cases" or "controversies," thus overburdening those words with a bulging content making them ever more technical without necessarily dissipating their ambiguity. Most of the tests of justiciability were thus largely identified with the phrase "cases and controversies" so that the broad definitions of [the nineteenth century] are now almost unrecognizable. Apart from the traditional grounds for refusing to review administrative findings, to pass on political questions, or decide abstract, hypothetical, fictitious, non-adversary or moot cases, cases have in recent years been dismissed on the ground that the plaintiff's interest was inadequate or that the issue was not sufficiently concrete to justify adjudication.

Borchard thus identified two problems: the perception (also reflected in Judge Scalia's comment) that the case-controversy language has been assigned "a bulging content" and the view that doctrines, developed as tools to manage constitutional litigation, had evolved into across-the-board restrictions that unduly narrow the judicial function in more mundane matters.[8]

Borchard was writing in part to defend his handiwork, the Federal Declaratory Judgment Act of 1934 and the many state declaratory judgment statutes he had supported, from the threat of invalidation posed by the adverse-party rule. Borchard understood that judicial power, in both Roman and civilian legal systems, included the use of uncontested adjudication and the issuance of declaratory judgments. Indeed, in an earlier defense of declaratory practice, Borchard pointed to the example of the declarator action of the Scottish Court of Session, a civil-law jurisdiction. The adverse-party rule of *Muskrat*, broadened and misapplied, might deprive American jurisprudence of an extremely useful procedure. By the early 1930s, the threat seemed quite real; such cases as *Willing v. Chicago Auditorium Association* had raised substantial doubts as to the power of federal courts to issue declaratory judgments.[9]

Borchard successfully fended off challenges to the declaratory judgment; one year after his article appeared, the Court ruled in *Aetna Life Insurance v. Haworth* that the exercise of judicial power in such matters was consistent with Article III. Yet Borchard identified broader themes that run through this book. As matters of concern, he identified the drift away from nineteenth-century understandings; the assignment of steadily expanding doctrinal content to the case-or-controversy language; and the eventual use of the new learning to question the constitutionality of forms of adjudication that, at least when viewed from the perspective of history and traditional practice here and abroad, have a strong claim to legality. Sure enough, litigants and scholars have mounted a series of adverse-party challenges to familiar forms of uncontested adjudication. The next chapter describes these attacks, their broad lack of success to date, and their worrisome potential.[10]

Notes

1. The Norris-LaGuardia Act, ch. 90, 47 Stat. 70 (1932) (codified as amended at 29 U.S.C. §§ 101–15 (2018)). The Supreme Court upheld the Act in *Lauf v. E.G. Shinner & Co.*, 303 U.S. 323 (1938) (finding that "[t]here can be no question of the power of Congress" to limit the ability of federal district courts to grant labor injunctions). *See* Felix Frankfurter & Nathan Greene, The Labor Injunction (1930), for a survey of the history of the labor injunction and major cases prior to the passage of the Act (along with an argument for adopting the terms of the bill). For a thoughtful treatment of Frankfurter's thought and work, *see* Clyde W. Summers, *Frankfurter, Labor Law and the Judge's Function*, 67 Yale L.J. 266 (1957). On the history of labor injunctions, *see* William K. Briggs, *Deconstructing "Just and Proper": Arguments in Favor of Adopting the "Remedial Purpose" Approach to Section 10(j) Labor Injunction*, 110 Mich. L. Rev. 127 (2011) (focusing on the exceptions allowing district courts to issue labor injunctions).

2. *See Crowell*, 285 U.S. 22 (disputed award made by United States Employees' Compensation Commission under the Longshoremen's and Harbor Workers' Compensation Act 33 U.S.C.A. 901–50). Other examples of administrative bodies empowered to handle disputes include the National Labor Relations Board (created pursuant to 29 U.S.C. §§ 151–69 (2018)) and the Norris LaGuardia Act, 29 U.S.C. ch. 6. *Erie v. Tompkins*, 304 U.S. 64 (1938). *See also* EDWARD A. PURCELL, BRANDEIS AND THE PROGRESSIVE CONSTITUTION: *ERIE*, THE JUDICIAL POWER, AND THE POLITICS OF THE FEDERAL COURTS IN TWENTIETH-CENTURY AMERICA (2000).
3. *Ashwander*, 297 U.S. 288 at 346 (Brandeis, J., concurring) (quoting *Chicago & Grand Trunk Ry.*, 143 U.S. at 345). *Id.*
4. Federal Declaratory Judgment Act of 1934, Pub. L. No. 73-343, 48 Stat. 955. *See* Coleman v. Miller, 307 U.S. 433, 460 (1939) (opinion of Frankfurter, J.) ("Judicial power could come into play only in matters that were the traditional concern of the courts at Westminster. . . ."); *see also* Willing v. Chi. Auditorium Ass'n, 277 U.S. 274, 290 (1928) (noting in Justice Brandeis's majority opinion that a resort to equity when no case or controversy existed was "a proceeding which was unknown to . . . English . . . courts").
5. HENRY M. HART JR. & HERBERT WECHSLER, THE FEDERAL COURTS AND THE FEDERAL SYSTEM 75–217 (1st ed. 1953).
6. Antonin Scalia, *The Doctrine of Standing as an Essential Element of the Separation of Powers*, 17 SUFFOLK U.L. REV. 881, 882 (1983).
7. Lujan v. Defenders of Wildlife, 504 U.S. 555 (1992). For an example of a later Scalia opinion arguing for limits on Congress, *see* Fed. Election Comm'n v. Akins, 524 U.S. 11, 29 (1998) (Scalia, J., dissenting). *See Windsor*, 570 U.S. 744 at 786 (Scalia, J., dissenting) (characterizing the adverse-party requirement not as a prudential requirement "that we have invented," but as an "essential element of an Article III case or controversy").
8. Edwin Borchard was memorialized posthumously in a volume of the *Yale Law Journal*, where his colleague and friend Charles Clark (himself a judge on the Second Circuit) wrote a tribute. Charles E. Clark, *Edwin Borchard*, 60 YALE L.J. 1071–72 (1951). For another short biography, *see* Herbert W. Briggs, *In Memoriam: Edwin M. Morchard, 1884–1951*, 45 AM. J. INT'L L. 708–09 (1951). Borchard contributed to a wide range of subjects, including the legality of declaratory judgments, *The Next Step beyond Equity: The Declaratory Action*, 13 U. CHI. L. REV. 145 (1946); *The Constitutionality of Declaratory Judgments*, 31 COLUM. L. REV. 561 (1931); government liability in tort, *Government Liability in Tort* (pts. 1–3), 34 YALE L.J. 129, 229 (1924); criminal justice reform, EDWIN M. BORCHARD, CONVICTING THE INNOCENT: ERRORS OF CRIMINAL JUSTICE (1932); and international law, *Treaty-Making Power as Support for Federal Legislation*, 29 YALE L.J. 445 (1920); *Shall the Executive Agreement Replace the Treaty?*, 53 YALE L.J. 664 (1944). Quoted passage appears in Borchard, *Justiciability*, 4 U. CHI. L. REV. 1, 4–5 (1936). Borchard was a progressive and an activist, advocating for criminal justice reform, serving on the ACLU's national committee, and publicly "signing on" to the amicus brief in *Korematsu v. United States*, 323 U.S. 214 (1944). Marvin

Zalman, *Edwin Borchard's Innocence Project: The Origin and Legacy of His Wrongful Conviction Scholarship*, 1 WRONGFUL CONVICTION L.R. 124, 132 (2020).

9. Declaratory Judgment Act, Pub. L. No. 73-343, 48 Stat. 955. Willing v. Chicago Auditorium Ass'n, 277 U.S. 274, 288 (1928) (Brandeis, J.) (refusing to allow exercise of equity jurisdiction over bill to remove cloud on title and casting doubt on the power of federal courts to issue declaratory judgments; finding that the defendants were not alleged to have committed any "hostile act or threat" or to have done anything which "hampered the full enjoyment of the present use and occupancy" of the premises).
10. *See Aetna Life Ins. Co.*, 300 U.S. 227 (1937).

7
The New Adverse-Party Rule Confronts Judicial Practice

After the adverse-party idea took hold at the dawn of the twentieth century, litigants wasted little time in contending that certain judicial practices failed the new dispensation. This chapter catalogs the various challenges that have arisen over the course of the past century. It begins with the government's challenge to appellate review of naturalization petitions during the 1920s and concludes with latter-day challenges to the FISA court's warrant practices and the uncontested adjudication of certain fee waiver requests. Lower courts sometimes go astray, but the Supreme Court has almost always upheld longstanding judicial practices against adverse party challenges.

7.1 *Tutun* and Naturalization

In *Tutun v. United States*, the Court would resolve a division in the lower courts as to whether a district court order adjudicating a naturalization petition was subject to appellate review. The relevant statute empowered the federal appellate courts to hear appeals from final decisions in "all cases." When his application for citizenship was denied, Tutun appealed. The government argued that his petition for naturalization was not a case within the meaning of the statute and thus did not come within the scope of appellate review.[1]

Rather than limit the analysis to the statutory language, Justice Brandeis's opinion tackled the more fundamental issue of how to define "cases" within the meaning of Article III. Thus, Justice Brandeis adverted to the fact that the congressional practice of assigning naturalization proceedings to the federal courts had begun in the 1790s and had never been questioned. What's more, Brandeis noted that "[i]f the proceeding were not a case or controversy within the meaning of Art[icle] III, § 2, this delegation of power upon the courts would have been invalid." Accompanying citation of authority clearly reveals that Brandeis saw no problem under the finality requirement of the

Cases Without Controversies. James E. Pfander, Oxford University Press. © James E. Pfander 2021.
DOI: 10.1093/oso/9780197571408.003.0008

1792 decision(s) collected in *Hayburn's Case* or under the non-advisory rule stated in *The Correspondence of the Justices* and later applied in *Muskrat v. United States*. Indeed, he recognized two possible obstacles to finality—the prospect of a second petition following the denial of the first and the prospect of a suit by the government to cancel a certificate of citizenship. Accepting these forms of judicial review of naturalization orders, Brandeis nonetheless concluded that an order granting or denying a petition for naturalization is "clearly a final decision."[2]

Next, Brandeis considered arguments that the practice of naturalization was essentially an administrative action and thus unfit for judicial cognizance. In evaluating the nature of the proceeding, Brandeis explained that citizenship under the naturalization law was no mere privilege:

> The applicant for citizenship, like other suitors who institute proceedings in a court of justice to secure the determination of an asserted right, must allege in his petition the fulfillment of all conditions upon the existence of which the alleged right is made dependent; and he must establish these allegations by competent evidence to the satisfaction of the court. In passing upon the application the court exercises judicial judgment. It does not confer or withhold a favor.

For Brandeis, then, the key to the case-like quality of the proceeding lay in the asserted claim of right and the exercise of judicial judgment in determining if the requisite showing had been made. Rooted in nineteenth-century definitions, the Brandeis formulation has important implications for understanding other instances of uncontested adjudication.[3]

Brandeis found that Congress has broad discretion in structuring the assertion of claims for naturalized citizenship. According to Brandeis, the United States may "create rights in individuals against itself and provide only an administrative remedy." Or it may provide a legal (i.e., judicial) remedy, but require that individuals first exhaust administrative remedies. Or it may create both administrative and legal remedies and give the individual a choice of which to pursue. Or it may "provide only a remedy" in federal court. Brandeis found that when Congress chooses the latter path by creating a regular mode of procedure, and when the individual invokes the established procedure in pursuit of a claim of right, "there arises a case within the meaning of the Constitution." A petition for naturalization, Brandeis concluded, "is clearly a proceeding of that character."[4]

It seems odd that the animating feature of Brandeis's opinion—that when Congress so provides, original ex parte claims to a federal right qualify as cases within the meaning of Article III—has largely disappeared from view. Recall that Brandeis was among the leading architects of the Court's justiciability doctrines and had insisted in other contexts on the importance of adverse parties. One might suppose that Brandeis's reputation as an adverse-party hawk would lend greater authority to his acceptance in *Tutun* of ex parte proceedings. But such has not been the case. Instead, scholars have tended to pigeonhole *Tutun* as a decision that stands for a proposition less threatening to adversary ideals than the one Brandeis articulated. Some point to the fact that Brandeis also invoked the lessons of history, adverting to the longstanding practice of naturalizing citizens as one that had never been questioned. And many, as we shall see, treat *Tutun* as a potential adversary case.[5]

But that reading is not persuasive. Although the "potential adversary" language had appeared earlier in *Muskrat* and *Pacific Railway Commission*, Brandeis did not suggest that *Muskrat* controlled. Nor did he suggest that his characterization of naturalization proceedings as "cases" turned on the possibility that an opponent might appear. Nor did he explain how much potential adverseness was enough or indicate that the actual appearance of the United States was necessary to bring the matter within the judicial power. Brandeis also did not contend that the congressional creation of a potential role for the United States was essential to make Tutun's claim a case; after all, the history of naturalization to which Brandeis referred did not feature an adversary, potential or otherwise. To be sure, beginning in 1906, applications for citizenship were to undergo relatively searching review. In addition to a hearing at which the court considered testimony from the applicant and witnesses, Brandeis called attention to the various ways in which the government could contest naturalization, both before and after the issuance of the certificate. But before 1906, the various congressional enactments defining the role of courts in naturalization did not specifically authorize intervention by the United States or any other party to contest the petitioner's application. One might conclude, along with other close readers of the *Tutun* decision, that the reference to the government as a possible adverse party was not central to the Court's holding that ex parte naturalization proceedings are cases within Article III and the statute conferring appellate jurisdiction.[6]

How then to square *Tutun* with Brandeis's separate opinion in *Ashwander*, ten years later, casting doubt on the ability of the federal courts to entertain hypothetical, feigned, and non-adverse proceedings? One can harmonize the decisions by noting that the typical uncontested naturalization petition does not provide a vehicle for the assertion of constitutional claims. Most litigation that follows the submission of a claim of right in the form prescribed by law, in the Marshall-Story formulation, will concentrate on the fact of the matter. In *Ashwander*, Brandeis was concerned that private parties might contrive litigation to challenge the constitutionality of federal law. Brandeis viewed the adverse-party requirement as a prudential rule, aimed at judicial self-governance in handling constitutional questions. He did not, as *Tutun* makes clear, view the rule as an entailment of Article III that foreclosed traditional forms of uncontested adjudication.[7]

7.2 Petitions for the Writ of Habeas Corpus and Other Common Law Writs

In upholding longstanding practice in ex parte naturalization matters, Justice Brandeis was only the first of many jurists to consider the legality of established practices that might seem to conflict with the Court's freshly minted adverse-party rule. Similar conflicts arose in connection with the two-stage practice that developed in connection with the extraordinary or "prerogative" writs of habeas corpus, mandamus, certiorari, and prohibition. Applications for all these common law forms of relief began with a first-stage ex parte petition, addressed to the court itself. No adverse party was initially joined or served. Instead, the petitioner asked the court to issue the writ to a specified respondent, requiring the respondent to appear and explain why the court should not issue the requested relief. If the court agreed that the first-stage petition disclosed a proper basis for relief, it would issue the writ in the form of a show-cause order to the respondent and the matter would move to its second stage with a judicial consideration of the merits of the petitioner's claim and any defenses the respondent raised. Notably, though, at the initial pre-merits stage, the court had the authority to dismiss the petition without first requiring the respondent to appear in the matter, perhaps on a finding that the petition was defective in law or fact. Hence the notion that these common law writs had an extraordinary quality: they issued not as a matter of course upon the petitioner's ex parte application but only in the exercise of the court's sound discretion.[8]

Supporters of an adverse-party requirement might question the power of a federal court to conduct the initial, ex parte evaluation of a then as-yet uncontested petition. And such questions have arisen from time to time. Indeed, in *Pacific Railway Commission*, where cases and controversies were first fused, Justice Field struggled with how to treat petitions for habeas corpus, which he evidently regarded as failing his new case-or-controversy requirement. After recounting the history of Article III and its modification in the Eleventh Amendment, the court included this curious assertion. Article III was said to specify "all the cases and controversies in which the judicial power of the United States can be exercised, except those arising on a petition for a writ of habeas corpus, which is regarded as a suit for one's personal freedom." The statement implies that the court viewed ex parte habeas petitions as failing the case-or-controversy test but as nonetheless cognizable as a federal judicial proceeding. The court doubled down a moment later, explaining that the "judicial power of the United States is therefore vested in the courts, and can only be exercised by them in the cases and controversies enumerated, and in petitions for writs of habeas corpus." With these statements, the court was apparently attempting to accommodate uncontested habeas petitions and its novel adverse-party rule by treating habeas as a separate category of suits for personal freedom too well established to overthrow. Sometime later, in a footnote, the Court quietly disavowed this approach and characterized habeas petitions as cases under Article III.[9]

One finds a modern and much less embarrassed echo of this habeas characterization in Justice Scalia's dissent from the Supreme Court's decision in *Hohn v. United States*. The Court in *Hohn* found that a habeas petitioner who applies to a federal appellate court under federal law for a certificate of appealability (COA) has presented a case for purposes of triggering the Court's own appellate jurisdiction over cases "in" the appellate court. Speaking for four members of the Court, Justice Scalia disagreed.

> An application for a COA, standing alone, does not have the requisite qualities of a legal "case" under any known definition. It does not assert a grievance against anyone, does not seek remedy or redress for any legal injury, and does not even require a "party" on the other side. . . . The adversity which the Court acknowledges is needed for a "case" . . . is not satisfied by the dispute between petitioner and respondent as to whether the COA should be granted—any more than a "case or controversy" for purposes of

initial federal-court jurisdiction is created by a dispute over venue, between parties who agree on everything else.

For Justice Scalia, then, the statutory reference to cases was best understood by reference to his view that Article III inflexibly limits adjudication to claims for redress of injuries brought against opposing parties. The initial, uncontested phase of the COA proceeding did not qualify.[10]

Whatever its wisdom as to COAs under modern provisions for habeas review, Justice Scalia's approach to the initial phase of applications for habeas, mandamus, and prohibition runs counter to a string of decisions from the nineteenth century. Consider the views of the Court in *Ex parte Milligan*, which upheld its (statutory) jurisdiction to review a lower court's denial of habeas relief at the initial (non-merits) phase of the proceeding. Much as did Justice Scalia, the party opposing appellate review argued "that the proceeding does not ripen into a cause, until there are two parties to it." The Supreme Court responded:

> This we deny. It was the *cause* of Milligan when the petition was presented to the Circuit Court. It would have been the *cause* of both parties, if the court had issued the writ and brought those who held Milligan in custody before it. Webster defines the word "cause" thus: "A suit or action in court; any legal process which a party institutes to obtain his demand, or by which he seeks his right, or supposed right".... "[Webster confirmed that] popular use of the word [cause], coincide[ed] nearly with case, from *cado*, and action, from *ago*, to urge and drive."
>
> In any legal sense, action, suit, and cause, are convertible terms.

Having concluded that Milligan's initial petition presented a case or cause within the judicial power, the Court acknowledged that the proceeding was ex parte. But that did not prevent an exercise of judicial power, either at the trial level or on appeal. Citing Chief Justice Marshall's definition of suit, the Court emphasized that the term encompasses "any proceeding in a court of justice by which an individual pursues that remedy which the law affords him." It was not the presence of disputing parties, but the individual's pursuit of the "remedy which [federal] law afforded him" that brought the matter within original and appellate jurisdiction.[11]

Focus on the claim of right in the individual petitioner's initial application also explains the viability of petitions for mandamus and prohibition relief.

The Court acknowledged this similarity in *Holmes v. Jennison*. In an 1840 opinion that focused on habeas claims, the Court explained that "applications for writs of mandamus and of prohibition . . . stand upon the same principles with the proceedings on a habeas corpus." Such proceedings did not follow the adverse party "forms of a suit at common law" but were nonetheless suitable for appellate review. By the time of *Ex parte Quirin*, a habeas decision from 1942, the rule was settled that a request for leave constituted a case in the district court over which the court of appeals could assert jurisdiction, even though the district court had denied the request. The Court reasoned that "[p]resentation of the petition for judicial action is the institution of a suit. Hence the denial by the district court of leave to file the petitions in these causes was the judicial determination of a case or controversy, reviewable on appeal to the Court of Appeals." Contrary to Justice Scalia's position in *Hohn*, adverse parties cannot be deemed essential to the creation of a justiciable proceeding.[12]

7.3 Uncontested Proceedings in Bankruptcy

Bankruptcy proceedings bear some resemblance to applications for the probate of an estate. An initial petition gets the proceeding underway, leading to the appointment of a trustee and the creation of a bankruptcy estate that brings the property of the debtor into the custody of the court. The presence of the debtor's property confers in rem jurisdiction and leads to mixed proceedings thereafter. Some of what happens in bankruptcy resembles ordinary dispute resolution between adversaries, as the debtor (or trustee) seeks to recover assets for the estate and creditors make claims, often but not invariably contested, on the available property. But much of what happens lacks contestation: in the course of bankruptcy administration, the court sorts out competing claims, applies rules of security and priority, and distributes assets to the creditors. For some time, bankruptcy practitioners have distinguished between proceedings in bankruptcy, which typically include forms of uncontested administration, and controversies in bankruptcy.[13]

Along the way, the court may approve applications for fees and plans of reorganization and issue instructions, on petition, to the trustee. Fees may be due to the trustee or to professional advisors (lawyers, investment managers, and accountants) hired to assist with the estate's management. Such fees may generally be paid from the estate if "reasonable," and the law usually calls upon the court to make an assessment of reasonableness. In many situations, no party to the estate's administration has an incentive to contest these fees. Perhaps as a result, bankruptcy law holds that the court has an independent duty to examine the fees, even in the absence of a specific challenge. In some respects, the dynamic surrounding the approval of such fees resembles that triggered by other uncontested settlement agreements and raises similar concerns.[14]

During the course of bankruptcy proceedings, courts grant formal approval to a variety of business decisions by debtors-in-possession agreed to in advance by interested parties. For example, the parties may wish to reaffirm a pre-petition contract that has been profitable for the debtor and the bankruptcy estate. In such a situation, the federal bankruptcy code requires the court to approve the contract before it can be given legal effect. In addition, court approval of the debtor's reorganization plan requires satisfaction of a laundry list of items. The court must hold a hearing on the plan's confirmation and take evidence and make findings on each item, regardless of whether the item has "been placed in issue by the parties."[15]

Petitions for judicial involvement may be contested, but they need not be so to enable the court to begin the proceeding and appoint the fiduciary. Thus, debtors may file an uncontested or voluntary petition in bankruptcy. Even in the absence of any dispute over amounts owed, such a petition will initiate the proceeding and occasion the creation of a bankruptcy estate. In such an uncontested proceeding, the court has the power to distribute the non-exempt assets (if any) among the creditors. If there are no assets, and no creditors appear, the court nonetheless has power to provide the debtor with a discharge (and fresh start).[16]

Legal commentators have long been puzzled as to how they might square the uncontested or administrative elements of bankruptcy proceedings with Article III's adverse-party requirement. Thus, Professor Jo Desha Lucas admitted in a 1976 letter to Congress that the constitutional position of "cases 'in bankruptcy'" is not "altogether free from doubt." Professor Nancy King observed that the bankruptcy jurisdiction statute distinguishes between the words "case" and "proceeding," in that cases commenced under the bankruptcy code differ significantly from "a typical civil action commenced in state or federal court to resolve a two-party dispute." Professor Charles Tabb describes bankruptcy cases as unique, ranging from "uncontested administrative tasks to full-scale adversarial litigation" with adversarial litigation comprising "only a small portion of a typical bankruptcy case." The

Advisory Committee on Bankruptcy Rules agreed, acknowledging that the "bankruptcy case is not, in and of itself, litigation involving a legal dispute in the traditional sense."[17]

Ralph Avery raised these issues in an article that described and questioned the power of federal courts to conduct uncontested proceedings in bankruptcy. A similar argument appeared in the early years of the twentieth century, shortly after the enactment of the Bankruptcy Act of 1898. In *Hanover National Bank v. Moyses*, the debtor had filed a voluntary petition in bankruptcy, seeking a discharge of his debts. In accordance with the procedure set forth in the statute, the court made its initial determination on the voluntary petition on an uncontested basis. After the court's formal approval initiated the proceeding, the statute provided for notice to known creditors and gave them a specified time to appear and assert their claims. Next, the statute provided for additional notice, and a waiting period, before the issuance of the debtor's discharge. The bank brought suit to re-establish an obligation that an earlier order in bankruptcy, if lawful, would have discharged.[18]

The bank argued that the voluntary bankruptcy proceeding was unconstitutional because it failed to provide for the initial joinder of and notice to all interested parties. In effect, the bank viewed the voluntary petition as creating a per se entitlement to a discharge; such proceedings were said to operate on creditors in personam, and were thus said to require personal service of notice. The Court rejected that argument, characterizing the proceedings as in the nature of in rem that would allow forms of notice at later stages. Lower courts thus had the power to adjudicate the *status* of the bankrupt petitioner as such in an initial voluntary petition. That triggered the machinery of the bankruptcy process, but it did not deprive interested creditors of their right to appear and contest. Like a prize proceeding in admiralty or a common form probate proceeding, the voluntary bankruptcy proceeding could lawfully begin as an uncontested matter and then evolve into a contest if other parties appeared. But the uncertain prospect of a later contest did not deprive the court of the power to decree in its absence.[19]

7.4 Trustees: Instructions, Distribution, and Discharge

The law abounds with trust relationships. Courts appoint executors to administer the estates of decedents, guardians to attend to the affairs of their wards, and receivers to manage equitable receiverships. In addition, state and federal laws, like the federal Employee Retirement Income Security Act (ERISA), call for the appointment of trustees and impose fiduciary duties in relationship to participants and beneficiaries. Despite the difference in titles, the responsibilities of these fiduciaries overlap to a degree. They typically owe a duty of loyalty to the estate; they must manage the trust's affairs for the benefit of the participants, heirs, legatees, or beneficiaries; and they must all avoid conflicts of interest that might cast doubt on their loyalty to their fiduciary obligations.[20]

Many of the constitutive decrees that courts issue in the course of overseeing trust administration occur in connection with ex parte proceedings. As we have seen, the executors and administrators of a decedent's estate were traditionally appointed by the court in ex parte common form proceedings. During the course of trust administration, doubts may arise as to what course of action a prudent trustee should take, doubts caused by uncertainty as to the content of the law or the meaning of a will or trust instrument. Courts of equity addressed these doubts by allowing the trustee to petition the court for instructions, often on an ex parte basis, in what has been known as the bill for instructions. Courts might also oversee the eventual distribution of the assets in the trust, approving a proposed course of action. Finally, at the conclusion of the trust's administration, the court may review and approve the trustee's accounts, thereby conferring a discharge that will approve the trustee's management of the trust's affairs. All such decrees propose to invest the trustee with a degree of immunity from subsequent breach-of-trust claims. Recent Restatements of the law recognize that these decrees enjoy a measure of preclusive effect, at least for those who receive proper notice.[21]

Requests for instructions and other applications for judicial approval of the administrative activities of trustees can present case-or-controversy problems for Article III courts. Consider the Seventh Circuit's response in *Harris Trust & Savings Bank* to the efforts of the trustees of some junk bond indentures to secure a declaratory judgment in the form of instructions as to which of two plans of action to pursue. One plan—declaring the bonds in default—might trigger a bankruptcy filing, a resultant loss of value, and suits by disgruntled investors if indeed the default declaration was wrong or premature. A second option—sitting tight—also posed risks of litigation in the event the bonds were underwater and the trustees failed to act. Undecided as to the best option, the trustees brought suit to compel the bond issuers to disclose needed information and to secure the court's instructions about which way to go. But the Seventh Circuit refused to allow the suit to proceed, concluding that the absence of a controversy deprived the district court of jurisdiction. Recognizing the judicial maxim that the "law ought not make trusteeship so hazardous that responsible individuals and corporations will shy away from it," the court found that the maxim did not confer jurisdiction to issue instructions. However unpleasant the vision of trustees without sufficient guidance, the court described as "more disturbing" the vision of a flood of litigation brought by trustees and others who plead indecision and ask for instructions.[22]

For a variety of reasons, however, one should not over-read *Harris Trust* as a flat prohibition against the issuance of federal judicial instructions. First, the district court had played no role in appointing the trustees to serve as such, thereby attenuating any right they might claim to seek instructions. Second, the trustees did not point to any provisions of positive federal law that conferred a right to seek instructions. Instead, the trustees relied on the Declaratory Judgment Act, which limits the judicial role to cases of "actual controversy" between the parties. In a different case, without those factors in play, a court might well agree to issue instructions, as Judge Richard Posner explained in a later decision. Posner first invoked tradition, explaining that courts have long given "instructions to trustees who have substantial questions concerning their duties." In light of that tradition, one could not "sensibly interpret" Article III as denying instruction power to federal courts, "now that so much trust litigation comes into these courts under ERISA." But Posner acknowledged that the instruction tradition "evolved in state courts untroubled by Article III's limitation of federal judicial power to actual cases or controversies." He therefore viewed it as "arguable that unless there is an actual controversy between trustee and beneficiary, . . . a federal court has no power to instruct the trustee on his duties."[23]

One might better accommodate the traditional bill for instructions with the limits of federal judicial power by recognizing the power of trustees to apply for instructions in situations in which their appointment as such results from federal law. Such applications, if authorized by federal statute, would qualify as claims of right in the form prescribed by law and would seek a legal decree immunizing the trustee from liability for actions taken in reliance on the instructions. Federal courts could surely moderate their willingness to grant instructions to avoid the perceived problems in *Harris Bank*. Exercising discretion, courts of equity have long refused to grant instructions as to matters assigned to the business judgment of the trustee. The Seventh Circuit had no reason to fear that its willingness to issue instructions in an appropriate case might lead to a flood of petitions from trustees perplexed about a doubtful business decision.[24]

Similarly, federal courts might recognize the viability of bills for instruction as a general matter without allowing their use as vehicles for contrived challenges to the constitutionality of federal law. That was apparently the position taken in 1935 by a Delaware district court, denying a bill for instructions filed by the trustee in bankruptcy of a public utility. The district court confirmed that trustees in bankruptcy reorganizations, "like other trustees under certain circumstances, are entitled to apply to the court for instructions as to the administration of their trust." Such instructions might extend to questions involving the proper interpretation of federal law and the extent of their powers and duties. But the court refused to allow a petition in which the trustees sought instructions in light their doubts as to the constitutionality of the recently enacted federal Public Utility Holding Company Act. Rather than seeking instructions as to the administration of a trust, the petition sought the judicial invalidation of an act of Congress without bringing the relevant government agency before the court. Such an ex parte challenge to constitutional validity was viewed, for reasons similar to those Brandeis articulated in *Ashwander*, as a departure from procedural decorum.[25]

7.5 Warrant Proceedings and the FISA Court

Warrant proceedings date from the colonial period and remain a commonplace feature of federal judicial practice today. To be sure, much of the workaday review of applications for search and arrest warrants now falls to federal magistrates rather than to Article III judges. But Article III courts continue to assess ex parte warrant applications in other areas. In the much-discussed context of national security, Article III FISA courts sit at a secure location at the Department of Justice in Washington, D.C., to consider ex parte applications for warrants authorizing the government to conduct certain kinds of foreign surveillance. Created by the Foreign Intelligence Surveillance Act of 1978, the FISA court of first instance and the FISA court of review employ judges from the Article III judiciary who have been designated to serve for specified terms by the Chief Justice of the United States. As with Hamilton's tax law of 1791, FISA does not provide the targets with notice of the application or with an opportunity to contest the showing made in support of the warrant. The government presents its case for surveillance in a closed-door, ex parte proceeding. In the event the court rejects the warrant application, FISA permits the government to appeal on an ex parte basis without joining an adverse party.[26]

Ex parte warrant proceedings before the FISA courts have been criticized as failing to satisfy the adverse-party requirement of Article III. One prominent early critic of the FISA court, and later D.C. Circuit Judge Laurence Silberman, viewed the secret, non-adversary character of the proceedings as inconsistent with Article III's case-or-controversy requirement. Some argue that the possibility of later adversarial proceedings addresses any shortcomings with ex parte FISA warrant practice. Others observe that FISA warrants rarely lead to criminal proceedings, making "razor thin" the fiction that their issuance may result in an adversary proceeding. Still others suggest that Congress should address the absence of any potential adversary by authorizing an after-the-fact suit for damages in which targets of certain FISA warrants could contest their legality. The inspector general's 2019 report on the selective way government officials and lawyers present evidence in support of FISA warrant applications has underscored worries with its non-adversary character. Critics argue for reforms that would build a measure of adversarial contestation into the process. So far, however, the Supreme Court has had no occasion to assess the constitutionality of ex parte practice before the FISA court.[27]

7.6 Consent Decrees, Settlement Class Actions, and Feigned Cases

The Court also has long overseen entry of consent decrees by the lower federal courts without suggesting that such decrees violate Article III. Typically, such decrees represent the negotiated resolution of a dispute between adverse parties. Unlike purely private settlements, however, the parties to a consent decree condition their agreement on the willingness of the district court to enter the decree as part of their settlement. The decree operates like an injunction: it specifies what the defendant(s) can and cannot do, and it often provides the district court with continuing authority to oversee compliance with its terms, punishing or threatening with contempt those who fail to comply with the decree. Scholars have questioned the propriety of consent decrees, reasoning that the parties' agreement as to the scope of relief may deprive the proceeding of the adverseness necessary to enable the court to decree. On this view of consent decrees, some state officials responsible for a particular institution (schools or prisons) may agree with the plaintiffs that more funds should be appropriated to improve conditions and may collude with the plaintiffs on a consent decree that obliges the state to provide the funds in question. Although the Court has taken this critique on board to some decree in decisions that allow the reopening of consent decrees, it has yet to embrace the claim that Article III deprives the federal courts of power to award this form of relief.[28]

As with consent decrees, Rule 23(e) of the Federal Rules of Civil Procedure imposes an inquisitorial role on district courts, obliging them to oversee and approve the terms of the settlement of any certified class action. Settlement-approval protocols have grown increasingly elaborate, as courts have come to recognize the threat an inadequate settlement can pose to the interests of absentees. In addition to the judicial role in approving the settlement of certified class actions, courts sometimes agree to entertain what have come to be known as "settlement class actions," disputes that were resolved by party agreement in advance of litigation. When the parties agree, they may simultaneously file a complaint and a proposed settlement, inviting the court to approve a resolution of the claims on terms that they have previously agreed upon. Such settlement class actions can pose threats of collusion and self-dealing; critics portray them as advancing "only the interests of plaintiffs' attorneys, not those of the class members."[29]

Apart from the threat to the due process rights of individual litigants, some settlement class actions have been described as violating Article III's adverse-party requirement. Redish and Kastanek draw a sharp line between pre-certification settlement agreements and more "traditional" post-certification settlements. The authors defend the judicial role post-certification on the ground that the federal courts enjoy ancillary power to dispose of the whole case following a settlement that renders the claims nonjusticiable. But they condemn settlement class actions because the parties commence proceedings only to seek judicial approval of a prearranged agreement and thus have no adverse interests giving rise to a justiciable controversy at the time of the action's initiation.[30]

Critics of consent decrees and class action settlement agreements do have a point. Indeed, the Court has signaled a concern with what one might call the holdover effects of consent decrees and has allowed newly elected or appointed officials to reopen or renegotiate old decrees. Similarly, best practices in the oversight of class action settlements have come to include a fairly searching judicial inquiry to protect absentees and ensure proper notice to all affected parties. In general, courts doubtless recognize that genuinely adverse parties can more reliably negotiate such agreed-upon resolutions than parties who collude in an effort to secure judicial approval. Scholars critical of consent decrees and class action settlements thus understandably invoke the nineteenth-century case of *Lord v. Veazie*, which recognized that feigned and collusive proceedings can pose a threat to the interests of unrepresented third parties.[31]

Careful review of the decision, however, reveals that *Lord v. Veazie* stops well short of foreclosing all feigned cases. To be sure, Justice Scalia in *Windsor* and others have viewed the Court's decision as an important early articulation of the adverse-party requirement. And, to be sure, in *Lord*, Chief Justice Roger Taney minced no words in decrying the parties' invocation of judicial power in collusive proceedings:

> It is the office of courts of justice to decide the rights of persons and of property, when the persons interested cannot adjust them by agreement between themselves,—and to do this upon the full hearing of both parties. And any attempt, by a mere colorable dispute, to obtain the opinion of the court upon a question of law which a party desires to know for his own interest or his own purposes, when there is no real and substantial controversy between those who appear as adverse parties to the suit, is an abuse which courts of justice have always reprehended, and treated as a punishable contempt of court.

In accordance with these views, the Court dismissed an appeal after it became clear that the parties were not true adversaries but had conspired in presenting a feigned case that was meant to secure an advantageous statement of the law for use against an unrepresented third party.[32]

Despite the potential for abuse, historians agree that feigned proceedings were a fairly commonplace tool of adjudication in the early Republic. Previous work identifies property disputes and tax cases as primary exemplars of feigned cases. For example, in *Hylton v. United States*, the officials of the Treasury Department structured a feigned dispute to obtain a test of the federal carriage tax. Similarly, in *Pennington v. Coxe*, the parties set up a wager agreement that would satisfy the amount-in-controversy threshold needed to procure review in the Supreme Court. Other well-known examples include *Fletcher v. Peck*, *McCulloch v. Maryland*, and *Martin v. Hunter's Lessee*, where fictitious parties were identified to secure a test of the constitutionality of state laws.[33]

One can best grasp the early appeal of feigned proceedings when one understands their similarity to a modern declaratory judgment action. Most feigned proceedings enabled parties to secure a definitive judicial clarification of law or fact as the basis for ordering their affairs. Thus, in *Hylton v. United States*, the parties genuinely disputed the constitutionality of the carriage tax; ownership of 150 carriages was feigned only to ensure access to the Court's docket. Similarly, in *Pennington v. Coxe*, the feigned wager between the parties was designed to secure access to a federal trial docket for a resolution of a genuine dispute. Taking account of these developments, the Court explained in *Lord v. Veazie* that amicable actions are "approved and encouraged, because they facilitate greatly the administration of justice."[34]

Yet the very idea of an agreed-upon dispute posed a threat to the interests of courts and third parties. Just as courts today issue declaratory judgments only in cases of "actual controversy," so too courts in the eighteenth and nineteenth centuries worried that litigants would present amicable cases to obtain a legal pronouncement for reasons other than to resolve a genuine disagreement about the law. Hence the idea, also expressed in *Lord*, that "there must be an actual controversy, and adverse interests." The Court attempted to ensure compliance with this adverse-party limit by threatening lawyers who brought improper feigned cases with contempt sanctions.[35]

Lord thus introduced the idea that parties may contrive amicable proceedings to obtain a declaration of their respective rights only in cases of genuine uncertainty as to the law applicable to their own circumstances. When the parties lack adverse interests, feigned litigation often aims to secure a precedent rather than to resolve a dispute. Feigned cases to procure advantageous precedents became particularly troublesome during the Gilded Age, as railroads and other regulated entities hit upon ingenious strategies to structure private litigation that would necessitate the adjudication of constitutional issues. In one such case, a railroad contrived to have a passenger bring suit for damages after seeking and being denied the opportunity to purchase a ticket at a new regulated rate. In other cases, friendly shareholders would initiate a derivative suit to block the corporation from purchasing bonds issued by a federal agency; and friendly trustees would request instructions as to the legality of a course of action in the face of feigned constitutional uncertainty. These were the cases Justice Brandeis cataloged in *Ashwander*, opposing contrived challenges to the constitutionality of government action.[36]

Still, the judicial obligation to proceed cautiously in the face of threats to other inadequately represented interests does not in itself deprive Article III courts of the power to decree in such matters. When a party demands a right apparently conferred by federal law (such as class action damages or improvements in prison conditions), the defendant cannot deprive the court of the power to decree by agreeing with the demand in question. Otherwise, creditors could never secure a judgment enforceable against the property of impecunious (but agreeable) debtors. That fundamental logic explains why federal courts have power to decree and confer legal rights on plaintiffs even where the parties agree as to the contours of the relief to be granted. Courts, dating back to Roman times, have registered contracts to ensure their recognition and more ready enforceability. Modern practice on cognovit notes, or confessions of judgment, similarly represents an agreed-upon judicial registration of an admitted legal right. To the extent these registration practices pose threats to the rights of third parties, they call for the recognition of due process protections.[37]

But the importance of third-party interests should not deprive the federal courts of their power to decree. Instead of blocking the exercise of jurisdiction, the threat posed to third-party interests in the consent decree and class action settlement contexts argues for a more searching form of inquisitorial judging. Courts conducting ex parte proceedings and overseeing agreed-upon settlements have a duty to verify and find the facts for themselves, rather than relying on self-serving statements from the parties. These fact-finding obligations may encourage the courts to impose duties of candor on the attorneys in such proceedings. Alternatively, as with prize litigation in antebellum America, courts may take steps to foster independent fact-finding through commissioners or magistrates, rather than relying on the submissions of the parties themselves. In the end, one can agree in part with the criticisms of consent decrees and settlement class actions and view them as demanding a more incisive form of inquisitorial judging than they often receive. But one should not conclude that the federal courts lack constitutional power to take on such responsibilities.

7.7 Trademark Seizure Orders

Although prize cases have fallen by the wayside, Congress has relied on federal courts to exercise similar functions in contemporary forfeiture proceedings. In 1984, for example, Congress amended the Lanham Act to authorize federal courts to issue ex parte seizure warrants aimed at the sellers of goods infringing on a valid trademark. Exercising this power, federal courts have issued broad ex parte seizure orders authorizing the owners of a trademark to take counterfeit goods off the market in the days surrounding major events.[38]

The statute contemplates post-seizure proceedings, during which the target of the seizure order may contest the order, and provides for the award of compensatory and punitive damages and attorneys' fees in cases of wrongful seizure. But many such seizures are never contested; the target neither challenges the seizure nor appears in court to reclaim the goods. A close student of the practice reports that many successful trademark owners use the seizure order simply to get the counterfeit goods off the street and do not pursue claims for damages against the sellers of the offending goods. Other scholars have charted the drift of seizure practice, away from its in personam roots to something that more closely resembles in rem proceedings, brought against the offending articles.[39]

The federal circuits have so far failed to speak with one voice about how to characterize ex parte seizure orders or about how to bring such orders within the scope of their appellate jurisdiction. (For obvious reasons, most of the appeals have been filed by trademark owners, contesting a district court's refusal to grant a requested seizure order.) Much of the litigation has proceeded on the assumption that plaintiffs, seeking to appeal from the denial of an ex parte seizure order, have in effect sought review of the denial of an injunction or temporary restraining order. The Ninth Circuit rejected the analogy, concluding that ex parte seizure orders sought something different from injunctive relief. But the Third and Sixth Circuits went the other way. An insightful dissent from the Ninth Circuit's decision contained the seeds of an approach to seizure orders that would bring them within the tradition of appellate review of uncontested petitions. The dissenting judge found appellate review proper by analogizing the appeal to a petition for mandamus (an established vehicle for the appellate review of the denial of ex parte petitions). The dissent also observed that one might treat the denial of the ex parte seizure application as a final decision, triggering the available of appellate jurisdiction. Insofar as the statute creates an entitlement to seizure ex parte, denial of relief will operate in most instances as a final judgment. Litigation might proceed following notice to the defendant, but the opportunity to secure counterfeit goods will have been lost.[40]

Congress built on the ex parte trademark seizure model in adopting federal protections for trade secrets. The Defend Trade Secrets Act of 2016 authorizes the owner of trade secrets to seek an ex parte civil seizure and forfeiture order in respect of goods produced in violation of a party's trade secret. Critics questioned the wisdom of conferring inquisitorial responsibilities on the federal judiciary in ex parte trade secret seizure cases. As one scholar observed, federal courts typically conduct their proceedings in adversarial settings and do not handle ex parte proceedings very well. That scholar predicted relatively high error rates and mistaken seizures as courts failed to conduct the searching assessments needed to learn the facts. So far, it appears that the ex parte seizure provision has been mostly ignored by trade secret litigants.[41]

Microsoft pioneered another ex parte seizure proceeding for use in the digital world. Recognizing that a network of Russian ransomware hackers, known as TrickBot, had gained access to a variety of servers and was poised to take action disrupting the November 2020 election, Microsoft successfully sought an ex parte order from the federal district court in Virginia. The order gave Microsoft a right to compel web-hosting providers to take TrickBot's operators offline. The petition was framed as an application for preliminary injunctive relief against a variety of John Does. But rather than proceed openly, Microsoft filed under seal and secured a show-cause order and preliminary injunctive relief without actually notifying or serving any of the Does with process. In effect, the district court allowed Microsoft to seek relief somewhat comparable to that courts now allow against counterfeit goods—an ex parte order allowing Microsoft to destroy malicious and disruptive software that infects the Microsoft operating system.[42]

7.8 Testimonial Immunity and Government Financial Benefits

In a variety of situations, somewhat analogous to its earlier provision for the submission of petitions for naturalized citizenship, Congress has set up a scheme of benefits that individuals claim through uncontested applications to the federal courts. Litigants and commentators have raised doubts about three such legislative programs: that for the approval of immunized testimony; that for the payment of investigative fees associated with federal habeas litigation; and that for the waiver or remission of fees for access to electronic court records through the federal PACER (public access to court electronic records) system. After a brief sketch of these programs and the doubts they engendered, this section describes the Supreme Court's decision to approve them.

7.8.1 Immunized Testimony

When witnesses claim a Fifth Amendment privilege against self-incrimination, they trigger a mechanism that allows the government to grant them immunity and compel them to testify. Building on an approach adopted in 1954 to regulate immunized testimony in the national security arena, Congress in 1970 created a three-sided mechanism for the approval of witness immunity grants. The process begins when the witness claims the privilege; if the government wishes to compel the testimony, the government attorney procures from higher-ups in Washington, D.C., a statement as to the importance of the testimony, and submits an application to the federal district court for an order recognizing the propriety of the requested immunity. In many instances, none of the parties disagree: the witness and the government both prefer that the grant of immunity be extended, and no one opposes the result.[43]

When the proceeding was extended to national security issues in the 1950s, a number of commentators questioned the constitutionality of the judicial role, arguing that the absence of any case or controversy deprived courts of the power to issue immunity orders. Professor Robert Dixon observed that that the parties (witness and government) often both agree about the wisdom of securing the witness's testimony and the need for immunity. Party agreement reduced the district court to doing little more than "ratifying" the government's request for an immunity order, and thereby deprived the proceeding of the necessary elements of a "case" under the Constitution. John Rogge made a similar argument, urging that the legislation imposed a "non-judicial" function on the federal courts in violation of Article III of the Constitution.[44]

The Supreme Court rejected such claims in *Ullmann v. United States*. Although the decision triggered a spirited dissent, none of the Justices questioned the majority's conclusion as to the power of the federal courts to pass on the government's application for the recognition of immunity. The Court had previously upheld congressional authority to empower government agencies to invoke the federal courts' subpoena power in support of agency investigations; that decision, *Interstate Commerce Commission v. Brimson*, rejected the position (advanced by Justice Field in *Pacific Railway Commission*) that the absence of a lawsuit in federal court debarred judicial assistance. Justice Frankfurter's opinion for the Court in *Ullmann* drew on *Brimson* in concluding that the admittedly limited judicial function in immunity cases did not deprive the courts of the power to decree. The decree itself was seen as a necessarily prelude to a judicial order compelling testimony that would, consistently with the somewhat similar conclusion in *Brimson*, facilitate the grand jury's investigative powers.[45]

7.8.2 Petitions for Government Financial Benefits

Federal statutes occasionally make financial benefits available to litigants and other individual petitioners upon application to the district courts. A series of recent decisions about appellate review of fee petitions offers a good illustration of the problems that have arisen in connection with such matters. The appellate courts have taken the view that ex parte decisions of the district courts should be regarded as merely administrative and thus as lying beyond the scope of their appellate jurisdiction. The question has arisen when individual lawyers seek review of the denial of an ex parte fee application under the Criminal Justice Act (CJA) and when members of the press have sought review of the denial of applications to district courts for waiver of the fees otherwise associated with access to the electronic database known as PACER.[46]

In both instances, federal law assigns the power to pass on the petition to the district court but says nothing specifically about appellate review of the district court's decision. Access to federal review thus turns on the meaning of the statute that generally confers appellate jurisdiction over the "final decisions" of the district courts. Although the federal appellate courts correctly recognize that Congress chose the term "decisions" in 1948 to encompass all "cases" in the district courts, they have nonetheless held that the term does not apply to administrative matters. As a result, the district courts often exercise final and unreviewable authority over PACER applications, CJA fee requests, and perhaps other ex parte applications.[47]

Yet the Supreme Court's 2018 decision in *Ayestas v. Davis* casts doubts on these denials of appellate review. Convicted of murder and sentenced to death in Texas, Ayestas sought to develop evidence in support of his claims of ineffective assistance of counsel. To do so, he filed an ex parte motion asking for financial assistance under 18 U.S.C. § 3599(f), which provides in relevant part as follows:

> Upon a finding that investigative, expert, or other services are reasonably necessary for the representation of the defendant, whether in connection with issues relating to guilt or the sentence, the court may authorize the defendant's attorneys to obtain such services on behalf of the defendant and, if so authorized, shall order the payment of fees and expenses therefor.

The district court denied both the funding request and the ineffective assistance claim, decisions the Fifth Circuit affirmed. When the Supreme Court granted review to resolve a conflict over the proper standard for the allowance of funding requests in such circumstances, Texas sought dismissal of the proceeding on the ground that the matter was administrative, not judicial.[48]

The Court squarely rejected the proffered administrative characterization and viewed the petition for funding support as plainly calling for a judicial decision. Hence it presented a case, the disposition of which was properly subject to appellate review. The Court first clarified that the ex parte character of the petition was not controlling; ex parte applications had long been viewed as coming within the scope of the judicial power. Here, the Court pointed to applications for a certificate of appealability as approved in *Hohn*, applications for search warrants, and applications to conduct foreign intelligence surveillance under FISA, among others. Second, the Court claimed to find a measure of party contestation in the proceeding: Texas had opposed the petition for funding and had litigated that matter through the federal court system. The Court paid no attention to the rather obvious fact that the money in question would come from the federal treasury, lessening the state's economic interest in contesting any allowance of fees. But lacking a stake in the financial cost of the investigation, the state of Texas nonetheless disputed the petitioner's application for habeas relief. That was adversity enough to satisfy the Court.[49]

While the Court distinguished requests for attorney's fees under the Criminal Justice Act and thus did not resolve their status as cases for appellate review purposes, its decision could broaden somewhat the role of federal courts in hearing uncontested applications. Indeed, the Court's handling of one curious feature of the statute reflects a willingness to accept unconventional arrangements. The statutory framework in *Ayestas* included a requirement that requests for funding in excess of $7,500 be approved by the chief judge of the circuit or another designated circuit judge. Texas argued that this unconventional decisional structure made the funding approval process obviously administrative. But the Court shrugged off the departure from the typically hierarchical structure of the federal judiciary, observing that, "if Congress wishes to make certain rulings reviewable by a single circuit judge, rather than a panel of three, the Constitution does not stand in the way."[50] *Ayestas* thus continues a trend, begun in *Tutun*, in which the Supreme Court has reaffirmed the cognizability of ex parte applications to claim a federal right in the face of challenges based on a progressive-era case-or-controversy requirement.

Part II has described a change in constitutional meaning. Moving away from an antebellum America that recognized uncontested naturalization petitions as "cases" proper for federal adjudication, Gilded Age jurists engrafted a requirement of contestation onto the reference to "cases" in Article III. The adverse-party requirement—developed to address concerns with the administrative state and the *Lochner*-inflected review of feigned constitutional questions—now applies across the board in precisely the way Professor Edwin Borchard feared. The contestation requirement threatens the power of the federal courts to manage a wide range of ordinary uncontested proceedings. So far, the Supreme Court has muddled through, confirming the viability of such practices without clarifying the nature and limits of Article III authority. But if the decision in *Ayestas* provides any guide, the future viability of ex parte practice may depend on the ability to argue that adverse parties or adverse interests lurk beneath the surface of nominally uncontested proceedings. The next part explores how the Court might square the historical practice of uncontested adjudication with latter-day adverse-party and injury-in-fact rules that threaten congressional authority over federal jurisdiction.

Notes

1. 270 U.S. 568 (1926). *Tutun* arose on appeal from a district court decision refusing to grant the application for naturalized citizenship. The government took the position

that naturalization proceedings were not "cases" within the statute conferring appellate jurisdiction over "final decisions" in "all cases" in the district court. *See* Brief of the United States at 9, Tutun v. United States, 270 U.S. 568 (1926) (No. 762); *id.* at 16–17 (acknowledging that naturalization proceedings were "cases" within "the legitimate scope of the judicial power," but arguing that they were not "cases" within the meaning of the statute conferring appellate jurisdiction). It was this contention that Justice Brandeis rejected, although he spent much of the opinion discussing in more general terms the nature of Congress's power to assign naturalization proceedings to the federal courts. *See id.* at 576–79. *Id.* at 579 ("all cases").

2. *Tutun*, 270 U.S. at 576. Brandeis acknowledged that the statutory definition of a case for purposes of appellate review might well be narrower than its meaning in other contexts. But reading the encompassing reference to "all cases" in context, Brandeis found no intention on Congress's part to limit appellate review over matters that he viewed as clearly "cases" at the district court level. *Id.* at 579. On the non-advisory rule, *see* Letter from Justices of the Supreme Court to George Washington (Aug. 8, 1793), in 6 DOCUMENTARY HISTORY OF THE SUPREME COURT at 755. *See Tutun*, 270 U.S. at 576 (citing Muskrat v. United States, 219 U.S. 346 (1911), and Hayburn's Case, 2 U.S. (2 Dall.) 409 (1792)). The current edition of the Hart & Wechsler casebook acknowledges the threat to finality posed by proceedings to reopen a naturalization order, but it distinguishes executive branch revision rejected in *Hayburn's Case* from motions to reopen that the parties address to the courts themselves. *See* Fallon et al., HART & WECHSLER at 85–94 (7th ed. 2015).
3. *Tutun*, 270 U.S. at 578 (citations omitted). Although the federal government's administrative infrastructure was not as well developed as it is today, Congress still had administrative structures other than the courts available: it could assign administration of naturalization petitions to the marshals (as it assigned responsibility for administering the census in the Census Act of 1790, § 1, 1 Stat. 101) or to the clerks of the district courts (as it did for registering copyrights in the Copyright Act of 1790). Its choice of personnel may have reflected its considered view of the nature of the judgment required. In the Copyright Act, which was adopted by the same Congress that enacted the Naturalization Act of 1790, Congress directed parties seeking a copyright to lodge copies of the work with the "clerk" of the district court (rather than with the judge of the court or the court itself). *See* Copyright Act of 1790, § 3, 1 Stat. 125. The Act stated in peremptory terms that the "clerk of such court is hereby directed and required to record the same forthwith, in a book to be kept by him for that purpose." *Id.*
4. *Tutun*, 270 U.S. at 576, 577.
5. *See* Robert J. Pushaw Jr., *Justiciability and Separation of Powers: A Neo-Federalist Approach*, 81 CORNELL L. REV. 393, 458 & n.309 (1996) ((describing Tutun v. United States, 270 U.S. 568 (1926), as a case in which Justice "Brandeis deferred to longstanding precedent that conflicted with the modern idea that Article III courts can act only if presented with an adversarial dispute"). For the view that Brandeis was simply capitulating to history, *see* Pushaw, *Justiciability*, at 458 n.309. For a discussion of *Hayburn's Case*, *see* chapter 9.

6. Perhaps the reference was inserted to mollify a devotee of the *Muskrat* opinion. Justice William Day, author of the opinion, died in 1923. Quoted in full, without citations, Brandeis's discussion reads as follows:

> The petitioner's claim is one arising under the Constitution and laws of the United States. The claim is presented to the court in such a form that the judicial power is capable of acting upon it. The proceeding is instituted and is conducted throughout according to the regular course of judicial procedure. The United States is always a possible adverse party. By section 11 of the Naturalization Act the full rights of a litigant are expressly reserved to it. Its contentions are submitted to the court for adjudication. Section 9 provides that every final hearing must be held in open court, that upon such hearing the applicant and witnesses shall be examined under oath before the court and in its presence, and that every final order must be made under the hand of the court and shall be entered in full upon the record. The judgment entered, like other judgments of a court of record, is accepted as complete evidence of its own validity unless set aside. It may not be collaterally attacked. If a certificate is procured when the prescribed qualifications have no existence in fact, it may be canceled by suit. It is in this respect . . . closely analogous to a public grant of land, or of the exclusive right to make, use and vend a new and useful invention.

Tutun, 270 U.S. at 578. On the inquisitorial nature of the judicial task in early naturalization proceedings, *see In re* an Alien, 7 Hill 137 (N.Y. 1845) (viewing the statute as requiring the court to satisfy itself through some form of inquiry that the applicant for citizenship had made out an appropriate case).

7. *Cf. In re* Cent. W. Pub. Serv. Co., 13 F. Supp. 239, 240 (D. Del. 1935) (refusing to adjudicate constitutionality of federal statute in connection with application by trustee for instructions; noting that it would violate "accepted canons of legal procedure" to invalidate a federal statute without the government's "being a party to the proceeding and without having its day in court").

8. The Constitution's Suspension Clause, *see* U.S. CONST. art. I, § 9, cl. 2, presumes the availability of habeas corpus, a judicial mode of securing a test of the legality of current detention that was incorporated into the practice of the state and federal courts. *See* James E. Pfander, *Jurisdiction-Stripping and the Supreme Court's Power to Supervise Inferior Tribunals*, 78 TEX. L. REV. 1433, 1443–44 & 1444 n.42 (2000). *See Ex parte* Quirin, 317 U.S. 1 (1942):

> While it is the usual procedure on an application for a writ of habeas corpus in the federal courts for the court to issue the writ and on the return to hear and dispose of the case, it may without issuing the writ consider and determine whether the facts alleged by the petition, if proved, would warrant discharge of the prisoner. [Nonetheless,] [p]resentation of the petition for judicial action is the institution of a suit. Hence denial by the district court of leave to file the petitions in these causes was the judicial determination of a case or controversy, reviewable on appeal to the Court of Appeals and reviewable here by certiorari.

Id. at 24 (citation omitted).

9. *See In re* Pac. Ry. Comm'n, 32 F. 241, 255 (C.C.N.D. Cal. 1887). Footnote 1 to the court's opinion, which appears in the middle of the habeas discussion, contains this

intriguing comment: "NOTE BY THE COURT. Probably the supposed exception stated is not really one; and that cases arising on a petition for a writ of *habeas corpus* are included in those mentioned in the judiciary article" (citation omitted).

10. Hohn v. United States, 524 U.S. 236 (1998). *Id.* at 256–57, (Scalia, J., dissenting) (footnote omitted). Justice Scalia's adoption of this framework is in some tension with his conclusion in *Printz v. United States*, 521 U.S. 898, 908 n.2 (1997), that non-adverse naturalization proceedings were "purely adjudicative" in character and that the dissent was wrong to contend that such work was nonjudicial.
11. *Ex parte* Milligan, 71 U.S. (4 Wall.) 2, 112 (1866) (emphasis in original). Quoted Marshall definition appears in *Weston v. City Council of Charleston*, 27 U.S. 449, 464 (1829). On the connection between case and cause, *see* Bylew v. United States, 80 U.S. 581, 595 (1871) ("The words 'case' and 'cause' are constantly used as synonyms in statutes and judicial decisions, each meaning a proceeding in court, a suit, or action. Surely no court can have jurisdiction of either a case or a cause until it is presented in the form of an action.").
12. Holmes v. Jennison, 39 U.S. 540, 564 (1840). *See Ex parte* Quirin, 317 U.S. 1, 24 (1942) (citation omitted).
13. On the mixed quality of bankruptcy cases, *see* Ralph Brubaker, *On the Nature of Federal Bankruptcy Jurisdiction: A General Statutory and Constitutional Theory*, 41 Wm. & Mary L. Rev. 743, 837 n.352 (2000), which recognizes that a "case commenced under the Bankruptcy Code differs substantially from a typical civil action commenced in state or federal court to resolve a two-party dispute" (quoting Lawrence P. King, *Jurisdiction and Procedure Under the Bankruptcy Amendments of 1984*, 38 Vand. L. Rev. 675, 676–77 (1985)). As Brubaker reports, the Advisory Committee on Bankruptcy Rules described "the bankruptcy case" as something different from "litigation involving a legal dispute in the traditional sense." *Id.* (quoting Committee on Rules of Practice and Procedure, Request for Comment on Preliminary Draft of Proposed Amendments to the Federal Rules of Bankruptcy Procedure, Judicial Conference of the U.S. 5 (1998)); *see also* Avery at 450 (noting that in bankruptcy, courts often act as "administrators of a congressionally mandated system rather than arbiters of disputes between litigating parties.").
14. In bankruptcy, administrative fees are accorded a relatively high priority for payment by the estate. *See* 11 U.S.C. § 507 (2012) (conferring priority on payment of administrative fees, which include the actual necessary costs and expenses of preserving the estate); David G. Epstein et al., Bankruptcy § 7-11, at 463 (1993) (noting that administrative fees include attorneys', accountants', and investment bankers' fees). *See* Avery at 434 (explaining that "each creditor individually has little reason to object" based on a consideration of the costs of objection and the likely recovery). *See id.* at 433. *See infra* section 7.6 on settlement class actions and accompanying notes.
15. *See* Avery at 422–23. *Id.* at 437.
16. A similar procedure obtained in probate proceedings. On the difference between contested and uncontested proceedings in probate, *see* John F. Winkler, *The Probate Jurisdiction of the Federal Courts*, 14 Prob. L.J. 77, 84–85 (1997) (distinguishing

between ex parte "common form" proceedings and disputed, or inter partes, "solemn form" proceedings).

17. *See* Brubaker at 743 n.352 (quoting Professor Jo Desha Lucas, Professor Nancy King, Professor Charles Tabb, and the Advisory Committee on Bankruptcy Rules).
18. Avery at 449–50. Hanover Nat'l Bank v. Moyses, 186 U.S. 181 (1902).
19. *Hanover Bank*, 186 U.S. at 192 (citing Shawhan v. Wherritt, 48 U.S. 627 (1849), for the treatment of proceedings in bankruptcy as "in the nature of proceedings *in rem*," and citing New Lamp Chimney Co. v. Ansonia Brass & Copper Co., 91 U.S. 656 (1875), for the view that "a decree adjudging a corporation bankrupt is in the nature of a decree *in rem* as respects the status of the corporation").
20. *See* George T. Bogert, Trusts 1 (6th ed. 1987) (defining trust as fiduciary relationship in which the trustee holds title of property subject to an equitable obligation to administer it for the benefit of another). On the appointment of equity receivers, *see* James L. High, A Treatise of the Law of Receivers § 1, at 2 (Chicago, Callaghan & Co. 3d ed. 1894) (describing the receiver as an impartial officer "appointed by the court to preserve the property or fund in litigation *pendente lite* when it does not seem reasonable to the court that either party should hold it"). On the duties of the equity receiver, *see* John W. Smith, The Law of Receiverships 3 (2d ed. 1900) (noting that the receiver "is not the agent . . . of either party to the action, but is uniformly regarded as an officer of the court"). The bankruptcy trustee represents the interests of the creditors, whereas the equity receiver acts on behalf of the court in administering an equity remedy. On the duties of the bankruptcy trustee, *see* David G. Epstein & Steven H. Nickles, Principles of Bankruptcy Law § 1.5, at 24–26 (2007) (distinguishing the bankruptcy trustee, as "the representative of the estate," from the U.S. trustee, a federal official who shares in the work of overseeing bankruptcy administration).
21. Judicial approval of the trustee's accounts will bind the beneficiaries and protect the trustee from future liability. *See* Bogert § 972: "for matters adequately disclosed in a trustee's account, approval of the account by a court having jurisdiction is binding on the parties, and will protect the trustee from liability with respect to such matters to beneficiaries who received proper notice and had an opportunity to be heard, both on subsequent accounts and in collateral proceedings or actions." *See also* Restatement (Third) Trusts § 83 cmt. c (for those who receive proper notice, the court's order approving the trustee's accounts "discharges the trustee from liability for matters appropriately disclosed"). On the right to secure instructions, *see In re* Cent. W. Pub. Serv. Co., 13 F. Supp. 239 (D. Del. 1935) (confirming that trustees under federal law, like other trustees under certain circumstances, are entitled to apply to the court for instructions as to the administration of their trust on such matters as the proper interpretation of applicable law and the extent of their powers and duties thereunder).
22. *See* Harris Trust & Savings Bank v. E–II Holdings, Inc., 926 F.2d 636, 639–41 (7th Cir.1991) (dismissing application for instructions for want of subject matter jurisdiction). The quoted maxim appears in *Dabney v. Chase Nat'l Bank*, 196 F.2d 668, 675 (2d Cir. 1952) (Hand, J.).

23. First Nat'l Bank v. A.M. Castle & Co. Emp. Trust, 180 F.3d 814, 819 (7th Cir. 1999) (Posner, J.)
24. Note, *Executors' and Trustees' Bills*, 44 YALE L.J. at 1440 (collecting authority for the proposition that courts prefer "not to decide a question which was left by the settlor to the fiduciary's judgment").
25. *In re* Cent. W. Pub. Serv. Co., 13 F. Supp. at 240.
26. *See* Note, *A Survey of the Qualifications of Magistrates Authorized to Issue Warrants*, 9 VAL. U. L. REV. 443 (1975). On the Chief Justice's role in designating members of the FISA courts, *see* Judith Resnik & Lane Dilg, *Responding to a Democratic Deficit: Limiting the Powers and the Term of the Chief Justice of the United States*, 154 U. PA. L. REV. 1575 (2006) (exploring the Chief's various powers and questioning whether they should vest in a single Justice or be shared); Theodore W. Ruger, *The Judicial Appointment Power of the Chief Justice*, 7 U. PA. J. CONST. L. 341 (2004).
27. For a standard dismissal of Article III concerns with the ex parte proceedings in FISA courts, *see* David J. Barron & Martin S. Lederman, *The Commander-in-Chief at Lowest Ebb—A Constitutional History*, 121 HARV. L. REV. 941, 1106 n.663 (2008), which collects authority upholding the power of Article III FISA courts to entertain ex parte applications for warrants to conduct foreign intelligence surveillance (citing In re Sealed Case, 310 F.3d 717, 732 n.19 (FISA Ct. Rev. 2002). Jennifer C. Daskal, *The Geography of the Battlefield: A Framework for Detention and Targeting Outside the "Hot" Conflict Zone*, 161 U. PA. L. REV. 1165, 1224 n.187 (2013) (quoting *Drones and the War on Terror: When Can the U.S. Target Alleged American Terrorists Overseas?: Hearing Before the H. Comm. on the Judiciary*, 113th Cong. 31 (2013) (written statement of Robert Chesney, Professor, Univ. of Tex. Law Sch.), http://judiciary.house.gov/_files/hearings/printers/113th/113-2_79585.pdf [http://perma.cc/MYC3-FRNT]) (observing that the possibility that a FISA warrant will ultimately be contested in an adversarial hearing is little more than a "razor-thin legal fiction")). Daskal at 1224 n. 187 (suggesting that "[t]o the extent that this fiction [the possibility of future adversary proceedings] is deemed key, it could be dealt with by creating an after-the-fact damages remedy and allowing litigants to contest the initial authorization during that process"). On reforms, *see* Charlie Savage, *Court Orders F.B.I. to Fix National Security Wiretaps after Damning Report*, N.Y. TIMES, Dec. 17, 2019 (reporting on two proposals to ensure greater contestation, one by the ACLU to install a third-party monitor to contest government submissions and one to allow those prosecuted to challenge the initial showing made before the FISA court).
28. *See* Swift & Co. v. United States, 276 U.S. 311 (1928). On the use of consent decrees, *see* Ross Sandler & David Schoenbrod, *From Status to Contract and Back Again: Consent Decrees in Institutional Reform Litigation*, 27 REV. LITIG. 115 (2007) (describing the use of consent decrees, especially in institutional reform litigation, and the threat they pose to state official control of state policy). States have challenged consent decrees, but the Court has reaffirmed their viability, concluding that district courts may enforce consent decrees against state officials. *See* Frew v. Hawkins, 540 U.S. 431, 442 (2004) (rejecting state's argument that Eleventh Amendment narrowed the enforcement of a consent decree). Nonetheless, the Court has been receptive to arguments

that changes in circumstances may require the district court to reconsider and update the terms of the decree. *See* Horne v. Flores, 557 U.S. 433 (2009) (recognizing the threat structural reform injunctions pose to state governance and applying *Frew's* flexible standard to the proposed reconsideration of declaratory and injunctive relief); *Frew*, 540 U.S. at 440–41 (noting state official authority to seek relief from consent decrees). *See* Morley, *Consent of the Governed or Consent of the Government?*, at 637 (expressing doubt as to the justiciability of all consent decrees, whether negotiated in advance of the lawsuit or after the litigation begins); Redish & Kastanek at 569–70 & n.100 (accepting consent decrees to terminate litigation that was properly adversarial when initiated, but treating *Swift's* approval of prenegotiated decrees as "aberration[al]").

29. *See* FED. R. CIV. P. 23(e). Following certification and the associated finding that members of the class will be adequately represented by the named plaintiff and class counsel, counsel has presumptive authority to settle the case for the class as a whole. Scholars have raised important doubts as to just how adequate in fact this representation often proves to be. *See, e.g.*, Susan P. Koniak, *Feasting While the Widow Weeps:* Georgine v. AmChem Products, Inc., 80 CORNELL L. REV. 1045 (1995). These doubts have spawned a variety of proposals, including proposals for an invigorated protection of the due process rights of individual litigants, *see* Martin H. Redish, *Class Actions, Litigant Autonomy, and the Foundations of Procedural Due Process*, 95 CAL. L. REV. 1573 (2007); for the encouragement of opt-out guarantees, *see* Alan Morrison & Brian Wolfman, *What the* Shutts *Opt-Out Right Is and What It Ought to Be*, 74 U.M.K.C. L. REV. 729 (2006); and for the imposition of limits on the preclusive effect of class settlements on absentees, *see* Henry P. Monaghan, *Antisuit Injunctions and Preclusion Against Absent Nonresident Class Members*, 98 COLUM. L. REV. 1148 (1998). In 2003, the Rules were amended to require the district court to hold a hearing and approve the settlement only if the court is satisfied that the settlement is "fair, reasonable, and adequate." *See* FED. R. CIV. P. 23(e)(1)(C).
30. *See* Redish & Kastanek at 547, 563, 588–89, 614–15. *Id.* at 590 (citing U.S. Bancorp Mortgage Co. v. Bonner Mall P'ship, 513 U.S. 18 (1994)).
31. *See Windsor*, 570 U.S. at 787–88 (Scalia, J., dissenting) (citing Lord v. Veazie, 49 U.S. (8 How.) 251, 255–56 (1850)). For scholarly reliance on *Lord*, *see* Morley, *Consent of the Governed*, at 661; Redish & Kastanek, at 567–70.
32. Lord v. Veazie, 49 U.S. (8 How.) 251, 255 (1850). *See id.*
33. For a treatment of collusive suits as a commonplace feature of the early Republic, *see* Bloch at 612. Hylton v. United States, 3 U.S. (3 Dall.) 171 (1796). For an account of *Hylton*, *see* Robert P. Frankel Jr., *Before* Marbury: Hylton v. United States *and the Origins of Judicial Review*, J. SUP. CT. HIST. 1 (2003). Pennington v. Coxe, 6 U.S. (2 Cranch) 33 (1804); *see also* Charlotte Crane, *Before* Marbury: Hylton v. United States *and the Origins of Judicial Review*, J. SUP. CT. HIST. 1 (2003) (explaining the wager contrivance in *Pennington*). Lindsay G. Robertson, *"A Mere Feigned Case": Rethinking the* Fletcher v. Peck *Conspiracy and Early Republican Legal Culture*, 2000 UTAH L. REV. 249, 255–60; 1 CHARLES WARREN, THE SUPREME COURT IN UNITED STATES HISTORY 146–47, 392–95 & n.1 (1926) (describing as feigned cases both *Hylton*

and *Fletcher*). *See also* James E. Pfander & Jonathan L. Hunt, *Public Wrongs and Private Bills: Indemnification and Government Accountability in the Early Republic*, 85 N.Y.U. L. Rev. 1862, 1884–87, 1894–1903 (2010) (describing the feigned case of Maley v. Shattuck, 7 U.S. (3 Cranch) 458 (1806), in which prominent early American statesmen like Thomas Jefferson, James Madison, and John Marshall played central roles in procuring a feigned judicial test of the legality of the capture of a vessel by officers of the United States during the Quasi-War with France). Harold J. Plous & Gordon E. Baker, McCulloch v. Maryland: *Right Principle, Wrong Case*, 9 Stan. L. Rev. 710, 725 (1957) (noting accusation that *McCulloch* was a feigned case).

34. Robertson at 262–63 (discussing *Hylton* and *Pennington*). *Lord*, 49 U.S. (8 How.), at 255 (stating that "such amicable actions . . . are always approved and encouraged, because they facilitate greatly the administration of justice," but that "there must be an actual controversy, and adverse interests").
35. *Id.* at 255. *Id.* Contempt was commonly used by the superior courts in England to punish lawyers for bringing improper feigned proceedings. *See* Bethany R. Berger, *"Power over This Unfortunate Race": Race, Politics and Indian Law in* United States v. Rogers, 45 Wm. & Mary L. Rev. 1957, 2000–01 (2004) (citing Hoskins v. Berkeley, 100 Eng. Rep. 1086, 1086 (K.B. 1791)).
36. *See Chicago & Grand Trunk Ry. Co.*, 143 U.S. at 345 (indicating hostility to "friendly" constitutional challenges to legislative enactments absent an "honest and actual antagonistic" relationship between the parties). After the parties agreed to the factual record, the railroad sought an instruction that the new law, restricting passenger ticket prices, violated its constitutional rights as a taking of property. When the state court refused the instruction, the railroad appealed. The Michigan state attorney general appeared to defend the state law and characterized the proceeding as a feigned case. Wellman v. Chicago & G.T. Ry. Co., 47 N.W. 489, 489–90 (Mich. 1890). The Court agreed, and expressed concern lest the parties construct an artificial factual record on which the constitutional evaluation was to be made. *See* Comment, *The Case-Concept and Some Recent Indirect Procedures for Attacking the Constitutionality of Federal Regulatory Statutes*, 45 Yale. L.J. 469 (1936) (describing the use of stockholder's suits and cases framed in reorganization proceedings as weapons in the battle between American business and the New Deal). *Cf. In re* Cent. W. Pub. Serv. Co., 13 F. Supp. 239 (D. Del. 1935) (refusing to adjudicate constitutionality of federal law in an ex parte petition for instructions).
37. The Roman and civil law practice of registering contracts is discussed in chapters 1.1 and 1.2. Cognovit notes have been described as "the outer limits of the parties' ability to contract out of procedural law" but have survived constitutional challenge. Stephen C. Yeazell, Civil Procedure 144 (6th ed. 2004); *see* D.H. Overmeyer Co. Inc., of Ohio v. Frick Co., 405 U.S. 174, 187 (1972) ("voluntary, knowing, and intelligently made" waiver does not violate due process on its face); Swarb v. Lennox, 405 U.S. 191 (1972) (same). Chapter 9 evaluates the due process concerns posed by uncontested adjudication. For an analysis of due process issues raised by cognovit notes, *see* Kevin E. Davis & Helen Hershkoff, *Contracting for Procedure*, 53 Wm. & Mary L. Rev. 507 (2011). The history of judgment by confession is described briefly in *D.H.*

Overmeyer Co., 405 U.S. at 176 and in Note, *Confessions of Judgment*, 102 U. PA. L. REV. 524, 525–28 (1954).

38. *See* Trademark Counterfeiting Act of 1984, Pub. L. No. 98-473, §1503, 98 Stat. 2178, 2179; 15 U.S.C. § 1116(d) (2012). *See generally* Daniel Grobman, Note, *Preemptive Ex Parte Seizure Orders and Substantive Relief: A Far Cry from Congressional Intent*, 33 CARDOZO L. REV. 1185 (2012) (describing the background and operation of trademark seizure orders). The statute specifies that "the court may, upon ex parte application, grant an order under subsection (a) of this section pursuant to this subsection providing for the seizure of goods and counterfeit marks." 15 U.S.C. § 1116(d)(1)(a) (2012).
39. *See* 15 U.S.C. § 1116(d)(8); *id.* at § 1116(d)(11) (2012). For a summary of seizure practice and its critics, *see* Grobman at 1194–95. On the availability of appellate review of ex parte seizure orders, *see* Vuitton v. White, 945 F.2d 569, 570 (3d Cir. 1991), which holds that an order denying an application for a 15 U.S.C. § 1116(d) seizure order constitutes a denial of a form of injunction and is immediately appealable. The Ninth Circuit arrived at the opposite conclusion in *In re* Lorillard Tobacco Co., 370 F.3d 982, 989 (9th Cir. 2004), dismissing the plaintiff's appeal of the denial of its ex parte seizure application for lack of subject matter jurisdiction. *But see* NBA Props. v. Does, No. 97-40609, 1997 WL 271311 (10th Cir. May 21, 1997) (reversing the district court's denial of an ex parte trademark seizure application). Steven N. Baker & Matthew Lee Fesak, *Who Cares About the Counterfeiters? How the Fight Against Counterfeiting Became an In Rem Process*, 83 ST. JOHN'S L. REV. 735 (2009).
40. The Ninth Circuit decision is *In re* Lorillard Tobacco Co., 370 F.3d 982 (9th Cir. 2004). For the Sixth and Third Circuit examples, *see* First Tech. Safety Sys., Inc. v. Depinet, 11 F.3d 641, 647 (6th Cir.1993). *Vuitton*, 945 F.2d 569 (3d Cir.1991). For the dissent in *Lorillard Tobacco*, *see* 370 F.3d at 989–94 (Callahan, J., dissenting). On the finality of the denial of ex parte orders, *see Vuitton*, at 571 (treating the district court's denial of ex parte relief as subject to appellate review); *In re* Vuitton et Fils S.A., 606 F.2d 1 (2d Cir. 1979) (recognizing that denial of ex parte relief was effectively dispositive of the plaintiff's attempt to secure the counterfeit property through pre-notice seizure).
41. *See* Defend Trade Secrets Act, Pub. L. 114-153, 130 Stat. 376; 18 U.S.C. § 1836. The ex parte forfeiture provision appears in Section 1836(b)(3)(d). Early reports suggest that the federal courts have been wary about granting such relief. *See* Eric Golman, *Ex Parte Seizures and the Defend Trade Secrets Act*, 72 WASH. & LEE L. REV. ONLINE 284, 299 (2015).
42. *See* Microsoft Corp. v. Does, No. 1:20-CV-00730-LO-JFA (E.D. Va. July 13, 2020) (order granting ex parte preliminary injunction under seal). For an account, *see* David E. Sanger & Nicole Perlroth, *Microsoft Takes Down a Risk to the Election, and Finds U.S. Doing the Same*, N.Y. TIMES (Oct. 12, 2020).
43. For an overview of the law governing immunized witness testimony, *see* Leonard N. Sosnov, *Separation of Powers Shell Game: The Federal Witness Immunity Act*, 73 TEMPLE L. REV. 171 (2000). The basic structure of current law was adopted in 1954 to govern congressionally compelled testimony as part of the investigations of Senator Joe McCarthy, among others. *See* Immunity Act of 1954, Pub. L. No. 600, 68 Stat. 745.

For accounts of the Act, *see* Robert G. Dixon Jr., *The Doctrine of Separation of Powers and Federal Immunity Statutes*, 23 Geo. Wash. L. Rev. 501 (1955); O. John Rogge, *The New Federal Immunity Act and the Judicial Function*, 45 Cal. L. Rev. 109, 127 (1957); and Comment, *Immunization of Congressional Witnesses Under the Compulsory Testimony Act: Constitutionality of the Function of the District Courts*, 22 U. Chi. L. Rev. 657 (1955). *See* Organized Crime Control Act of 1970, Pub. L. No. 91-452, 84 Stat. 922 (codified as amended at 18 U.S.C. § 6003 (2012)). For an overview and criticism of the 1970 law, *see* Sosnov at 182–205. Dixon notes the fact of party agreement in the immunity cases, noting that the parties often both agree about the wisdom of testimony and the need for immunity. Dixon at 529–30 (describing the court's role as reduced to "ratifying the government's request for an immunity order").

44. *See, e.g., id.* at 531–32 (arguing that judicial immunity order cannot be "case" under Constitution); Rogge at 127, 132–33 (characterizing the act as imposing a "non-judicial function" on the courts in violation of Article III); Comment, *Immunization of Congressional Witnesses*, at 671 (criticizing judicial role on separation of powers grounds).
45. Ullman v. United States, 350 U.S. 422, 434 (1956) (Frankfurter, J.). *Id.* at 440 (Douglas, J., dissenting). *See id.* at 434 (citing Interstate Commerce Comm'n v. Brimson, 154 U.S. 447 (1894)).
46. *See, e.g., In re* Application for Exemption from Elec. Pub. Access Fees by Jennifer Gollan and Shane Shifflett, 728 F.3d 1033, 1035–36 (9th Cir. 2013).
47. The district court's jurisdiction is defined in 28 U.S.C. § 1291. On the appeals courts' inability to review administrative-type ex parte applications, *see In re* Marcum L.L.P., 670 F.3d 636, 638 (5th Cir. 2012); *see also* United States v. Stone, 53 F.3d 141, 143 (6th Cir. 1995). *See, e.g., In re* Application for Exemption, 728 F.3d 1033, 1039–41 (9th Cir. 2013). *See* 15A Wright & Miller, at § 3903. *See also In re* Carlyle, 644 F.3d 694 (8th Cir. 2011) (non-adversarial proceeding); United States v. Walton (*In re* Baker), 693 F.2d 925 (9th Cir. 1982) (same). For a description of the cases, *see* Matthew Heins, Note, *An Appeal to Common Sense: Why "Unappealable" District Court Decisions Should Be Subject to Appellate Review*, 109 Nw. U. L. Rev. 773 (2015).
48. Ayestas's motion cited in *Ayestas*, 138 S. Ct. 1080 at 1087.
49. *Id.* at 1091 (citing, in addition to those mentioned in the text, its earlier approval in *Ullmann* of applications for an order granting a witness immunity in exchange for self-incriminating testimony and its approval in *Monsanto* of motions to freeze defendant's assets pending trial).
50. *Id.* at 1092.

PART III

SYNTHESIS: CASES, CONTROVERSIES, AND LITIGABLE INTERESTS

Louis Brandeis in an expansive mood. Although Justice Brandeis sought, like Frankfurter, to constrain the law-saying power of the federal courts in constitutional cases by insisting on genuine contestation between opposing parties, he followed the lead of nineteenth century jurists in upholding the federal judicial role in adjudicating uncontested naturalization applications.
Photo credit- Bain News Service.

This part considers how to best synthesize the lessons of history and modern practice. Chapter 8 begins with the now-obvious point: Article III distinguishes cases from controversies. Cases include both contested disputes and uncontested applications to claim a right in the form prescribed by law; controversies, by contrast, encompass only disputes between the parties specified. Recovery of the distinction between cases and controversies makes sense of much of what we know about nineteenth-century practice, explaining both the existence of federal jurisdiction over uncontested matters of federal law and the absence of jurisdiction over constitutive matters of state law that appear in probate and domestic relations proceedings. But the distinction also challenges modern justiciability doctrines, including both the adverse-party rule and the rule of standing law that limits federal judicial power to those seeking redress for an injury in fact inflicted by an opposing party. Petitions for naturalization, like many other uncontested petitions, set up a claim of right that satisfies the nineteenth-century definition of cases, but they do not seek redress for an injury as required by the modern framework.

Chapter 9 considers the views of scholars who defend the idea that, nineteenth-century practice to the contrary, Article III should be read to impose some sort of adverse-party requirement. On the most sophisticated version of this defense, a general requirement of party-adverseness persists, and the existence of potential adversaries or lurking adverse interests may suffice to justify the exercise of some forms of otherwise-uncontested adjudication. Yet the potential-adversary thesis, the product of Justice Field's revisionist gloss on the definition of cases, does not fit well with the available historical evidence. Perhaps most importantly, it lacks an organizing theory that can make sense of the text and continuing judicial practice and can apply consistently across the categories of judicial power.

Chapter 10 attempts to resolve the tension between modern justiciability doctrines and the reality of uncontested adjudication. The chapter argues that the Supreme Court should use a new construct—the litigable interest—to assess the viability of claims brought to federal court. Building on the Marshall-Story definition of cases, litigable interests would encompass federal claims of right in the form prescribed by law. Such a formulation would extend federal question jurisdiction to adverse-party disputes and to uncontested adjudication, while preserving the important difference between contested and uncontested matters. Thus, the Court could accommodate Justice Brandeis's concern with collusive efforts to procure constitutional rulings and still preserve the workaday role of federal courts in run-of-the-mill uncontested cases.

Having put forward an account of Article III that defends the constitutionality of such practices, chapter 11 provides a primer for federal courts called upon to play the inquisitorial role that uncontested adjudication requires of them. Courts should accept their obligations under statutes that assign them such a role only where the petition seeks to assert a claim of right under federal law, when it calls upon the district court to make a suitably final determination of the question, and when it demands the exercise of judicial rather than ministerial judgment. Once they accept the legitimacy of their role, federal courts should adopt procedures aimed at improving their fact-finding capacity in ex parte proceedings.

Chapter 12 generalizes, using the history of uncontested adjudication to explore debates over how best to interpret our aging Constitution. Rather than proposing to return in originalist fashion to the approach of an earlier day, chapter 12 suggests that we incorporate the lessons of history through a form of constructive constitutionalism rooted in epistemic humility. Such an approach would allow the Supreme Court to honor both the text and tradition that gave rise to uncontested adjudication and still preserve core elements of its modern justiciability doctrine.

8

Uncontested Adjudication and the Modern Case-or-Controversy Rule

Uncontested adjudication casts doubt upon three core elements of modern "case-or-controversy" jurisprudence. First, those who file original petitions to set up an uncontested claim of right do not necessarily allege an injury in fact, despite Supreme Court decisions that treat such allegations as essential to the presentation of a case or controversy that satisfies the requirements of Article III. Second, original petitioners do not join adverse parties, despite language that treats the adverse-party requirement as one of constitutional dimension. Third, original petitioners may have the right to present uncontested claims as "cases" arising under federal law to the federal judiciary, but they may not have the same power with respect to "controversies," where state law supplies the rule of decision and the jurisdiction of the federal courts depends on the alignment of parties in opposition to one another. The proposed distinction between cases and controversies departs from the many decisions that have conflated the two terms in speaking of a one-size-fits-all case-or-controversy requirement. This chapter summarizes the challenges uncontested adjudication poses to the Court's injury-in-fact and adverse-party rules and to its assumption that these ideas apply with equal force to all "cases" and "controversies" that appear on the jurisdictional menu of Article III.[1]

8.1 Uncontested Proceedings and Injury in Fact

The Court has frequently reiterated its three-part test for Article III standing and just as frequently emphasized the importance of the first element: injury in fact. By emphasizing the injury-in-fact requirement in such familiar cases as *Allen v. Wright* and *Lujan v. Defenders of Wildlife*, the Court has sought to narrow the universe of potential litigants to those who have a concrete stake in contesting the legality of the defendant's conduct. Rather than permitting

Cases Without Controversies. James E. Pfander, Oxford University Press. © James E. Pfander 2021.
DOI: 10.1093/oso/9780197571408.003.0009

those with a generalized grievance, shared with all, to mount claims in federal court, the Court's injury-in-fact requirement forecloses suit by anyone who has not herself suffered a concrete injury. As a practical matter, the injury-in-fact rule serves to restrict the availability of some citizen suits and to protect the executive branch from some agency-forcing litigation that would interfere with law enforcement discretion. This tendency to limit judicial oversight of executive enforcement discretion partly explains the Court's occasional invocation of the separation of powers as a concern that animates its injury-in-fact jurisprudence.[2]

The Court has not only defined standing in terms of a required injury in fact—it has ruled out standing for those who have an evidently concrete interest in the outcome. Thus, the Court found in *Vermont Agency of Natural Resources v. United States* ex rel. *Stevens* that the interest of a *qui tam* relator, a bounty-hunting party suing under the False Claims Act to challenge government fraud, did not confer standing:

> There is no doubt, of course, that as to this portion of the recovery—the bounty he will receive if the suit is successful—a *qui tam* relator has a "concrete private interest in the outcome of [the] suit." But the same might be said of someone who has placed a wager upon the outcome. An interest unrelated to injury in fact is insufficient to give a plaintiff standing. The interest must consist of obtaining compensation for, or preventing, the violation of a legally protected right. A *qui tam* relator has suffered no such invasion—indeed, the "right" he seeks to vindicate does not even fully materialize until the litigation is completed and the relator prevails. This is not to suggest that Congress cannot define new legal rights, which in turn will confer standing to vindicate an injury caused to the claimant. As we have held in another context, however, an interest that is merely a "byproduct" of the suit itself cannot give rise to a cognizable injury in fact for Article III standing purposes.

While the Court upheld the cognizability of *qui tam* actions, it did so on the basis that the relator should be viewed as the assignee of the government's interest in redressing the injury the government itself had suffered.[3]

Most parties who assert a claim of right in the form of an original uncontested application to a federal court have not, perhaps needless to say, suffered an injury in fact. Consider the government official petitioning to secure a search warrant. It is certainly conceivable that the target of the search has committed a crime, and it is certainly true that the public prosecutor acts as the public's representative in seeking redress for such harms. But the warrant application does not seek to redress an injury; it seeks only formal legal approval to conduct an investigation. Or consider a foreign national who is petitioning for the recognition of a claimed right to citizenship. Such a petitioner resembles the bounty hunter in *qui tam* litigation: the interest to be vindicated through such an application for citizenship "does not . . . fully materialize until the litigation is completed and the [petitioner] prevails." The interest that underlies the petition does not arise from any injury inflicted on the foreign national by a prospective defendant; it simply arises from the decision of Congress to authorize a judicial decree of naturalization on showing that the petitioner meets certain specified federal law requirements.[4]

It thus seems clear that the injury-in-fact requirement, as articulated in recent cases, cannot coexist with the acceptance of the (injury-free) applications to register or claim a legal right that lie at the heart of the historical practice of uncontested adjudication. Courts agreeing to naturalize citizens (which federal courts have done since 1790) were not applying a thoroughgoing injury-in-fact requirement as a condition of entering the decree sought. It would therefore seem to follow that, in the early Republic, the injury-in-fact requirement was not viewed as an immutable limitation on the power of the federal courts. Indeed, the idea appears to have entered the Court's jurisprudence in 1970. Such a latter-day arrival certainly offers no definitive proof against the wisdom of the injury-in-fact construct; it simply raises questions about the Court's claim that standing doctrine derives from the understandings of the Framers or the original meaning of Article III.[5]

8.2 Uncontested Adjudication and the Adverse-Party Rule

Unlike the injury-in-fact requirement, the adverse-party requirement enjoys a measure of support in the history of antebellum American litigation. It arose originally as a limit on the use of feigned cases, a procedure by which two parties with a genuine disagreement about the law (and a genuine interest in the outcome) manufactured a dispute to procure the equivalent of a modern-day declaratory judgment. As we saw in chapter 7, the Court articulated these limits in *Lord v. Veazie*, generally approving of the use of feigned cases to secure something comparable to declaratory relief but criticizing the parties for having manufactured a dispute to obtain a decree for use against an unrepresented third party. The solution, according to the Court, was to limit the use of the device to matters involving a "real and substantial controversy between those who appear as adverse parties to the suit." Parties who feigned cases for selfish or collusive purposes—that is, those who lacked genuine adverse interests—were subject to contempt sanctions.[6]

Justice Brandeis articulated a similar concern with feigned cases after recognizing that corporate parties in the *Lochner* era had contrived disputes over the constitutionality of state and federal law in order to procure declarations of unconstitutionality. It was in this context that Brandeis issued his famous proclamation in support of genuinely adversarial proceedings. As we saw in chapter 6, Brandeis's argument against contrived tests of constitutionality proved quite influential. Not only do adverse-party concerns continue to inform constitutional adjudication, but one year after Brandeis wrote, Congress adopted legislation requiring notice to the government whenever private litigation draws into question the constitutionality of state or federal law.[7]

The embrace of the adverse-party requirement reflects deeply held ideas about the legitimacy of judicial review and the importance of adverse presentations to frame the issues for decision. As for legitimacy, the Court's iconic defense of judicial review in *Marbury v. Madison* turned on the claim that such review was essential to enable the Court to decide a litigated dispute. As for the framing of issues, the Court has often reminded us that it performs its function of law-exposition best when the parties to the dispute have the concretely adverse interests necessary to encourage them to make effective opposing arguments. One can certainly raise questions about the degree to which the Court's current management of its (discretionary) appellate docket always conforms to the dispute-resolution (as opposed to the norm-articulation) ideal. But most of the matters on which the Court opines feature nominal, and often genuinely antagonistic, opponents. One recent case with nominal opposition, that between the United States and Edith Windsor, occasioned a dissent from Justice Scalia, who would have dismissed the proceeding for want of the adverse parties that he understood Article III to require.[8]

The tradition of uncontested proceedings, however, casts doubt on the view that Article III imposes an inflexible adverse-party requirement that applies to all matters brought before the federal courts. Indeed, in upholding the case-like quality of a naturalization petition, Justice Brandeis placed a good deal of emphasis on history and tradition: "The constitutionality of this exercise of jurisdiction has never been questioned. If the proceeding were not a case or controversy within the meaning of Art. III, § 2, this delegation of power upon the courts would have been invalid." While Justice Brandeis mentioned in passing the possibility that the United States could appear to contest any particular naturalization proceeding, he did not suggest that such an appearance was necessary to permit the proceeding to go forward. Instead, he emphasized the obligation of the court: to conduct open proceedings, to examine the petitioner and witnesses under oath, and to enter a judgment. Plainly, then, he expected the court to perform the searching inquiry that we associate with inquisitorial adjudication.[9]

Justice Story said much the same thing in explaining the nature of prize litigation, an offshoot of seagoing warfare in the nineteenth century. In prize proceedings, as more fully described in chapter 2, the court's commissioners collected evidence and took depositions on which the court would make its decision as to whether the captured ship was to be condemned as good prize and sold by the marshal. While it was possible that an opponent would appear, in many instances the claim of prize was factually sound and no one would appear to contest the matter. Nonetheless, the district court had the power to decree in uncontested matters and its judgment was binding.[10]

Justice Story understood that the procedure used in prize litigation had its roots in civil law and did not rely on the forms and modes of practice associated with the common law. Indeed, he described prize proceedings as "modelled upon the civil law" and indicated that they could not be "more unlike than those in the Courts of common law." Accordingly, Story explained that it was simply not necessary that "adverse parties should be before the court" in a prize proceeding. Party adverseness was unnecessary because the court itself acted as the "general guardian of all interests which are brought to its notice." One can scarcely find a clearer defense of the inquisitorial role of a federal court in hearing uncontested matters or a clearer refutation of the idea that Article III inflexibly demands adversary presentations.[11]

8.3 Uncontested Proceedings and the Meaning of Cases and Controversies

One final point should be made about the Court's handling of the so-called "case-or-controversy" requirement. The Court has repeatedly linked its standing and adverse-party doctrines to Article III's textual reference to "cases" and "controversies," and it has tended to equate the two terms in defining judicial power by reference to historical practice. A representative sample appears in Justice Scalia's opinion in *Vermont Agency of Natural Resources v. United States* ex rel. *Stevens*: "That history is particularly relevant to the constitutional standing inquiry since, as we have said elsewhere, Article III's restriction of the judicial power to 'Cases' and 'Controversies' is properly understood to mean 'cases and controversies of the sort traditionally amenable to, and resolved by, the judicial process.'" Scalia here echoed Justice Frankfurter's view that "[j]udicial power could come into play only in matters that were the traditional concern of the courts at Westminster and only if they arose in ways that to the expert feel of lawyers constituted 'Cases' or 'Controversies.'"[12]

The history of uncontested adjudication casts doubt on the Court's easy assumption that the terms "cases" and "controversies" mean much the same thing and impose an equally demanding injury-in-fact and adverse-party requirement on all matters brought before the Article III courts. In truth, the history of federal practice suggests a sharp distinction in the meaning of the terms. The examples of original uncontested proceedings from the nineteenth century—naturalization proceedings, prize cases, bankruptcy petitions, warrant applications—all arose under federal law and thus constituted "cases" within the meaning of Article III. When, by contrast, an original application for an uncontested adjudication was rooted in state law, the federal courts refused to hear the matter. As we saw in chapters 3 and 4, the probate exception forecloses the federal courts from hearing certain probate matters. One can best explain that exception as reflecting the Court's conclusion that matters governed by state law were cognizable in federal court only where a "controversy" or dispute had arisen between citizens of different states. For much of the nation's history, probate proceedings began with an uncontested application for the admission of a will to probate in the common form and did not present a controversy within the meaning of Article III.[13]

Nineteenth-century jurists distinguished, for adverse-party purposes, between "cases" in Article III (those arising under the constitution, laws, and treaties of the United States and those of admiralty and maritime jurisdiction) and "controversies" between parties specified in Article III. As for cases, nineteenth-century opinion held that a simple application to a federal court to assert a federal claim of right in the forms prescribed by law was all that was required. This formulation was broad enough to encompass both disputes between opposing parties (contentious jurisdiction) and original uncontested applications for the assertion of rights, such as petitions for naturalization. Plaintiffs invoking federal judicial power over "controversies," by contrast, were required to present the court with a claim against one of the opposing parties specified in Article III.

8.4 Reclaiming the Distinctive Meaning of Cases and Controversies

Others have questioned the willingness of modern jurists to equate "cases" and "controversies" in speaking of a one-size-fits-all "case-or-controversy" requirement. After all, the Court's conflation of cases and controversies runs afoul of the commonplace presumption that legal drafters use different terms to convey different meanings. That presumption deserves application here, given that Article III uses cases and controversies in two different contexts: the term "case" is generally used where a grant of jurisdiction depends on the subject matter of the action, whereas the term "controversy" is used exclusively where the grant of jurisdiction depends on the identity of the parties opposing one another.[14]

Building on these distinctions, scholars have proposed a variety of explanations for the difference in usage. Thus, some argue that "cases" may be the broader of the two and may include both civil and criminal matters, whereas the narrower "controversies" may include only disputes of a civil character. Professor Robert Pushaw has questioned this civil–criminal distinction in the course of arguing that the terms may actually describe two different functions of the federal judiciary. For Pushaw, cases that implicate federal law invite the federal courts to play an expositional role, whereas controversies simply call upon the federal courts to provide an unbiased forum for the adjudication of disputes between specified opponents. While scholars tend to agree that controversies differ from cases, no consensus has yet emerged to explain the distinguishing feature of jurisdiction over cases.[15]

This book's account of uncontested adjudication helps to explain the obvious difference in usage between the terms "cases" and "controversies" and to account for the presence of ex parte proceedings on federal dockets. On the view taken in this book, and in keeping with nineteenth-century conceptions of a "case," Congress may assign and federal courts may accept responsibility for the adjudication of uncontested suits to claim rights under federal law. So understood, the definition of "cases" surely includes both criminal and civil matters and at the same time contemplates a special function for federal courts. As we have seen, uncontested adjudication crops up on both the civil and criminal side of the federal docket. Just as federal bankruptcy proceedings require federal judicial administration of the bankruptcy estate, so too do federal criminal matters frequently lead to the issuance of ex parte search or arrest warrants, uncontested applications to grant immunity for certain testimony, and the entry of convictions on the basis of agreed-upon guilty pleas. The term "case," particularly as defined by Marshall and Story, extends broadly enough to encompass all such proceedings. Article III controversies, by contrast, require a dispute between designated opponents and exclude original petitions for the performance of the adjudicative functions associated with non-contentious jurisdiction.[16]

This book thus takes Professor Pushaw's suggested definition of "cases" in a new direction, emphasizing less the power of federal courts to expound the law than their power to adjudicate claims of right assigned to them by Congress despite the lack of a controversy. A "case," on this view, might properly arise under federal law or admiralty jurisdiction, without invariably entailing the joinder of adverse parties. Federal courts might plausibly be given—and, as we have seen, often have been given—the authority to exercise judicial judgment in federal law "cases" on an ex parte or uncontested basis. That was certainly the view of the Court in *Tutun*, which concluded that naturalization petitions gave rise to "cases" within the meaning of Article III, and it is a view that permits theory to cohere with text and practice.[17]

Notes

1. On the Court's continuing adherence to standing doctrine, *see* Clapper v. Amnesty Int'l USA, 568 U.S. 398, 409 (2013) (reciting the familiar three-part test for standing). On concrete adverseness, *see* Massachusetts v. EPA, 549 U.S. 497, 517 (2007) ("At bottom, 'the gist of the question of standing' is whether petitioners have 'such a personal stake in the outcome of the controversy as to assure that concrete adverseness which sharpens the presentation of issues upon which the court so largely depends for illumination"' (quoting Baker v. Carr, 369 U.S. 186, 204 (1962)).
2. *See* Allen v. Wright, 468 U.S 737, 754 (1984) (denying standing to plaintiff class to the extent they simply sought to assert an interest in having the government comply with the law); Lujan v. Defenders of Wildlife, 504 U.S. 555, 574–76 (1992) (denying

standing to members of an environmental group who had too little direct contact with the habitat in question to plausibly claim an injury in fact from projects that threatened the habitat). Other cases demand relatively clear threatened injury. *See* Clapper v. Amnesty Int'l USA, 568 U.S. at 409 (quoting Whitmore v. Arkansas, 495 U.S. 149, 158 (1990) for the proposition that "threatened injury must be *certainly impending* to constitute injury in fact" and that "[a]llegations of possible future injury" will not suffice). In such cases as *Allen* and *Lujan*, the Court has made clear that it views with suspicion citizen suits brought to compel a government agency to regulate a third party more rigorously. The oft-expressed linkage between standing and separation of powers reflects this concern with interference in the enforcement discretion of the executive branch. *See Allen*, 468 U.S. at 761 (identifying executive branch primacy in law enforcement, as reflected in the Take Care Clause, as among the reasons why the Court hesitated to permit suit against a government agency to compel it to regulate others); *see also Lujan*, 504 U.S. at 577.

3. *See* Vermont Agency of Nat. Res. v. United States *ex rel.* Stevens, 529 U.S. 765 (2000). For the text of the False Claims Act, *see* 31 U.S.C. § 3729 (2012). The quoted language appears in *Vermont Agency*, 529 U.S. at 772–73 (alteration in original) (citations omitted). On the Court's reliance on assignment to uphold standing, *see id.* at 773 ("[T]he assignee of a claim has standing to assert the injury in fact suffered by the assignor").
4. *Id.*
5. *See* Ass'n of Data Processing Serv. Orgs., Inc. v. Camp, 397 U.S. 150, 152 (1970) ("The first question is whether the plaintiff alleges that the challenged action has caused him injury in fact, economic or otherwise."). For the context in which "injury in fact" entered the lexicon, *see* Caleb Nelson, *"Standing" and Remedial Rights in Administrative Law*, 105 VA. L. REV. 703 (2019).
6. *See* Lord v. Veazie, 49 U.S. (8 How.) 251 (1850). On the declaratory quality of feigned cases, *see id.* at 255 (describing the use of a feigned case for proper law-clarification purposes as "approved and encouraged" to facilitate the "administration of justice"). Gradually, as declaratory judgments came to be accepted in "cases of actual controversy" between the parties, 28 U.S.C. § 2201 (2020), the feigned case slipped into desuetude. Today, the parties to a genuine disagreement about the legal rules applicable to their circumstances may secure declaratory relief and have little reason to feign a dispute. *See* Pfander & Birk, *Article III Judicial Power*, at 1438.
7. On the use of the adverse-party requirement to limit judicial review to constitutional cases in which the parties joined issue on the question at hand, *see Muskrat*, 219 U.S. 346 (1911). *See also* Pennsylvania v. West Virginia, 262 U.S. 553, 605–23 (1923) (Brandeis, J., dissenting). For cases limiting judicial review in friendly proceedings, *see Ashwander*, 297 U.S. at 345 (Brandeis, J., concurring) (noting a reluctance to allow constitutional challenges by way of stockholder's suit); *cf.* Smith v. Kan. City Title & Tr. Co., 255 U.S. 180, 199–202 (1921) (upholding jurisdiction over private suit to block corporate investment and reaching the merits of challenge to constitutionality of congressional authority). On the use of derivative suits by an out-of-state shareholder to procure access to federal court on the basis of diversity, *see* John C. Coffee Jr. & Donald E. Schwartz, *The Survival of the Derivative Suit: An Evaluation and a Proposal*

for Legislative Reform, 81 COLUM. L. REV. 261, 266–71 (1981), which discusses *Dodge v. Woolsey*, 59 U.S. (18 How.) 331 (1855). For the legislation requiring notice to governments interested in defending statutes from constitutional challenges, *see* Act of Aug. 24, 1937, Pub. L. No. 75-352, § 1, 50 Stat. 751, 751 (1937) (codified as amended at 28 U.S.C. § 2403). For background on the adoption of the statute requiring notice to the government of pending constitutional challenges, *see* Raoul Berger, *Intervention by Public Agencies in Private Litigation in the Federal Courts*, 50 YALE L.J. 65 (1940).

8. *See* Marbury v. Madison, 5 U.S. (1 Cranch) 137, 178–80 (1803) (judicial review justified by reference to the need to resolve a dispute in accordance with applicable law). *See* Poe v. Ullman, 367 U.S. 497, 503 (1961) ("[T]he adjudicatory process is most securely founded when it is exercised under the impact of a lively conflict between antagonistic demands, actively pressed."); Heather Elliot, *The Functions of Standing*, 61 STAN. L. REV. 459, 469–75 (2008). *See* Henry Paul Monaghan, *On Avoiding Avoidance, Agenda Control, and Related Matters*, 112 COLUM. L. REV. 665, 707–08 (2012) ("[T]he [Supreme] Court still disclaims any freestanding authority to pronounce on issues of constitutional law. . . . A live controversy of some kind must still exist."). For doubts that modern certiorari practice limits the Court to its historic role in dispute resolution, *see* Edward A. Hartnett, *Questioning Certiorari: Some Reflections Seventy-Five Years After the Judges' Bill*, 100 COLUM. L. REV. 1643, 1733–35 (2000). For Justice Scalia's dissent on the grounds of adverseness, *see Windsor*, 570 U.S. at 784–85 (2013).
9. Tutun v. United States, 270 U.S. 568, 576–77 (1926).
10. Justice Story was a close student of prize litigation, presiding over many of the issues that arose in New England as the circuit justice for that region and writing the rules of prize litigation that prevailed in the district courts there. *See* R. KENT NEWMYER, SUPREME COURT JUSTICE JOSEPH STORY: STATESMAN OF THE OLD REPUBLIC 100 & n.86, 408 (1985). Justice Story also reportedly ghostwrote a note on prize practice that appeared in Henry Wheaton's first volume of reports. *See* Arlyck at 11 n.13, 239. *See id.* at 234 (describing the declaration of war and the authorization to issue commissions to privateers). For an account of prize litigation during the War of 1812, *see* chapter 2 and notes; Arlyck at 260–66. On the distribution of proceeds, *see id.* at 258–59. On the absence of party-based contestation, *see id.* at 261 (reporting based on archival research that in many instances "libels filed against prizes of war went unopposed"). *See* HENRY WHEATON, A DIGEST OF THE LAW OF MARITIME CAPTURES AND PRIZES 274–76 (1815).
11. On Justice Story's role in prize litigation during the War of 1812, *see* Arlyck at 232–42, 265 n.81 (quoting Justice Story's opinion in *The Schooner Adeline*, 13 U.S. (9 Cranch) 244, 284 (1815)). Arlyck reports that "prize proceedings were largely nonadversarial; that is, in most cases the only parties to the proceedings were the captors seeking condemnation of the vessel and cargo as good prize." Arlyck attributes the lack of adverse-party presentations to the simple notion that the owners had nothing to litigate. *Id.* at 264.
12. *See* Vermont Agency, 529 U.S. at 774 (2000) (quoting Steel Co. v. Citizens for Better Env't, 523 U.S. 83, 102 (1998)). *See also* Coleman v. Miller, 307 U.S. 433, 460 (1939) (opinion of Frankfurter, J.).

13. For the Court's most recent attempt to explain the contours of the probate exception, *see* Marshall v. Marshall, 547 U.S. 293 (2006). For a more detailed account of the inability of the federal courts to take cognizance of uncontested state law probate matters, *see* James E. Pfander & Michael J.T. Downey, *In Search of the Probate Exception*, 67 VAND. L. REV. 1533, 1558–60 (2014). *See generally* chapter 3.3 (discussing nineteenth-century authority).
14. For statements of the canon in the statutory context, *see* 2A NORMAN J. SINGER, SUTHERLAND'S STATUTES AND STATUTORY CONSTRUCTION § 46:6 (7th ed. 2010) ("Different words used in the same, or a similar, statute are assigned different meanings whenever possible") (footnote omitted); Sosa v. Alvarez-Machain, 542 U.S. 692, 711 n.9 (2004) (describing the presumption that different words in the same statute mean different things). For a more general statement, *see* ANTONIN SCALIA & BRYAN A. GARNER, READING LAW: THE INTERPRETATION OF LEGAL TEXTS 170 (2012) ("[W]here [a] document has used one term in one place, and a materially different term in another, the presumption is that the different term denotes a different idea.").
15. William A. Fletcher, *The "Case or Controversy" Requirement in State Court Adjudication of Federal Questions*, 78 CAL. L. REV. 263, 266–67 (1990) (quoting definitions of case and controversy by St. George Tucker and Joseph Story); James E. Pfander, *Rethinking the Supreme Court's Original Jurisdiction in State-Party Cases*, 82 CAL. L. REV. 555, 604–17 (1994). Pushaw, *Article III's Case/Controversy Distinction*. Pushaw later described his thesis as follows:

    > In federal question, admiralty, and foreign officer "Cases," the judiciary's main role would be to "expound" (i.e., interpret and apply) laws having national and international significance. By contrast, in "Controversies," federal judges would serve chiefly as neutral umpires in resolving bilateral disputes involving the designated parties.

    Robert J. Pushaw Jr., *Congressional Power over Federal Court Jurisdiction: A Defense of the Neo-Federalist Interpretation of Article III*, 1997 B.Y.U. L. REV. 847, 851. For a criticism of Pushaw's law-declaration thesis, *see* David Engdahl, *Intrinsic Limits of Congress' Power Regarding the Judicial Branch*, 1999 B.Y.U. L. REV. 75, 149 n.278 (1999) (arguing that the law-declaration model of the judicial role did not appear in federal jurisprudence until the twentieth century); John Harrison, *The Power of Congress to Limit the Jurisdiction of Federal Courts and the Text of Article III*, 64 U. CHI. L. REV. 203, 229–30 (1997) (criticizing Pushaw's account as lacking direct evidence and failing to fit with available structural evidence). Somewhat in contrast to Pushaw's account, this book suggests that cases, unlike controversies, contemplate forms of uncontested adjudication in which the federal judiciary functions as an inquisitorial fact-finding and law-application body. While federal courts might expound the law in such uncontested proceedings, this book suggests that they should proceed cautiously when asked to do so.
16. For the suggestion that non-contentious jurisdiction includes causes both criminal and civil, *see* Layton B. Register, *Spanish Courts*, 27 YALE L.J. 769, 772 (1918), which states:

> The civil affairs of the courts of first instance are either contentious or non-contentious. The non-contentious jurisdiction consists of uncontested or ex parte acts, and includes categories both civil and criminal. The contentious jurisdiction comprises contested causes and includes all civil and commercial actions which . . . can not be brought before the municipal courts.

For our suggested distinction between original and ancillary non-contentious jurisdiction, *see* chapter 11.1.

17. Pushaw was quite right to discern an important distinction in the meaning of cases and controversies. But he did not address ex parte proceedings and did not include ex parte matters in his account of "cases" that lack attendant disputes. *See* Pushaw, *Article III's Case/Controversy Distinction*, at 480–82 (arguing that English courts expounded the law in such matters as advisory opinions, prerogative writs, and relator and informer actions). Nor did he suggest that his account of the meaning of cases would solve the puzzles that ex parte proceedings present when integrated into a legal system primarily devoted to dispute resolution. *Cf. id.* at 526–30 (arguing that his case-exposition theory would help resolve issues of mootness, ripeness, and standing).

9

Evaluating Defenses of a Requirement of Adverse Interests

Despite the lessons of history, many argue that Article III incorporates an "adverse-party" requirement. Consider the claim Justice Scalia put forward in his dissenting opinion in *United States v. Windsor*. Urging that the basis for federal court jurisdiction over that case disappeared once the United States announced that it agreed with the legal position of its party opponent, Justice Scalia repeatedly spoke of "the requirement of party-adverseness," the idea that an Article III case or controversy requires "disagreement between the parties." Critics of practices such as federal judicial engagement with warrants, with bankruptcy administration, and with the oversight of settlements and consent decrees frequently claim that these practices fail the requirement of party adverseness.[1]

9.1 Woolhandler's Pivot to Adverse Interests

Perhaps the strongest defense of an adverseness requirement appears in the work of Professor Ann Woolhandler, published in response to an earlier account of non-contentious jurisdiction under Article III. Agreeing that many uncontested proceedings pose no Article III difficulty, Professor Woolhandler defends adverseness by reformulating the requirement as one of "adverse interests." That allows her to explain how individuals who agree as to the resolution of a particular legal problem can nonetheless secure a judicial decree confirming their shared conception. What matters, for Woolhandler, is not whether the parties contest claims in court but whether they have possibly adverse interests that can be adjusted either through litigation or through settlement. Adverse interests, then, allow Woolhandler to bring uncontested practices within the framework of the more limited conception of adverseness that she seeks to defend. Abandoning as indefensible much of the lore that has grown up around the view that there must be actual

Cases Without Controversies. James E. Pfander, Oxford University Press. © James E. Pfander 2021.
DOI: 10.1093/oso/9780197571408.003.0010

(and actively) *adverse parties* to every federal court action, Woolhander's adverse interest construct seemingly admits that the adverse-party requirement does not pose a constitutional limit on federal court jurisdiction and seemingly disavows Justice Scalia's dissenting opinion in *United States v. Windsor*.[2]

Woolhandler applies her adverse-interest construct to the in rem features of admiralty practice. She shows that potential adverse interests doubtless underlay much in rem litigation, even though the suit proceeded against the property before the court and did not require the identification of and notice to particular adversaries as a condition of adjudication. Woolhandler shows that, in many instances, adverse parties learned of the pendency of suit and could come forward or not as they saw fit to dispute the claims being made. All that makes sense, but in a good many cases, nonetheless, prize claims went forward without the slightest contestation whatsoever. In such cases, the federal admiralty courts proceeded on an inquisitorial basis, collected evidence through depositions, and registered claims of right against property. Therefore, party contestation was not essential to ground jurisdiction. Moreover, in the many cases where no adverse party appeared or mounted a contest, the existence of adverse interests did nothing to change the fact that the actual adjudication was uncontested. Such suits lacked the "concrete adversity" and the vigorous opposing submissions that provide the rationale for an adverseness requirement.[3]

Woolhandler also tackles the problem of feigned cases. She agrees that such cases were not, contrary to widespread assumptions, invariably problematic from an Article III perspective. Indeed, when the parties genuinely differed on a legal point, the feigned case could provide them with a mechanism for securing the functional equivalent of a declaratory judgment. Yet feigned cases do present potential problems, particularly when the parties contrive a dispute in order to injure a third party or to procure a constitutional declamation on the basis of an incomplete record. Woolhandler usefully extends feigned-case wisdom and offers a new set of categories—merits collusion and jurisdictional collusion—to help readers keep separate the various forms of collusive litigation. "Jurisdictional collusion" is aimed at procuring the resolution of a genuine dispute, as opposed to the more problematic form of merits collusion. Woolhandler's new, more refined categories help explain the eventual rejection of feigned cases by federal courts. What Woolhandler calls collusion on the merits takes place when parties who agree as to the result use a feigned action to obtain some external advantage.[4]

9.2 The Challenges of an Adverse-Interest Approach

While Woolhandler's adverse-interest construct points to results broadly consistent with a conception of Article III that encompasses some uncontested claims, it cannot explain much of the evidence from the nineteenth century. Consider, for example, the history of uncontested adjudication of petitions for naturalized citizenship. The naturalization example offers strong support for the claim that federal courts can adjudicate without contestation or adverse interests. Professor Woolhandler agrees that the petitions themselves do not appear to present adverse interests, and she admits that they count as the "best example."[5]

But having made this concession, Woolhandler works to downplay the significance of naturalization petitions by contending that they had never been formally upheld in the face of an explicit jurisdictional challenge until 1926, at which time the United States had been installed as a potential adverse contestant. While this might work as a lawyer's argument, it does not make good sense as history. As a matter of historical fact, the First Congress assigned this uncontested work to the federal courts and that such federal judges as John Marshall and Joseph Story (and everyone else, of course) performed it without raising a doubt as to its legitimacy for over one hundred years. They treated their decisions, moreover, as binding adjudications of a claim of right and defined Article III "cases" in terms that would embrace their docket of uncontested work. Only after Justice Field introduced the idea of required contestation in the Gilded Age (abandoning the Marshall-Story definition of a case to propose an alternative) did it suddenly occur to parties and jurists that Article III might disable the federal courts from hearing naturalization petitions in the absence of an adverse party. It was this latter-day revisionism—revisionism that Professor Woolhandler continues to press—that led to the Supreme Court's 1926 decision in *Tutun v. United States*. There, as we have seen, Justice Brandeis offered a resounding reaffirmation of noncontentious judicial power over naturalization and explicitly validated the exercise of such power in its purest form as practiced since the 1790s.[6]

What, then, should one make of the naturalization example? Much depends on how one frames the question. If one seeks to place the naturalization example within a system committed to and based on adversary proceedings, then one might, as Professor Woolhandler does, conjecture that Justice Brandeis gestured to the United States as a potential adversary in an effort to refrain from abrogating a longstanding, if anomalous, district court practice. But if one begins with the recognition that antebellum jurists embraced a wide range of uncontested proceedings, in addition to naturalization petitions, one might view the possible adversary construct as a fundamental change in the definition of a "case," introduced by Justice Field during the Gilded Age. One might, in short, view the extensive catalog of uncontested proceedings in the nineteenth century as the more relevant baseline for purposes of evaluating the significance of naturalization.[7]

Professor Woolhandler disagrees. Having distinguished away such close cousins as pension applications, petitions for remission or mitigation of forfeitures, and prize proceedings, she frames naturalization as an "outlier," an aberration that does not, alone, suffice to carry the burden of disproving her refashioned adverse-interest requirement. Woolhandler, in short, accepts the early twentieth century as her baseline and treats the judicial rhetoric of that period as the key to understanding the nature of party adverseness. But she does not grapple with the history of uncontested adjudication as a familiar element of the learned eighteenth-century lawyer's lived experience. Nor does she set out to defend the adverse-interest requirement on policy grounds as a useful adaptation that focuses the energies of the federal judiciary on its important work as a forum for the resolution of disputes and explication of law. Her account thus imagines a distinctive form of living constitutionalism, drawn not from text or history but from the doctrinal changes that emerged in the latter part of the nineteenth and early part of the twentieth centuries.[8]

One can see the difference in approach most sharply revealed in an assessment of *Hayburn's Case*. Conventional wisdom treats the refusal of some circuit justices and district judges to hear uncontested applications for veterans' pension benefits in the early Republic as a reflection of dual concerns with the absence of finality (executive revision) and, based entirely on speculation, with the absence of properly aligned parties. Some of the letters that the judges wrote in explaining their refusal to do the work described the task at hand as work not of a "judicial nature." Evaluating that language from a latter-day perspective informed by conventional statements of the adverse-party requirement, many modern scholars have assumed that the circuit judges were articulating a requirement of party adverseness. Yet a competing explanation better accounts for that language. Some judges were expressing concern that it was improper (and perhaps undignified) to view the wounds of a veteran in the course of adjudicating benefit claims. Attorney General Edmund Randolph met the judges' complaint with a seemingly persuasive argument that judges at common law were called upon to view wounds in the course of adjudicating mayhem claims. Randolph's apparent invocation of the precedent of mayhem claims, as recorded in Justice James Iredell's notes of the oral argument, particularly when coupled with a notable lack of argument about the absence of an adverse party, strongly implies that the "not of a judicial nature" objection was rooted in concerns about an offense to judicial dignity rather than an unarticulated concern about adverseness.[9]

Moreover, one supposes that, if circuit court judges and justices considered uncontested applications for government pensions as work of a nonjudicial nature, they would have considered uncontested naturalization petitions equally problematic. One might doubt the coherence of the party adverseness interpretation given the absence of any clear reference to concerns about adverseness and the willingness of the same judges and justices to hear entirely non-adverse naturalization petitions. Finally, one might observe that the litigation in the Court itself entailed an ex parte submission on behalf of Hayburn that did not feature the joinder of any opposing party. (Edmund Randolph's appearance as counsel on behalf of on Hayburn's pension application has been shown to have addressed earlier doubts not as to the presence of party adversaries but as to Randolph's authority to proceed without a client and without specific presidential authority in his capacity as the Attorney General.) No Justice was recorded as having questioned this configuration of litigants.[10]

Instead of coming to grips with the evidence, Professor Woolhandler restates the standard assumption that the Supreme Court was concerned with the lack of party adverseness in pension proceedings. But the fact that the Supreme Court later invalidated the work of judges as "commissioners" does not, as Woolhandler contends, help to establish an adverse-party reading of this series of events. The Court's refusal to validate the decisions of circuit judges serving as self-styled judicial commissioners could have reflected a variety of considerations: the fact that the statute assigned the task of reviewing pension claims to the "courts" rather than to the judges themselves; the fact that the decisions of the judges were still subject to improper executive revision; the fact that Congress lacks power to appoint commissioners by legislative act (an interpretation that gains support from Congress's later adoption of curative legislation that empowered district judges either to do the work themselves or to appoint commissioners). While modern scholars have instinctively embraced the interpretation, one cannot treat an unelaborated concern about the "judicial nature" of pension work as driven by the absence of adverse parties unless one weighs competing evidence in the historical record.[11]

Professor Woolhandler treats Chief Justice Taney's decision in *United States v. Ferreira* as rejecting uncontested proceedings and as confirming her interpretation of the events reported in *Hayburn's Case*. Both assertions are hard to square with the *Ferreira* decision itself, which, like the circuit court opinions collected in *Hayburn's Case*, viewed the absence of finality as the controlling objection to the exercise of federal judicial power. Indeed, in a most revealing aside, *Ferreira* appears to have subtly acknowledged the propriety of judicial power to "administ[er] the law" in uncontested ex parte benefit applications.[12]

Ferriera grew out of a claims-processing treaty, in which the United States agreed to establish a tribunal to hear claims by civilians seeking compensation for U.S. military operations in what was then Spanish Florida. (After statehood, the claims were handled by the federal judge in Florida.) Questions arose as to the nature of the tribunal and as to whether the United States could appeal as a party from a decision awarding money to a claimant. According to the Court, the statute implementing the treaty called for initial review of the claimant's submission, the issuance of an award, and the transmittal of the evidence and the award to the Secretary of the Treasury, who was to pay the amount specified if satisfied that the award was "just and equitable."[13]

The Court was certainly aware that the typical claim would arrive at the district court's chambers as an ex parte submission, rather than an *inter partes* dispute. Counsel for one of the parties highlighted the point, contending that whether or not the United States appeared as a formal party on the record, these claims were " 'cases,' within the legal meaning of the term." What blocked the right of appeal, according to counsel, was the provision for review by the Secretary of the Treasury. The Court took precisely that position, acknowledging the ex parte character of the proceedings in the language Professor Woolhandler quotes, but focusing on the absence of judicial finality in refusing to entertain the appeal. Thus, the Court explained that the evidence and award were not filed or "recorded" in the district court, but were to be transmitted to the Executive to take effect only upon decision of the Secretary. The claims process thus differed from naturalization proceedings, in which decisions of the federal court were final and binding, were entered into the record of the federal court, and were to control future judicial proceedings.[14]

The Court's acknowledgment that ex parte proceedings lay well within federal judicial power came after a lengthy discussion of the similarities between the Florida procedure and the problematic procedure in *Hayburn's Case*. For the Court, the problem with both proceedings was clear: their nonfinal character made them "entirely alien to the legitimate functions of a judge or court of justice." The proceedings thus had "no analogy to the general or special powers ordinarily and legally conferred on judges or courts to secure the due administration of the law." In this revealing passage, the Court acknowledged counsel's suggestion that ex parte claims were proper "cases" for judicial determination; the Court was saying that federal courts can administer the law in "special" ex parte proceedings, but only when the proceeding yields a final judgment. In the end, then, the Court said nothing to support Professor Woolhandler's interpretation, and much to confirm that ex parte proceedings (like naturalization petitions) can appear as cases proper for adjudication in Article III courts.[15]

Professor Woolhandler examines a few other antebellum practices but does not show that their legitimacy was thought to turn on the presence of adverse interests. Consider, for example, the example of warrant applications as an instance of uncontested adjudication. Federal courts issue legally meaningful decrees on the basis of ex parte submissions that do not involve any party contestation. Professor Woolhandler admits the truth of the assertion, but argues that warrants were not dispositive of all issues and did not necessarily foreclose subsequent contestation. True enough. For example, as Woolhandler notes, if execution of the warrant failed to turn up evidence, the target might contest some of the warrant's features in a subsequent proceeding or might bring suit against the complainant (or informant) for having provided false evidence in support of the warrant's issuance. While certainly conceivable, these possible spin-off claims do not alter the fact that the *constable* could claim legal protection from a trespass action when acting pursuant to lawful warrant. Moreover, the possibility that the target might later institute an adverse proceeding does nothing to imbue the warrant application proceeding with the benefits of adversarial litigation, or even to mimic the form of an adversary proceeding. Any lurking interests would not find expression in submissions made to the court or magistrate in connection with a warrant application.[16]

Nor does Professor Woolhandler grapple with the implications of uncontested proceedings in American state courts, whose general jurisdiction embraces a wider variety of subject matters than those encompassed by the federal courts. In the eighteenth century, state courts regularly entertained uncontested petitions for adjustment of status and judicial certification of transactions such as probate proceedings in the common, or uncontested, form. Today, state courts continue to preside over such matters, as well as over petitions for name changes, adoptions, and other uncontested matters of family law. To be sure, the Court-created justiciability doctrines have come to be viewed as more demanding in certain respects than the judicial limits that may apply to some state courts, and state precedents have no binding force in federal court. Nonetheless, state practice illuminates the way lawyers in the early Republic understood the nature of judicial power generally and helps to explain why assignments of uncontested work to the federal judiciary did not raise eyebrows in antebellum America.[17]

9.3 Toward a Theory of Adverse Interests

Professor Woolhandler deserves credit for undertaking the proposed recharacterization of the adverse party requirement. But she fails to supply the kind of detailed framework that would enable readers to evaluate her proposed recharacterization. Here one might invoke Professor Akhil Amar's idea that it takes a theory to beat a theory. To be plausible and fairly comparable to its competitors, a theory should offer an account of the text and history of Article III, an account of judicial and legislative practice under that Article, and perhaps a normative justification for the lines drawn. Woolhandler does none of these things, aside from offering a rich and very useful discussion of federal judicial practice. One cannot say with confidence what limits her theory would impose, where they come from, or what sorts of practices would succeed and fail under her assessment. As a consequence, readers cannot conduct a comparative evaluation of how well our two competing theories "fit" with surrounding judicial practices and longstanding institutional commitments.[18]

One possible account of adverse interests would essentially read the requirement out of Article III altogether. Thus, one could reinterpret the naturalization (and veterans' pension) proceedings of the early Republic as cases in which the United States government (as the possible adversary) has consented in advance to the entry of a default judgment as to any finding of citizenship (or award of pension benefits) that the judge agrees to enter upon an ex parte application. Though not a formal party, the government, on this view, might be seen as revoking its consent in the small set of cases in which it learns of an award that was entered in error. Such revocation could then set the stage for an action to recover the pension or a proceeding to vacate the naturalization decree. The government has a potential interest adverse to all claimants on its largesse and poses a threat to institute adverse litigation. Professor Woolhandler, for her part, indicates that she would not embrace so far-reaching a view, apparently due to concerns with the lack of formal notice to the adversary.

But Professor Woolhandler would not apparently require formal notice to the possible adverse party in every instance. For example, she rationalizes the practice of issuing warrants on ex parte application by observing that the targets of such warrants frequently learn of them upon execution and can contest their entry at that later stage. Where no such notice through execution occurs (as with the issuance of FISA warrants), Woolhandler refrains from endorsing the practice as permissible. Hence, post-hoc notice and the prospect of contestation can save a proceeding that might otherwise be problematic. What then does she make of prize and capture proceedings in admiralty, which made no pretense of specifically notifying the possibly adverse claimants in advance and offered no mechanism by which an unlucky former owner could contest an erroneous declaration of good prize upon later learning of the seizure? Woolhandler tells us that potentially interested parties were theoretically notified by seizure of the vessel in keeping with the (in rem) procedural due process rules of the day, even if many potentially interested parties did not receive notice as a practical matter. But she does not explain how the un-notified potential adversary in a prize proceeding can represent an adverse interest more effectively than the un-notified potential adversaries who have been targeted for foreign intelligence surveillance.[19]

By the same token, Professor Woolhandler does not consider whether the type of forum in which the potential contest might unfold should be weighed as a factor in her analysis of potential adverse interests. Justice Field took the position that a federal commission's investigative proceeding did not provide for contestation of the kind that would support a federal judicial role in the issuance of subpoenas; on this view, one might limit federal courts to the issuance of subpoenas only in support of their own contested proceedings rather than as an adjunct to proceedings elsewhere. Woolhandler does not say whether Justice Field was right to dismiss such potential adverseness on the basis that it would unfold outside the Article III judiciary. Nor does she take a position as to whether the adverse proceedings of foreign courts might provide an adverse-interest basis for an original petition to a federal court for the issuance of letters rogatory (essentially subpoenas to collect evidence in the United States for use before foreign tribunals).[20]

In essence, then, Professor Woolhandler presents a more elegant version of potential adversary theories that have cropped up in the literature from time to time. Many scholars have considered only a piece of the available evidence, criticizing the exercise of uncontested adjudication as a violation of Article III and treating counterexamples as anomalies. That was the approach taken by Ralph Avery, for example, in highlighting certain uncontested features of bankruptcy administration. Woolhandler embraces bankruptcy administration and equity receiverships as appropriate exercises of judicial power even in the absence of contestation, and would apparently reject Avery's view of Article III limits. But like other scholars, she continues to dismiss naturalization (and other examples) as anomalous because her theory cannot account for or explain it.[21]

In contrast, this book's framework for uncontested adjudication could apply to (and account for) a range of situations. So long as Congress acts pursuant to its enumerated powers in creating a right and assigns the federal courts final authority over applications by parties to claim such a right, federal courts can entertain uncontested applications to register claims to the right in question. Procedural due process will ensure notice to interested parties and will invalidate any scheme (such as feigned or collusive litigation) that threatens to injure the rights of nonparties. By assigning the question to Congress to resolve as a matter of policy, one can rationalize the cases in terms of the exercise of congressional discretion, rather than judicial power. To be sure, one might encourage Congress to limit the non-contentious role of the federal courts, especially when federal agencies can readily perform the work. And one might well encourage the courts to refrain from making far-reaching legal pronouncements in the context of uncontested adjudication. Chapter 11 builds on these concerns in proposing guidelines for federal courts to use in the course of handling uncontested matters.[22]

9.4 The Relevance of the Text

Professor Woolhandler similarly fails to come to grips with the text of Article III either to defend her adverse-interests account or to refute a suggested distinction between contested and uncontested adjudication.

Early interpretations of the word "Case" in Article III, as a claim of right in the forms prescribed by law, were capacious enough to encompass both forms of adjudication. By contrast, the word "Controversy" connotes a dispute between party opponents identified in Article III and seems to rule out non-contentious jurisdiction. Couple this textual evidence of distinct meaning with evidence from practice: federal courts consistently took up non-contentious chores in federal question "cases," and refused to do such work in connection with state law "controversies." Indeed, the probate exception derived in part from the requirements of contestation embedded in the term "Controversies." The conflation of the terms cases and controversies first occurred in the late nineteenth century, in an apparent effort to impose a new requirement of contestation in federal question cases.[23]

Professor Woolhandler does not dispute any of this head on and thus fails to address the possibility that Article III requires contestation only as to controversies and not as to cases. She does observe that scholars have proposed alternative distinctions, including the suggestion that the term "Controversies" includes only matters of a civil nature and thus differs from the more inclusive reference to "Cases" of both a criminal and civil nature. But one can accept such suggested distinctions without rejecting the claim that the judicial power in cases, but not in controversies, extends to both contested and uncontested proceedings. Cases may differ from controversies in a number of respects. In any case, the work by earlier scholars on the case–controversy distinction was published long ago. It misses the point to treat earlier scholarship (which does not address this book's new evidence as to the meaning of cases in Article III) as having rejected a theory that was unavailable at the time the scholars on whom Woolhandler relies did their work.[24]

9.5 History and Legal Method

In contrast to this book's account of uncontested adjudication, Professor Woolhandler does not explicitly ground her construct in historical sources. Instead, Woolhandler offers her adverse interest theory as a way to align some uncontested federal court proceedings with contemporary conceptions of the judicial power. Woolhandler does not point to historical sources that identify an "adverse interest" subspecies. Even if both conventional federal controversies and certain of the ex parte cases on which she focuses could be reconceptualized as involving adverse interests, she fails to show that observers from the eighteenth century considered the existence of adverse interests as central to the judicial cognizability of those cases. Woolhandler identifies no source from the eighteenth or early nineteenth century that seeks to defend naturalization or other early forms as proper instances of adverse-interest contestation.[25]

To the contrary, the historical evidence suggests that many of the practices Professor Woolhandler now defines as supported by adverse interests were explained in the eighteenth century as instances of uncontested adjudication. For example, even though potential adversaries presumably lurk in the background of any uncontested application for probate of a will, Blackstone's *Commentaries* recognizes the category of non-contentious jurisdiction in a brief discussion of probate practice. Discussing the matter of non-contentious jurisdiction at somewhat greater length, Thomas Wood's eighteenth-century treatise described consent as the key to distinguishing contentious and non-contentious jurisdiction. Wood treats emancipation, manumission, and adoption as instances of non-contentious jurisdiction and then refers to "several other legal Acts granted by the Judge upon request, and by consent of all Parties." Woolhandler regards these matters of consensual adjustment as reflecting the resolution of a conflict between parties holding adverse interests. But that's not the way eighteenth-century thinkers explained the judicial role in overseeing consensual adjustment. It seems more likely that the Framers shared the eighteenth-century understanding than a revisionist understanding put forth one or two centuries later.[26]

Apart from offering little historical support, Professor Woolhandler does not advance any explicit normative arguments in the course of defending her suggested adverse-interest requirement. Nor does she explain the methodological basis on which she would regard such a requirement as constitutionally compelled by Article III. Indeed, the absence of normative or policy-based justifications for such a requirement, or for its selective relaxation in particular cases involving relatively remote adverse interests, suggests that Woolhandler writes with a view toward defending a conventional, latter-day understanding of Article III adjudication. On the antebellum view of the Article III case, parties do not need an injury in fact to pursue a claim in federal court. Redress of injuries was certainly one form of adjudication known to the Framers, but it did not exhaust the category.[27]

Professor Woolhandler previously defended the Court's standing jurisprudence on historical grounds. As in her response to uncontested adjudication,

Woolhandler and Caleb Nelson offered a qualified defense of standing law against challenges based on evidence that historical practice was inconsistent with the notion that Article III adjudication has always been limited to those making claims for redress of injuries in fact. The earlier paper accorded a good deal of weight to evolving judicial practice in the late nineteenth and early twentieth centuries and sought to distinguish counterexamples as uncommon or anomalous even as it sought to restate the conventional wisdom in more readily defensible terms. Perhaps Woolhandler maintains a continuing commitment to the view that history does not defeat modern standing doctrine. After all, acceptance of non-contentious jurisdiction means that the injury requirement, so central to modern standing doctrine, does not accurately describe many uncontested cases that appeared on the dockets of early state and federal courts.[28]

But such an approach to scholarship on the meaning of Article III raises questions about the normative justification for, and workability of, the regime the author seeks to defend. Consider, for example, the problem of deciding when the interest of a potential adversary achieves the degree of concreteness needed to satisfy the demands of Article III. Many authors have invoked the construct of the potential adversary as a way to square uncontested practices with the presumed applicability of an adverse-party requirement. But these authors, like Professor Woolhandler, rarely explain how concrete or specific a possible adverse interest must be to satisfy the supposed Article III standard. Does litigation yielding a consent decree qualify? How about a settlement class action? Must the holder of an adversarial interest be notified of the proceeding and invited to participate? Or do more remote prospects of adversarial participation suffice?[29]

One might begin to answer such questions with a normative account of the purposes served by an adverse-interest or adverse-party requirement. But Professor Woolhandler does not offer such an account. How then should courts and litigants draw a line between the sufficiently and insufficiently adverse interest? Should they align themselves with Justice Kennedy's *Windsor* opinion in viewing the adverse-party requirement as one the Court might dispense with on the basis of prudential considerations, or follow Justice Scalia's lead in viewing the requirement as a crucial element of Article III? Neither the practices that Woolhandler catalogs nor the reasons they arose help to resolve that puzzle.[30]

Nor does Professor Woolhandler evaluate the application of her construct of adverse interests to other matters within Article III such as the provision for jurisdiction over controversies between citizens of different states. Controversies seemingly require a dispute between opponents and differ from cases on this score. Extending that idea, the distinction between "cases" and "controversies" may, as we have seen, help to explain the inability of the federal courts to entertain matters falling within the so-called probate and domestic relations exceptions. Because state law typically provides the rule of decision for such matters, they come to federal diversity dockets as "controversies" between citizens of different states. But some of the state court proceedings within the categories in question, such as common-form probate proceedings and certain domestic relations matters (for example, marriage; adoption; custody and guardianship appointments) proceed on an uncontested basis. Either no contest has emerged (as in common-form probate proceedings) or the parties come to court to register an agreed-upon change in legal status, as with adoption proceedings. The absence of any "controversy" between disputing parties helps to explain why these non-contentious matters do not qualify for adjudication under Article III (at least so long as they remain governed by state law). On the theory defended in this book, however, a decision by Congress to federalize the substantive law would allow such matters to be brought to federal courts as "cases."[31]

From Woolhandler's vantage point, adverse interests might be said to lurk beneath the surface of these nominally uncontested matters of probate and family law. Sometimes, a dispute breaks into the open, necessitating the transformation of a common-form probate proceeding into a formal will contest. But often the adverse interests (between the birth mother, say, and the adoptive parents or between the administrator of the estate who institutes probate in the common form and some of the estate's potential beneficiaries) are submerged or compromised. The absence of an open controversy would foreclose the exercise of party-based jurisdiction, thus helping to explain why these matters fall outside Article III. How would Professor Woolhandler treat the potential presence of adverse interests in evaluating party-based jurisdiction? If the possibility of contestation creates adverse interests sufficient to meet the Article III requirement, then perhaps the Constitution would allow federal courts to exercise diversity jurisdiction over uncontested matters of state law on the theory that the potential for adversary litigation creates the sort of "controversy" necessary to satisfy the party-based heads of Article III jurisdiction. On that view, Congress could assign common-form probate matters or other uncontested matters of state law to the federal diversity docket, assuming the potential contestants were citizens of different states. Such a "case-or-controversy" requirement would apply the same adverse interest construct across the Article III menu, but would produce results so unusual as to cast doubt on Woolhandler's account. The adverse-interest construct fails to explain the available evidence as well as this book's suggested distinction between cases and controversies.[32]

Notes

1. *See, e.g.*, Richardson v. Ramirez, 418 U.S. 24, 36 (1974) ("While the Supreme Court of California may choose to adjudicate a controversy simply because of its public importance, and the desirability of a statewide decision, we are limited by the case-or-controversy requirement of Art. III to adjudication of actual disputes between adverse parties."). Scalia's quoted language appears in *Windsor*, 570 U.S. at 785 (Scalia, J., dissenting). *See* Pfander & Birk, *Article III Judicial Power*, at 1379 (discussing Silberman testimony arguing that federal courts could not constitutionally oversee ex parte applications for foreign surveillance warrants because of their non-adversarial character). *See* Avery, *Article III and Title 11* (arguing that certain non-contentious features of bankruptcy administration may violate Article III). *See* Morley, *Consent of the Governed or Consent of the Government?* (contending that consent decrees lack the adverseness necessary to warrant judicial involvement).
2. *See* Ann Woolhandler, *Adverse Interests and Article III*, 111 Nw. U. L. Rev. 1025, 1032–40 (2017). *Id.* at 1032–40. For Justice Scalia's view, *see Windsor*, 570 U.S. at 784–86 (Scalia, J., dissenting).
3. *See* Woolhandler at 1036–40. Indeed, the eventual demise of in rem jurisdiction reflects the Supreme Court's acceptance of the idea that a suit against property effectively operates as "a proceeding against the owners of that property." Shaffer v. Heitner, 433 U.S. 186, 205 (1977). *See* Woolhandler at 1037–40. *See* Pfander & Birk, *Article III Judicial Power*, at 1420 n.349. *See id.* (quoting Justice Story's recognition that adverse parties need not appear to ground Article III jurisdiction because the court acts as the "general guardian" of all interests brought to its attention); Arlyck at 264–65. On the rationale of requiring adverse presentations, *see* Wright & Kane, Law of Federal Courts, § 12, at 60 (noting the "risk that comes from passing on abstract questions rather than limiting decisions to concrete cases in which a question is precisely framed by a clash of genuine adversary argument exploring every aspect of the issue" (citing United States v. Fruehauf, 365 U.S. 146 (1961); Golden v. Zwickler, 394 U.S. 103 (1969))).
4. On the attendant problems of feigned cases, *see* the discussion of *Lord v. Veazie* in chapter 7.6. *See* Pfander & Birk, *Article III Judicial Power*, at 1433–40. *Id.* at 1434–38. *See* Woolhandler at 1047–54 (distinguishing jurisdictional from merits collusion aimed at procuring the resolution of a genuine dispute from the more problematic form of merits collusion).

5. On the history of naturalization petitions, *see* chapters 2.1 (antebellum practice) and 7.1 (nineteenth-century practice). *See* Pfander & Birk, *Article III Judicial Power*, at 1361–63, 1393–1402. For the "best example" concession, *see* Woolhandler at 1056.
6. *See* Woolhandler at 1061–65. *See* Act of Mar. 26, 1790, ch. 3, 1 Stat. 103. *Tutun* is discussed in chapter 7.1. *See* Pfander & Birk, *Article III Judicial Power*, at 1414–21, 1421–24. For Justice Brandeis's validation of the naturalization example, *see Tutun*, 270 U.S. 568, 576–78 (1926).
7. The historical development from antebellum to nineteenth-century practice is discussed in Part II. *See* Pfander & Birk, *Article III Judicial Power*, 1401, 1421–24. *Id.* at 1359–91.
8. Woolhandler at 1065. *Cf.* David A. Strauss, *Common Law Constitutional Interpretation*, 63 U. Chi. L. Rev. 877 (1996) (advocating a common law understanding of the development of constitutional doctrine).
9. *See* Hayburn's Case, 2 U.S. (2 Dall.) 409 (1792). For Woolhandler's account, Woolhandler at 1056–58 & n.154 (citing the work of Russell Wheeler and Susan Low Bloch). Justice Iredell's notes of the oral argument in *Hayburn* are collected in 8 Documentary History of the Supreme Court at 547–50 & n.1 (2007). Although Justice Iredell often took copious notes, *see* 5 Documentary History at 164–93, 214–17 (collecting the Justice's extensive notes on his views about the susceptibility of states to suit and his account of the argument in *Chisholm v. Georgia*, 2 U.S. (2 Dall.) 419 (1793)), we do not know how well he captured the discussion or whether his notes reflect the views of the Justices or the arguments of counsel. In describing "objections" to the pension statute, Justice Iredell's notes read as follows:

   Objections.

   1. Not of a Judicial nature.
   2. Not to be exercised in a Judicial manner.

   As to the first, it must be found in the Constitution all Laws under the United States &c.
   Contracts equally valid &c.
   Pensioners. all public Services
   Congress have done nothing more than to direct [the pensioners'] titles to be re-examined
   In effect a Suitor.
   Petitions of Right & *Monstrans de droit* Destitute of forms of Writ_
   Suit_ a Demand of any thing.
   A more dignified mode of becoming a Defendant 2. Not to be executed in a Judicial way.
   Examples.
   To inspect wounds in the case of *Mayhems*.
   Substance only to be regarded where a Sovereignty permits itself to be sued.
   Forms may be disregarded where Parties agree.

   8 Documentary History at 548–49.

10. For the clarification of a long-mooted scholarly debate over the power of Randolph to proceed in the Supreme Court without a client, *see* Maeva Marcus & Robert Teir, Hayburn's Case: *A Misinterpretation of Precedent*, 1988 Wis. L. Rev. 527 (1988)

(concluding that the issue in the Court focused on Randolph's authority to represent the government by virtue of his office).

11. Woolhandler at 1058–60 (quoting terms of curative legislation). The curative 1793 legislation made a number of changes. In particular, it avoided the finality problem by instructing the district judge to collect evidence under oath and send the evidence along to the Secretary of War and ultimately to Congress, which reserved to itself the power to make any "proper" order. *See* An Act To Regulate the Claims to Invalid Pensions, ch. 17, § 2, 1 Stat. 324, 325 (1793) (calling on the Secretary of War to make a report based on the evidence submitted as would enable Congress to "take such order thereon, as [it] may judge proper"). In addition, the task of inspecting wounds and disabilities was transferred from federal judges to physicians, who were expected to offer their opinion as to the extent of the claimant's disability. *See* Act of March 23, 1792 § 2, 1 Stat. 243. In a portion of Chief Justice Taney's opinion in *United States v. Ferreira*, 54 U.S. (13 How.) 40, 45 (1852), the Court identified problems with the legislative appointment of federal judges to serve as commissioners as a potential argument against the viability of the assignment by statute of nonjudicial work to the federal judiciary.
12. *See* Woolhandler at 1027 n.4, 1058 (asserting that their ex parte character was a factor in the Court's conclusion that treaty claims were not Article III cases). *See Ferreira*, 54 U.S. at 51–52.
13. *Id.* at 45. *See id.* at 47.
14. *Id.* at 44. Counsel made the point in an effort to show that ex parte proceedings were proper subjects of the judicial power. On counsel's view, appeals would lie from decisions adverse to claimants, but not from those adverse to the government. *Id.* at 46–47. For this account of the naturalization process, *see* chapter 2.1.
15. *See Ferreira*, 54 U.S. at 49–51. *Id.* at 51. Professor Woolhandler treats the *Ferreira* Court's appendix, containing information on the 1794 unpublished decision in *United States v. Todd*, as support for interpreting *Hayburn's Case* to express concern with the absence of adverse parties. *See* Woolhandler at 1059. To be sure, the *Todd* decision invalidated a pension award under the 1792 legislation, holding that the decisions of judges as self-styled commissioners were not lawful adjudications. *See Ferreira*, 54 U.S. at 53. There were at least two reasons for that conclusion: that the Act assigned the power to the "court" rather than to the judges as such (and thus ruled out action by the judges out of court) and that the appointment of commissioners requires action by the President, rather than legislation by Congress. Taney invoked *Todd* to highlight his concern with legislative appointment of judges as commissioners. Nothing in his opinion, or in his account of *Todd*, expresses doubts about the power of federal courts to enter judgments in ex parte proceedings, so long as the proceedings comply with the requirement of judicial finality. Woolhandler has much to say about commissioners and judicial power, but fails to adduce a single case in which the Court has condemned as improperly ex parte a procedure in which the lower courts were empowered to enter a final judgment.
16. *See* chapter 2.2 for an account of warrant proceedings in the early Republic. *See* Pfander & Birk, *Article III Judicial Power*, at 1375–78. Woolhandler at 1043–46.

17. So-called common form probate applications by the administrator of the probate estate were legally effective in clothing the administrator with the power to act and did not require party-contestation to take effect. *See* Pfander & Downey, *In Search of the Probate Exception*. *See also* chapter 4.2. Matters of state law have a place on Article III dockets only if they satisfy the controversy requirement (or qualify for the exercise of supplemental jurisdiction), something uncontested probate applications fail to do. On the exercise of non-contentious jurisdiction in family law matters and the origins of the so-called domestic relations exception to Article III, *see* Pfander & Damrau, *A Non-Contentious Account of Article III's Domestic Relations Exception*. *See* Hollingsworth v. Perry, 570 U.S. 693, 713–15 (2013).
18. *See* Akhil Reed Amar, *The Two-Tiered Structure of the Judiciary Act of 1789*, 138 U. Pa. L. Rev. 1499, 1566 (1990) (suggesting that one should conduct a comparison of competing Article III theories under a preponderance of the evidence standard to determine which theory is more plausible).
19. Woolhandler at 1119–20. Pfander & Birk, *Article III Judicial Power*, at 1462–63 (noting that, "unlike the targets of other warrant proceedings, most FISA targets will never learn that the surveillance has been carried out" because the surveillance is carried out covertly and the warrant proceedings are classified). Chapter 7.5 discusses the FISA court's proceedings in more detail. Woolhandler at 1046. *Id.* at 1039–40.
20. *See In re* Pac. Ry. Comm'n, 32 F. 241, 257–59, 257 n.1 (C.C.N.D. Cal. 1887). *Cf.* chapter 5.1 (discussing Justice Field's opinion).
21. On bankruptcy, *see* chapter 7.3. *See* Avery, *Article III and Title 11*, at 418 n.137. *See* Woolhandler at 1033–35. *Cf.* Hart & Wechsler 85–86; Morley, *Consent of the Governed or Consent of the Government?*, at 668–70. Woolhandler at 1065.
22. *See* chapters 10 and 11 for a development of this framework. *See also* Pfander & Birk, *Article III Judicial Power*, at 1440–55; *id.* at 1455–71 (applying framework to applications for certificates of appealability by habeas corpus petitioners, the "probate exception" to federal court jurisdiction, extradition proceedings, FISA courts, and more). *Id.* at 1440–45. *See id.* at 1453–55.
23. For the earlier Marshall-Story account of cases, *see* chapter 4. On nineteenth-century changes in meaning, *see* chapters 5 and 6.
24. Woolhandler at 1028 n.9 (listing John Harrison and Daniel Meltzer as scholars who endorse this view). *See generally* Pfander, *Rethinking the Supreme Court's Original Jurisdiction in State-Party Cases* at 604–12 (distinguishing cases from controversies). Of course, some scholars did anticipate our conclusions in suggesting that cases and controversies meant different things in Article III. *See* Pushaw, *Article III's Case/Controversy Distinction*, at 450.
25. *See, e.g.*, Woolhandler at 1036–40 (conceptualizing prize cases as default judgments in an in rem suit as consistent with procedural due process requirements of the time).
26. 3 Blackstone, at *98. *See* Wood at 293. Chapter 1.3 and notes trace the legal landscape with which the Framers were familiar.
27. Pfander & Birk, *Article III Judicial Power*, at 1452 ("In deploying non-contentious jurisdiction, Congress can create individual rights and enable individuals to bring an ex parte action in federal court to secure formal recognition of the right in question.

Such individuals have not suffered an 'injury-in-fact'; rather, they seek to establish a legal interest through the assertion of their claim."); *see also* Pushaw, *Justiciability and Separation of Powers*, at 485–90 (refuting the claim that standing requires an injury in fact).

28. *See* Ann Woolhandler & Caleb Nelson, *Does History Defeat Standing Doctrine?*, 102 MICH. L. REV. 689 (2004). *But cf.* Raoul Berger, *Standing to Sue in Public Actions: Is It a Constitutional Requirement?*, 78 YALE L.J. 816 (1969) (showing that the personal interest requirement of modern standing doctrine lacks historical support in both early English and American legal tradition); Steven L. Winter, *The Metaphor of Standing and the Problem of Self-Governance*, 40 STAN. L. REV. 1371, 1406–09 (1988) (arguing that standing law's injury-in-fact requirement was at odds with the early willingness of federal courts to hear suits brought by informers who sought bounties rather than redress of injuries personal to themselves). *See* chapters 1.1–1.3 for a discussion of Roman, European, and colonial non-contentious procedures.
29. Pfander & Birk, *Article III Judicial Power*, at 1393–96.
30. *Compare Windsor*, 570 U.S. at 756–62 (Kennedy, J.) (describing adverse-party requirement as prudential), *with id.* at 784–85 (Scalia, J., dissenting) (portraying adverse-party requirement as an element of Article III).
31. Chapter 4.2 and accompanying notes provide an account of the case–controversy distinction in the state-law context of probate and family law. *See* 28 U.S.C. § 1332(a) (2012) (conferring diversity jurisdiction); *id.* § 1652 (prescribing state law as the rule of decision, except where otherwise provided). For the argument on federalization of substantive law, *see* Pfander & Damrau at 149; Pfander & Downey at 1577.
32. *See* Pfander & Downey at 1553. *See* Woolhandler at 1036–46 (describing the potential for adverse argument in prize, remission, and warrant cases to provide the necessary adverseness to satisfy Article III).

10

Uncontested Adjudication and Standing to Sue

Just as this book's proposed account of cases and controversies casts doubt on a thoroughgoing adverse-interest requirement, so too does it undermine the claim that Article III limits adjudication to those seeking redress for an injury in fact. This chapter proposes to formulate a new, more historically defensible basis for the judicial assessment of standing to sue—one that would focus on whether the plaintiff has a "litigable interest," rather than an injury in fact. Borrowed from one account of standing law, and adapted in light of historical practice, the construct of a litigable interest would encompass claims by those seeking redress for injuries in fact as well as by plaintiffs who assert rights in uncontested proceedings, who assert bounty claims, and who bring suit on behalf of the public in appropriate circumstances. Adoption of the litigable interest construct would enable the Supreme Court to relax its across-the-board injury requirement and thereby bring the law of standing into better alignment with the increasingly case-specific state of the doctrine.[1]

In developing its litigable interest test, the chapter begins with *Spokeo, Inc. v. Robins* and with the concurring suggestion of Justice Clarence Thomas that standing law differs in suits brought to enforce public and private rights. While Justice Thomas correctly identified a disparity in the doctrine, he takes a too narrow view of the historical ability of litigants to mount public or popular actions. His error lies in the assumption that the common-law forms of action exhaust the historical forms of litigation in place at the time of the Framing. In the Roman or civil-law tradition—a tradition that informed the development of practice in the courts of equity and admiralty—popular actions were available to interested members of the public without any showing of personal injury. After describing Scotland's representative experience with the civil law *actio popularis*, or popular action, this chapter suggests that history offers a straightforward basis for regarding private litigants as having a litigable interest in the enforcement of public rights.[2]

Cases Without Controversies. James E. Pfander, Oxford University Press. © James E. Pfander 2021.
DOI: 10.1093/oso/9780197571408.003.0011

10.1 The Public–Private Distinction in *Spokeo*

The Court's 2016 decision in *Spokeo, Inc. v. Robins* addressed Congress's power to authorize private individuals to pursue so-called "no injury" class actions: suits to recover penalties for noncompliance with federal consumer protection laws. Firms supporting Spokeo, an internet search firm that collects financial and other information on individuals, sought a broad ruling foreclosing such claims (and the class actions they engender). Consumer groups preferred a ruling upholding the Ninth Circuit's decision that individuals always have standing to pursue claims for violation of a statute that confers rights on them personally. On that broad view, litigants would need only allege a violation of the statute without showing any injury specific to themselves. Scholars took heed: the case raised the prospect that the Court might deploy Article III as a constitutional limit on the power of Congress to create new rights enforceable through private litigation. A strict reading of the injury-in-fact rule might also undermine a variety of claims (such as those for trespass and nominal damages) that the common law conventionally allowed litigants to pursue without a showing of harm.[3]

The Court reaffirmed the injury requirement, but did less than was hoped and feared. Emphasizing that injuries must be both particularized (or individual) and concrete, the Court vacated the Ninth Circuit decision on the basis that it had failed to give the concreteness requirement sufficient attention. Violation of a statute, without more, would not necessarily result in any injury to Robins, or to the class he proposed to represent. True, Congress can recognize new rights and authorize individuals to sue for their violation. But Spokeo's publication of an individual's incorrect zip code, for example, would not ordinarily cause any harm and was not a proper subject of federal litigation. The Court held that congressional say-so alone will not suffice; harm must be real ("de facto") as well as legally actionable under the statute. Two Justices dissented on the ground that Robins's complaint adequately alleged genuine harm resulting from the publication of false information that might hurt his job prospects.[4]

Writing in concurrence with the majority, Justice Thomas expressed a willingness to rethink the monolithic character of the injury-in-fact requirement. Justice Thomas began as did his colleagues: by reaffirming the centrality of history. Standing doctrine was said to limit the judicial power to matters "of the sort traditionally amenable to, and resolved by, the judicial process." For Justice Thomas these limits derived from "the traditional, fundamental limitations upon the powers of common-law courts." Building on scholarship by Woolhandler and Nelson and that by Andrew Hessick, Justice Thomas explained that the common law evaluated the plaintiff's right to sue "depending on the type of right the plaintiff sought to vindicate." In the arena of private rights, the common-law courts were willing to adjudicate bare allegations of a rights violation, and nothing more. In many instances, as in suits for trespass, infringement of intellectual property, and unjust enrichment, no showing of damage or harm was required and the suit could proceed on the basis of an invasion of legal right.[5]

Justice Thomas explained, however, that for violations of "public rights," "[c]ommon-law courts . . . have required a further showing of injury." Ordinarily, the government alone had authority to vindicate a harm inflicted on the public at large. In the small collection of cases in which private plaintiffs could sue for a violation of public rights, they had to show that the violation caused them some special harm. Here, Justice Thomas invoked the example of nuisance litigation and quoted William Blackstone for the proposition that only claimants who alleged special damage were permitted to proceed on behalf of the public, "lest 'every subject in the kingdom'" "harass the offender with separate actions." Justice Thomas then generalized: the law of standing demands a stronger showing of injury in fact as a predicate for public law litigation than for private rights litigation, and it "applies with special force when a plaintiff files suit to require an executive agency to 'follow the law.'" These sorts of public-law claims, according to Justice Thomas, threaten to embroil the judiciary in political disputes and thus occasion the separation-of-powers concerns that have been cited to justify a more stringent injury-in-fact requirement. Private suits to enforce private rights, by contrast, do not intrude on the political branches and thus may proceed without a showing of actual injury apart from the violation of the right itself.[6]

Justice Thomas deserves credit for attempting to rationalize the law of standing by recognizing that the Court has applied its injury-in-fact requirement with varying force depending on the context. Scholars have increasingly recognized the fragmentary character of standing law. Evan Lee and Josephine Ellis showed that the redressability requirements have been relaxed in procedural rights cases; Richard Fallon traced the very different way the Court has applied standing rules across different substantive areas of law; Hessick drew a distinction between private and public rights litigation and the stringency of the injury-in-fact requirement in those different settings. But two related features of Justice Thomas's approach to standing law pose problems. First, the repeated emphasis on the work of the common-law courts necessarily hides from view the adjudicatory practices of the civil-law-inflected courts of equity and admiralty. Uncontested adjudication was a creature of civil law; most common-law proceedings were contested *inter partes* disputes. By limiting his gaze to common-law practice, Justice Thomas ignored the civilians, and the voluntary forms of adjudication they embraced, just as Justice Brandeis narrowed his historical focus to exclude declaratory judgment practice in Scotland. When it comes to standing, at least in Justice Thomas's telling, the common law has conquered equity, not the other way around.[7]

The emphasis on common-law forms may blind the Court to uncontested practices in equity and obscure the very different way in which the civilians managed the right of individuals to judicial process. Consider, in this vein, the distinction Christopher Columbus Langdell drew between the practice in courts of common law and that in courts of equity. Langdell recognized the existence of uncontested adjudication but viewed it as a creature of equity. He thus explained that the "jurisdiction of a court of [common] law is contentious only, that is, it is strictly limited to deciding controversies." By contrast, Langdell explained, the power of the chancellor in a court of equity is not "limited to deciding controversies." To illustrate the point in equity, Langdell invoked the power of the trustee to apply to the chancellor for instructions. Such bills did not, in Langdell's telling, seek to resolve a contest over the trustee's "misconduct" but instead to clarify the nature of the trustee's duty and to secure "the assistance and protection of the court."[8]

If Langdell was right to distinguish common-law proceedings from those in equity, then a mode of historical analysis that focuses solely on common-law practices will give a false picture of judicial power. Common-law assumptions about the nature of the adversary system cannot account for uncontested proceedings in equity (proceedings that often lacked both an injury in fact and an adverse party). Likewise, too strong an emphasis on common-law forms today may obscure the civilians' historic willingness to embrace the right of private individuals to bring public actions. As noted earlier, the Romans developed a popular action or *actio popularis* that enabled private individuals to sue on behalf of the public interest. The recognition of such a right to sue, though qualified in important respects, provides an important historical precursor to modern public law litigation. The next section briefly recounts the roots of the Scottish version of the *actio popularis*, as it developed in the Scottish Court of Session in the eighteenth century. At a minimum, the history complicates the proposed distinction between private and public rights that informed the work of Woolhandler and Nelson. More intriguingly, the Scottish practice suggests a basis for incorporating a qualified version of the public action into the book's proposed conception of the litigable interest.[9]

10.2 Civil Law and the Example of Scotland

The treatment of the Roman law *actio popularis* by the Scottish Court of Session may provide a useful building block for the construction of a more nuanced, historically inflected body of standing law. The Court of Session served as Scotland's highest court in civil-law matters, exercising jurisdiction over suits in law and equity. By the eighteenth century, the Court of Session had long agreed to entertain what Abram Chayes would later describe as "public law" litigation: that is, suits brought to declare and clarify the commonly held or public rights of individuals in cases where government bodies appeared as interested parties. Practice before the Court of Session came to include features that resemble the law of standing that later arose to define and constrain the work of the courts of the United States.[10]

For starters, the Scots developed a separate set of rules to govern the standing of parties in the ordinary course of private litigation. The Court of Session framed this standing inquiry in terms of the plaintiff's (or pursuer's) "title" and "interest" to sue. To pursue a claim, a plaintiff was required to show that she had both an interest in the relief being sought and title to pursue the claim. Not everyone with an interest (or something to gain) could initiate an action; instead, Scots law limited court access to those with title, which served as a concept that restricted suit to those with a clear legal right to pursue the claim. Scots private law ruled out third-party standing for those seeking to enforce the rights of another party, which the Scots, following Roman law, called *jus tertii*. Despite these private-law standing limits, the Scots recognized an exception for a "popular action," or what the Scots referred to (again following Roman law) as an *actio popularis*. The *actio popularis* authorized any person to pursue a claim on behalf of the public in cases in which a public delict or wrong might otherwise go unredressed. The Scots version of the *actio popularis* empowered an individual to mount a claim, often in an action for a declaratory judgment, when the defendant (often a public body) had impinged on rights held in common by a variety of individuals. None of the would-be plaintiffs had a clear title to sue in cases of such widespread and somewhat diffuse injury, yet the Court of Session formulated rules enabling one or more of them to pursue the claim in order to avoid a defect of justice. The conception of the Court of Session as a court of equity, acting in the last resort, helped to justify such *actio popularis* proceedings in the eighteenth century. Indeed, the Court of Session seems to have recognized that the rules of standing applicable to private litigation must give way to allow public actions to proceed.[11]

The decision to allow a single champion to step forward on behalf of the public posed a threat of duplicative litigation and necessitated some form of coordination or preclusion. In some circumstances, *actio popularis* decrees were given some preclusive effect in subsequent litigation, at least where there was a "sufficient identity of interest" between earlier and later litigants. A twentieth-century source states that, for an *actio popularis*:

> [T]he answer to the question as to whether there is such community of interest as to make a previous decision *res judicata* as against the parties to a subsequent action, would appear to depend largely upon whether there is or is not a contract expressed or implied between the parties to the proceedings or their authors or ancestors.

In an action for a public right-of-way, "where certain parties appear or are called as representing the interests of the general public," the general public is bound by the decision in the earlier suit. But an action by the magistrates of Edinburgh regarding use of a public market was not thought to preclude a second proceeding by members of the general public.[12]

The Court of Session thus struck a balance between competing models of public and private law litigation. Recognizing the importance of title and interest to sue in private matters, the Court of Session acted to prevent a failure of justice by relaxing those strictures for public actions. At the same time, Scots law qualified the pursuit of public or popular actions to limit the assertion of duplicative claims. Scots law thus anticipated some features of public law litigation that have made their way into statute books in the United States. The citizen-suit provisions of some environmental statutes, for example, authorize a plaintiff to litigate public rights claims against a private defendant. But those statutes qualify the right to sue by providing for a measure of governmental oversight (thereby helping to ensure adequate representation of the public interest). And they may accord a degree of nonparty preclusive effect to the decision, thereby shielding the defendant from the threat of repetitive litigation on the same claim. That threat, of course, was among those Justice Thomas highlighted in repeating Blackstone's concern with vexatious litigation.[13]

Cases in the United States from the first half of the nineteenth century come at the problem of the public action from a perspective remarkably similar to that of the Scots. In *People* ex rel. *Case v. Collins*, the New York Supreme Court allowed representatives of the public who lacked any specific injury to seek a mandamus to compel the town's commissioners to perform their duty in laying out a local road or highway. The court acknowledged that, in matters of private right, the suitor must show her "title to relief" or face dismissal of the claim as a stranger. In a "matter of mere public right, however, it is otherwise; here the people are the real party." The courts had long issued mandamus at the suit of representatives of the people at large; after all, "the wrongful refusal of the officers to act is no more the concern of one citizen than another." Distinguishing private from public right, the court quoted with approval the explanation that courts allow such public action proceedings to "prevent a failure of justice." In the end, then, parties without private title or interest were permitted to pursue their claims on behalf of the public as a whole for reasons essentially identical to those that informed the Scots law of the *actio popularis*.[14]

10.3 Standing and the Idea of Litigable Interests

How can we best incorporate the lessons of history and modern practice into a body of law that would govern the individual's right to invoke the judicial power of the United States? Instead of conflating cases and controversies and inflexibly demanding injuries in fact, the Court should ask if the plaintiff can assert a "litigable interest." Such a litigable interest formulation need not inflexibly limit the federal courts to the adjudication of claims for redress of injuries. Indeed, the litigable test could accommodate the adjudication of contested and uncontested claims, recognizing both as asserting claims of right in the form prescribed by law.

The litigable interest construct would allow courts to tailor access to federal court in a way that takes account of the historic distinction between cases and controversies and the rich variety of proceedings on federal dockets. A litigable interest may arise from conduct that inflicts a compensable injury, to be sure, but it can arise in other ways. Modes of litigation vary as well, especially across the law-equity divide. Common-law forms were (as Langdell reminded us) often contentious and would often entail the assertion of a claim for redress of injuries inflicted by the defendant. Equitable and civil-law forms covered more ground, including suits for redress or prevention of injuries and such uncontested proceedings as the trustee's application for instructions, the petition for appointment of a guardian, the initiation of common form probate proceedings, the administration of an estate, and the assertion of uncontested prize claims. Neither concrete injuries nor adverse parties were essential for these forms of equitable proceeding; it was enough that the party asserted a recognized claim of right. By restoring its earlier emphasis on the assertion of claims of right, the Court could revisit its across-the-board injury requirement. By applying a litigable interest test that takes account of the differences between "cases" and "controversies," moreover, the Court could limit the uncontested work of the federal courts to federal question "cases" and continue to insist on full adversary proceedings in matters governed by state law (and thereby reaffirm the probate and domestic relations exceptions to Article III).[15]

Apart from the fact that it better coheres with recognized elements of traditional judicial practice, the litigable interest standard nicely matches the linguistic formulations of early accounts of what it means to bring a "case" in federal court. As we have seen, both Chief Justice Marshall and Justice Story explained that a "case" under federal law consists of the assertion of a claim of right in the forms prescribed by law. The litigable interest standard would build on the Marshall-Story formulation by requiring that plaintiffs who wish to invoke the judicial power set up a claim of right (an "interest") in accordance with the forms prescribed by law ("litigable"). The definition would encompass the assertion of claims seeking redress for an injury as well as ex parte claims to a benefit conferred by federal law, such as petitions for naturalized citizenship.

Use of the litigable interest standard would presume substantial deference to Congress's decisions about when federal courts may entertain original applications to register a claim in uncontested proceedings. Such a deferential approach nicely tracks the model Justice Brandeis offered in *Tutun v. United States*. When Congress chooses to create a federal judicial remedy, as in the case of naturalization, and the individual invokes the established judicial mode, Brandeis found that a case arises "within the meaning of the Constitution." In short, when Congress creates a right and an uncontested mode for the assertion of that right, individuals enjoy a litigable interest in pursuing the right in federal court.[16]

While one can thus quite readily tailor the litigable interest standard to the assertion of uncontested federal claims, the application of the standard to contentious matters will doubtless pose a series of tricky puzzles. We might begin, as the Scots had done and Justice Thomas did in *Spokeo*, by distinguishing the enforcement of private rights from public actions. *Spokeo* appears to present a problem in private rights and thus would seem to call for substantial deference to Congress's power, more perhaps than the majority was willing to grant. The *Spokeo* majority recognized that Congress had created both a federal right to accuracy in credit reportage and a federal right to sue for violations of the right. The majority viewed the actions of Congress as highly influential, at least where those actions promoted de facto injuries (to rights of privacy and reputation) to the status of legal cognizability. But the majority did not regard the claim for violation of a statutory right as sufficient in itself to establish standing, even in the context of private litigation. Beneath the surface of the Court's relatively searching assessment of the plaintiff's standing lay a concern with the use of the so-called "no-injury" class action as a device to aggregate small claims. Such aggregation confronts defendants with substantial liability, perhaps out of proportion to the reputational threat their conduct posed.[17]

One might argue that class action–style litigation, by creating a bounty for successful claim(s) typically payable to the attorney, can lead to relatively intensive enforcement efforts in today's world, perhaps more intensive than a federal agency might pursue. Building on this perception, one might also argue that such intensive enforcement interferes with agency enforcement discretion in a way that undercuts the ability of the executive to "Take Care" that the laws be faithfully executed. Such an argument complicates Justice Thomas's assumption that matters of private right do not implicate the separation of powers. But such an argument fails to recognize the substantial control Congress can properly exercise over the manner in which it divides enforcement authority between federal agencies and private actors. True, the Federal Trade Commission has been assigned enforcement authority under the Fair Credit Reporting Act (FCRA), the statute at issue in *Spokeo*. But Congress specifically created a private right of action allowing individuals affected by an erroneous credit report to recover a specified award of damages. Moreover, Congress has on occasion assigned exclusive enforcement authority to the agency, thereby apparently foreclosing private litigation under the FCRA. So long as one accepts the power of Congress to regulate industry and calibrate enforcement intensity by allocating enforcement authority between federal agencies and private suitors, one has difficulty seeing a role for the Court in treating the congressionally approved existence of private enforcement authority in *Spokeo* as improperly invading executive discretion.[18]

Nor can one articulate a persuasive argument for judicial leadership in updating the regulatory infrastructure in light of technological change. True, Justice Samuel Alito observed in the *Spokeo* majority opinion that the FCRA was enacted "long before the advent of the Internet." But the passage of time does not normally justify the judicial recalibration of statutory remedial systems. For one thing, Congress and the participants in the civil rules advisory process have better access to the kind of information that should inform refinements of credit reporting rules and the class action litigation process. The civil rules process has grown far more open in the past generation, with public meetings and an opportunity for interested parties to comment on proposed rules. Legislative assemblies benefit from the constant demands placed upon them by interested parties who press members to address (and thus to learn about) the latest technological developments. For all of the many virtues the justices bring to their job, they do not display special expertise in the technology of data aggregation or the threat it poses to consumer reputation and privacy; indeed, many observers would rate the justices' technological savvy as woefully inadequate. Couple the Court's lack of knowledge with its lack of lawmaking legitimacy and one finds little justification for judicial leadership in updating the FCRA or the use of class actions to enforce the Act. When Congress creates litigable interests in private regulatory programs, the Court has little justification for second-guessing that decision.[19]

In the context of public law litigation, where conclusions seem somewhat more elusive, a more flexible litigable interest standard might better focus the rules of standing. Today, the injury requirement often serves as a limit on the ability of private suitors to mount claims on behalf of the public. Government action often threatens the environment, but not just anyone can bring suit to protect the habitat of the Nile crocodile or the Asian elephant. Only those with some proximity to the source of environmental degradation can be said to have suffered the kind of injury necessary to allow the suit to proceed. The injury rule thus screens out some litigants who appear to have little personal incentive to bring the suit to a successful conclusion. But notwithstanding its screening function, the rule provides little assurance that the properly "injured" suitor will pursue the claim effectively in court or that the resulting decision will take adequate account of the public interest. By enlarging the inquiry to consider the representational adequacy of the proposed suitor, and making such adequacy a part of the inquiry into the presence of a litigable interest, the Court could focus public law litigation on the factors most likely to protect the public from feckless or duplicative litigation.[20]

Similarly, the litigable interest formulation can accommodate the lessons of Scottish practice. As we have seen, the Scots demanded that litigants establish their title and interest to sue; the suggested inquiry into the presence of litigable interests captures both features of Scots' practice. While title and interest were rather inflexibly required for most private litigation, the Scots relaxed their conception of title and interest to sue to allow individuals to mount popular actions. In doing so, the Scots were embracing a right to sue that arose from equity's concern with providing a remedy for violations of the public's rights that would otherwise escape review. Just as the Scots asked if the claimant had title and interest to sue—an inquiry specific to the nature of the claim asserted—so too might the Court begin to ask if a claimant invoking Article III had asserted a litigable interest, or a claim of right in the form prescribed by law. Such an interest might not invariably require an injury, especially where Congress has taken steps to protect the government's enforcement primacy and the defendant's interest in the avoidance of duplicative litigation.[21]

Notes

1. *See* Woolhandler & Nelson at 708–09, 716–18, 721, 723.
2. Spokeo, Inc. v. Robins, 136 S. Ct. 1540 (2016). *Id.* at 1550–51 (Thomas, J., concurring) (emphasizing traditional powers of common-law courts); *cf.* Abram Chayes, *The Role of the Judge in Public Law Litigation*, 89 Harv. L. Rev. 1281, 1292–96 (1976) (identifying an equitable core in public law litigation). *See infra* section 10.2 on the example of Scotland.
3. *See, e.g.*, Brief of the Chamber of Commerce of the United States of America and the International Association of Defense Counsel as *Amici Curiae* in Support of Petitioner, *Spokeo*, 136 S. Ct. 1540 (No. 13-1339), 2014 WL 2536508. *See, e.g.*, Brief for *Amici Curiae* Lawyers' Committee for Civil Rights Under Law and National Fair Housing Alliance in Support of Respondent, *Spokeo*, 136 S. Ct. 1540 (No. 13-1339), 2015 WL 5316997. *See* F. Andrew Hessick, *Standing, Injury in Fact, and Private Rights*, 93 Cornell L. Rev. 275, 280–82 (2008) (describing trespass and nominal damage claims as lacking injuries in fact); *see also* Brief of Restitution and Remedies Scholars

as Amici Curiae in Support of Respondent, *Spokeo*, 136 S. Ct. 1540 (No. 13-1339), 2015 WL 5302537 (describing a series of restitutionary claims in which the suit seeks to recover the unjust gain to the defendant without regard to the injury suffered by the plaintiff).

4. *See Spokeo*, 136 S. Ct. at 1548 (reaffirming injury requirement). *See id.* 1550, 1549, 1548–50 (concreteness and de fact nature of injury). *Id.* at 1555–56 (Ginsburg, J., dissenting).
5. *Id.* at 1550 (Thomas, J., concurring). *Id.* (quoting Vermont Agency of Nat. Res. v. United States *ex rel.* Stevens, 529 U.S. 765, 774 (2000)). *Id.* at 1550–51 (quoting Honig v. Doe, 484 U.S. 305, 340 (1988) (Scalia, J., dissenting)). *See id.* at 1551, 1553 (first citing Woolhandler & Nelson at 693; then citing Hessick at 317–21). *See id.* at 1551.
6. *Id.* at 1551–52. *Id.* at 1551 (quoting 3 Blackstone at *219). *See id.* at 1552 (identifying separation-of-powers concerns as the justification for a more stringent injury requirement in publications). *See id.* at 1553.
7. *See* Evan Tsen Lee & Josephine Mason Ellis, *The Standing Doctrine's Dirty Little Secret*, 107 Nw. U. L. Rev. 169, 174 (2012). *See* Richard H. Fallon Jr., *The Fragmentation of Standing*, 93 Tex. L. Rev. 1061, 1063, 1071–80 (2015). *See* Hessick at 277; *see also Spokeo*, 136 S. Ct. at 1553 (citing Hessick at 317–21). When discussing procedural codes after the merger in 1938, we have become accustomed to thinking of equity as having conquered common law. *See* Stephen N. Subrin, *How Equity Conquered Common Law: The Federal Rules of Civil Procedure in Historical Perspective*, 135 U. Pa. L. Rev. 909, 922 (1987) (providing a history of the drafting of the merger of law and equity in the 1938 Federal Rules of Civil Procedure and emphasizing the degree to which equitable practices came to dominate those of the common law). Both discovery practice and multiparty joinder in the post-merger litigation of our "one form of action," *see* Fed. R. Civ. P. 2, bear strong equitable influences. *See* Subrin at 922 (identifying pleading, discovery, and joinder as three areas of practice in which the equitable forms of practice were particularly influential in the post-merger procedural rules); *cf.* Geoffrey C. Hazard Jr., *Forms of Action Under the Federal Rules of Civil Procedure*, 63 Notre Dame L. Rev. 628, 632–34 (1988) (describing the impact of the new regime on old notions of joinder and discovery).
8. C.C. Langdell, A Summary of Equity Pleading 34 (2d ed. 1883). *Id.* at 40.
9. Roman law held that an individual could pursue a popular action, or what the Romans called an *actio popularis*, on behalf of the public interest. The Digest of Justinian 47.23.1–4 (Alan Watson et al. eds., 1985). *See generally* James E. Pfander, *Standing to Sue: Lessons from Scotland's* Actio Popularis, 66 Duke L.J. 1493 (2017).
10. On the jurisdiction and structure of the Court of Session, *see* Pfander & Birk, *Article III and the Scottish Judiciary*, at 1653–56. *See* Chayes at 1302 (highlighting the more active, inquisitorial role of the judge in public law proceedings as compared to the more passive dispute-resolving role of the judge in private law litigation). On the key elements of public law litigation, *see* Steffel v. Thompson, 415 U.S. 452, 463–65 (1974), which identifies: (1) federal question jurisdiction under 28 U.S.C. § 1331 (2012); (2) constitutional tort claims under 42 U.S.C. § 1983; and (3) officer suability under

Ex parte Young, 209 U.S. 123 (1908), as the cornerstones of modern public law litigation. *See* R.S., *The Scotch Action of Declarator*, 10 L. MAG. 173, 194 (1849) (describing the Scots' declarator and distinguishing Blackstone's emphasis on the importance of adversaries from the Scottish ideas of John Erskine, who saw the need for a declaration of rights before they were denied or called into question). On the willingness of the Scots to allow private parties to interplead with the Crown, *see* J.D.B. Mitchell, *The Royal Prerogative in Modern Scots Law*, *in* PUBLIC LAW 304, 304 (J.A.G. Griffith ed., 1957), which traces the suability of the Crown in Scotland to legal developments in the 1540s. Lord Kames characterized as an "established maxim, That [*sic*] the King, with whom the executive part of the law is trusted, has no part of the judicative power." HENRY HOME, LORD KAMES, HISTORICAL LAW-TRACTS 286 (2d ed., Lawbook Exch. Ltd. 2000) (1758).

11. *See* HENRY HOME, LORD KAMES, ELUCIDATIONS RESPECTING THE COMMON AND STATUTE LAW OF SCOTLAND 127, 213, 216 (1777) (defining title as evidence of a right and interest as the receipt of some benefit from the action). Modern sources largely echo Lord Kames in defining title and interest. *See, e.g.*, MUNGO DEANS, SCOTS PUBLIC LAW 170 (1995) (describing title and interest to sue as common-law principles synonymous with standing or *locus standi*). Determination of whether a plaintiff had an interest "was relatively simple [and] required that the actor—either plaintiff or defendant—receive some benefit from the action," whereas "title was frequently used to describe a formal claim to legal ownership of the right in question" and "was a more complicated, or at least more variegated, concept." Pfander, *Standing to Sue*, at 1516–17. *See* KAMES, ELUCIDATIONS, at 214 (*jus tertii*). Lord Bankton, author of a well-regarded eighteenth-century treatise, connected the practice of popular actions ("in which any person whatever, capable of suing, may prosecute the party") to Roman and Scots historical practice. 2 ANDREW McDOUALL, LORD BANKTON, AN INSTITUTE OF THE LAWS OF SCOTLAND IN CIVIL RIGHTS 610 (R. Fleming 1751) (footnote omitted). The Court of Session took an extremely broad view of its *nobile officium*, or equitable power, to depart from the strict mandates of the law and proceed according to what it considered "just[] and fit." GEORGE MACKENZIE, THE INSTITUTIONS OF THE LAW OF SCOTLAND 233–34 (1694). In cases in which law did not provide an established remedy or was otherwise inadequate, the Court of Session had "recourse from strict law to equity, even in the matter of judgment; and in more cases they may recede from the ordinary form and manner of probation, whereof there are many instances commonly known." JAMES DALRYMPLE, THE INSTITUTIONS OF THE LAW OF SCOTLAND 570 (3d ed. 1759). For a modern account of the origins and current application of the *nobile officium*, *see* STEPHEN THOMSON, THE NOBILE OFFICIUM: THE EXTRAORDINARY EQUITABLE JURISDICTION OF THE SUPREME COURTS OF SCOTLAND 6–17 (2015).

12. 7 GREEN'S ENCYCLOPAEDIA OF THE LAW OF SCOTLAND 292 (John Chisholm ed., 1912) (citing nineteenth-century cases). *See also* LORD CLYDE & DENIS J. EDWARDS, JUDICIAL REVIEW 386 (2000) ("The decision in an *actio popularis* decided against one

member of the public will be *res judicata* against all other members of the public."). Green's Encyclopaedia at 292.

13. Environmental statutes authorize suits broadly. *See, e.g.*, 33 U.S.C. § 1365(a) (2018) (authorizing "any person" to file suit to enforce the Clean Water Act); 42 U.S.C. § 7604(a) (2018) (the same authorization in the Clean Air Act). The statutes require the plaintiff to notify the Department of Justice of the proposed commencement of an action and broadly authorize governmental intervention. *See* 42 U.S.C. § 7604(b)–(c). The statutes also limit the ability of private litigants to pursue claims when the government has taken the lead. *See* 33 U.S.C. § 1365(b)(1)(B) (barring commencement of private suit when "Administrator or State has commenced and is diligently prosecuting" an enforcement action); 42 U.S.C. § 7604(b)(1)(B) (barring the same under the Clean Air Act). For a description of the statutory scheme, *see* Friends of the Earth, Inc. v. Laidlaw Environmental Services (TOC), Inc., 528 U.S. 167, 174–75 (2000). For cases that attempt to sort out problems of preclusive effect in the context of public rights environmental litigation, *see Sierra Club v. Two Elk Generation Partners, Ltd. Partnership*, 646 F.3d 1258, 1271–72 (10th Cir. 2011), a citizen suit under the Clean Air Act barred by the state's prior litigation of alleged environmental violation; *Ellis v. Gallatin Steel Co.*, 390 F.3d 461, 473–74 (6th Cir. 2004), a suit in the context of the Clean Air Act. Also note *Headwaters Inc. v. United States Forest Service*, 399 F.3d 1047, 1050 (9th Cir. 2005), which concluded that claim preclusion did not bar individual from challenging forest service compliance with the National Environmental Policy Act, 42 U.S.C. §§ 4321–70, despite prior litigation in which public's interest was pursued by others. *Spokeo, Inc.*, 136 S. Ct. at 1551 (quoting 3 Blackstone at *219).
14. People *ex rel.* Case v. Collins, 19 Wend. 56 (N.Y. Sup. Ct. 1837). *Id.* at 64–65 (emphasis omitted). *Id.* at 65 (quoting Rex v. White, Cas. t. Hardw. 92).
15. *See supra* section 10.1 endnote 7 and accompanying text. *See* Pfander & Birk, *Article III Judicial Power*, at 1368, 1371, 1372, 1436, 1457. On the probate exception, *see* chapter 9.2 endnote 17.
16. *Tutun*, 270 U.S. 568 (1926); *see also* John F. Manning, *Foreword: The Means of Constitutional Power*, 128 Harv. L. Rev. 1, 73, 83 (2014) (similarly calling for deference to Congress's decisions about when and by what means an individual can invoke federal judicial power). *Tutun*, 270 U.S. at 576–77. *Id.* at 577.
17. *See Spokeo, Inc.*, 136 S. Ct. at 1545, 1549 (observing that allegation of bare statutory violation, without accompanying harm, will not suffice, but recognizing the importance of congressional judgment in evaluating whether intangible harm meets the test of concrete injury). The remand left open the possibility that the plaintiff could be said to have alleged concrete injuries. *See id.* at 1550. The dissenters thought the requisite allegations had already been made. *Id.* at 1556.
18. The Court has often justified the injury-in-fact requirement of standing doctrine on its view that private enforcement of public actions may interfere with agency enforcement discretion in violation of the Take Care Clause. *See, e.g., Lujan*, 504 U.S. at 577. *See* Stephen B. Burbank & Sean Farhang, Rights and Retrenchment: The Counterrevolution Against Federal Litigation 7–9 (2017) (describing the work of consumer rights and other public interest advocates to secure legislation that

was meant to empower private enforcement of federal rights as a way to supplement or bypass agency enforcement). *See* 15 U.S.C. § 1681s (2012) (conferring power on the Federal Trade Commission to enforce the Fair Credit Reporting Act). *See* 15 U.S.C. § 1681n(a). *See id.* §1681m(h)(8)(B) (declaring that a specific section "shall be enforced exclusively under section 1681s of this title by the Federal agencies and officials identified in that section").

19. *Spokeo*, 136 S. Ct. at 1545. For a description of this more open rules advisory process and an argument for rule-making primacy in contrast to lawmaking by judicial decree, *see generally* Lumen Mulligan & Glen Staszewski, *The Supreme Court's Regulation of Civil Procedure: Lessons from Administrative Law*, 59 UCLA L. REV. 1188 (2012), which describes the modern rulemaking process and arguing that it outperforms the judicial process as a forum for the creation of procedural law. The 115th Congress considered legislation that would curtail some features of class action litigation, tending to confirm the view that legislative attention to the consumer-business balance has not waned over the years. H.R. 985, the Fairness in Class Action Litigation Act of 2017, was introduced on February 9, 2017, by Representative Bob Goodlatte (R-VA), chair of the House Committee on the Judiciary. The U.S. House of Representatives passed the bill (as amended) in March 2017 by a vote of 220–201; it is now pending in the U.S. Senate where it has been referred to the Committee on the Judiciary. If enacted, H.R. 985 would make dramatic changes in class action practice. *See, e.g.*, Karson Thompson, Note, *Luddites No Longer: Adopting the Technology Tutorial at the Supreme Court*, 91 TEX. L. REV. 199, 202–09 (2012) (collecting examples of the Justices' lack of technological sophistication). The argument for congressional primacy flows directly from the long post–New Deal tradition of judicial deference to economic regulation. *See* Williamson v. Lee Optical of Okla., Inc., 348 U.S. 483 (1955) (rejecting Due Process and Equal Protection challenges to consumer-protection legislation). *See, e.g.*, *The Supreme Court, 2015 Term—Leading Cases*, 130 HARV. L. REV. 437, 446 (2016) (discussing *Spokeo* and calling for judicial deference to the congressional policy judgment as to individual's right to sue).
20. *See Lujan*, 504 U.S. 555 (1992). *See id.* at 565–66. Realists have criticized the legal fictions to which strict adherence to form for its own sake can sometimes give rise. Brian Tamanaha has documented the turn-of-the-century frustration with "legal proceedings . . . shot through with deliberate falsehoods" and subsequent turn to realism. BRIAN Z. TAMANAHA, BEYOND THE FORMALIST-REALIST DIVIDE: THE ROLE OF POLITICS IN JUDGING 47–48 (2010). Formalism "misses the real meaning and character of the law and ses the relations of men to property and to each other, only as they are established by printed rules." *Id.* (quoting JEROME FRANK, LAW AND THE MODERN MIND 54 (1930)). Realism, as many academic "isms," has been defined in many ways and may be subdivided into many schools. *See* Brian Leiter, *Positivism, Formalism, Realism*, 99 COLUM. L. REV. 1138 (1999). However, realism may be defined most basically in its commitment to flexibility and "the underlying facts of the case." *Id.* at 1148. *See generally* JOHN HENRY SCHLEGEL, AMERICAN LEGAL REALISM AND EMPIRICAL SOCIAL SCIENCE (1995); Brian Z. Tamanaha, *Understanding Legal Realism*, 87 TEX. L. REV. 731 (2009).

21. The Court of Session evaluated the merits of the claim at the same time it considered whether to recognize title and interest to pursue a popular action. *See, e.g.*, Merchant Co. v. Magistrates of Herriot's Hosp. (1765), *in* 8 WILLIAM MAXWELL MORISON, THE DECISIONS OF THE COURT SESSION FROM ITS INSTITUTION UNTIL THE SEPARATION OF COURT INTO TWO DIVISIONS IN THE YEAR 1808, DIGESTED UNDER PROPER HEADS, IN THE FORM OF A DICTIONARY 5752 (1811) (acknowledging the pursuer's lack of conventional title and interest to sue, but emphasizing the absence of an alternative remedy). Under modern class action practice, the federal courts take similar account of the merits in deciding whether to certify the plaintiff class. *See, e.g.*, Wal-Mart Stores, Inc. v. Duke, 564 U.S. 338, 351–52 (2011) (acknowledging that rigorous assessment of class certification may overlap with evaluation of the merits of the plaintiffs' claims). *See Vermont Agency*, 529 U.S. 765 (describing elements of the False Claims Act that gave the federal government a right to supervise the litigation and offered the defendant some protection from duplicative litigation).

11

A Practical Guide to Uncontested Adjudication

Although the application of the litigable interest construct effectively synthesizes history, text, and practice, one might worry that its adoption might increase the share of uncontested matters on the dockets of the federal courts. Such expanded ex parte adjudication could present a series of concerns. First, one might worry that the resolution of uncontested claims does not represent the best use of scarce federal judicial capacity, especially in a world in which Congress has broad power to assign such chores to federal agencies instead. Second, one might worry that the federal courts would fail to attend carefully to the uncontested matters on their dockets, privileging disputes and slighting ex parte prisoner petitions and applications for waiver of PACER fees. Finally, one might fear that the inquisitorial muscles of the federal judiciary have atrophied over time, as the rhetoric of adverse-party contestation has led federal judges to view uncontested matters as beneath their dignity or perhaps their pay grade. Judges in such a world may not conduct their inquisitions with the rigor necessary to ensure just outcomes.

These concerns with federal judicial capacity and responsiveness surely demand that Congress act as a good steward of judicial resources. To be clear, this book does not argue that the legislature should assign more uncontested work to the federal judiciary. In circumstances where agencies can do the work, Congress should ordinarily rely on them and offer disappointed litigants access to a federal forum for review of agency errors. But in some situations, Congress might understandably assign uncontested work to the judiciary, taking advantage of litigation economies or judicial experience and independence or both. In providing for federal judicial determination of petitions for PACER fee waivers or habeas investigation fees, Congress may have recognized that the federal courts were well informed about the issues at hand. In creating the FISA court to evaluate the government's application for foreign surveillance warrants, Congress chose to implement the Fourth Amendment's neutral magistrate requirement with independent Article III

Cases Without Controversies. James E. Pfander, Oxford University Press.
DOI: 10.1093/oso/9780197571408.003.0012

judges. Over time, as these decisions have accumulated, the federal courts have acquired a fairly substantial docket of uncontested matters.

Viewing uncontested judicial work as both constitutionally permissible and to some extent unavoidable, this chapter offers a primer or how-to guide for the proper adjudication of any uncontested matters Congress assigns to the federal judiciary. It first explores how such matters can be brought into conformity with such bedrock features of federal adjudication as the due process rights of interested parties and the requirement of judicial finality. Next, it examines the practical side of uncontested adjudication and explores the way federal appellate courts should oversee the uncontested judgments of the district courts. The chapter concludes with practical suggestions for the federal judicial consideration of pro se prisoner petitions, perhaps the single most important source of uncontested adjudication on federal dockets today.

11.1 Constitutional Limits on Uncontested Adjudication

Three important constitutional principles restrict the scope of uncontested adjudication in federal court. First, original petitions to register an uncontested claim of right must implicate federal law and must proceed in the "form prescribed by law." That is, they must qualify as "cases" within the meaning of federal jurisdiction. Second, the court must protect due process rights by ensuring that any interested third parties receive notice of the proceeding and an opportunity to be heard. Just as state courts should ensure some kind of notice to parties with interests in common form probate proceedings, federal courts must attend to third-party interests. Third, federal courts should proceed with the matter only when it calls for the exercise of judicial power in circumstances in which the court's decree will operate as a final judgment.[1]

11.1.1 Federal Cases and the Nature of Original and Ancillary Proceedings

In defining the scope of federal judicial power, federal courts will find it useful to distinguish "original" petitions in which a plaintiff sets up an uncontested claim and "ancillary" jurisdiction over non-contentious matters that arise in the course of other proceedings properly before the court. Many examples of uncontested adjudication arise in the shadow of a dispute between actual or potential adversaries. Consent decrees settle disputes between contending parties, just as guilty pleas resolve criminal charges, and equity receiverships provide relief to creditors whose legitimate claims cannot be satisfied. Bankruptcy proceedings involve the potentially conflicting claims of creditors to an estate insufficient to satisfy them all. Default judgments enter in connection with litigation to secure an unmet demand from a party who has failed to answer the court's summons. In all of these instances, the power of the federal courts to proceed on an uncontested basis arises from their duty, in any proper case, to provide parties with the relief to which applicable law entitles them. Just as commentators have observed in describing consent decrees as ancillary to the resolution of pending disputes, much of the uncontested work of the federal courts takes place in the shadow of potential or actual contention.[2]

While federal courts can exercise ancillary jurisdiction over the uncontested aspects of any proceeding that has been properly brought in federal court, the exercise of original jurisdiction over uncontested proceedings must meet a more stringent test. Although Chief Justice Marshall did not say so expressly, the second element of his definition—the requirement that cases must implicate the Constitution, laws, treaties, or admiralty jurisdiction of the United States—imposes an important limit on the scope of original non-contentious jurisdiction. As we have seen, the federal courts may hear uncontested "cases" that seek to vindicate a claim of federal right, but that power does not extend to "controversies" defined by the alignment of the parties. Controversies really do require opposing parties, as many commentators have observed. The paradigm example of such a controversy, a diversity dispute between citizens of different states, helped to define the early contentious work of the federal courts. Inasmuch as a controversy connotes a dispute between parties, the federal courts have no constitutional authority to exercise original non-contentious jurisdiction over matters of nonfederal law.

Apart from ruling out uncontested adjudication of claims based in nonfederal law, the Marshall definition of a litigable interest requires the party seeking to invoke the non-contentious jurisdiction of the federal courts to follow the form "prescribed by law." This element of the definition properly captures the primacy of Congress in defining the scope of non-contentious jurisdiction. Congress can, as Justice Brandeis observed in *Tutun*, assign administrative matters to federal agencies or to federal courts or create a system of shared responsibility among them. While the federal courts rightly presume that Congress intends to preserve judicial review of final agency action, no similar presumption should operate in favor of first-instance judicial resolution of non-contentious claims. Federal courts, on this view, should accept congressional assignments of uncontested work but should not seek out such assignments through the "alchemy" of statutory interpretation. Nor should they develop a counterpart to their disputed (and to some extent disavowed) power to recognize the existence of implied rights of action to enforce federal statutes that contain no explicit right of action. It does not make sense to fashion an implied right of action that would enable private parties to register a claim of right in a judicial proceeding instead of one brought before the proper agency. (Nor does it seem likely that the federal courts would clamor to create such a doctrine.)[3]

Once jurisdiction has attached to a proceeding, parties may invoke the ancillary jurisdiction of the federal courts over uncontested proceedings. For such proceedings, a broader array of federal practice can provide a form "prescribed by law." Default judgments have roots deep in the legal tradition. Generalizing from the power to issue default judgments, courts exercise the power to register settlement agreements and enter guilty pleas. In all of these instances, the federal courts proceed in ancillary non-contentious jurisdiction and do so without any specific grant of original authority from Congress. Still, congressional approval of these practices can be easily inferred from the available legal materials. In the case of default judgments, the Rules Enabling Act confers rulemaking authority on the Supreme Court that culminates in the promulgation of rules that take effect unless Congress disapproves of them. The foundation for default judgments in Rule 55 would thus enjoy ample support in a controlling legal text. The judicial role in uncontested bankruptcy proceedings, in the entry of plea agreements, and in the registration of settlements enjoys a similar foundation in positive law.

11.1.2 The Requirement of Finality

Apart from the elements embedded in the Marshall-Story formulation of a "case," the federal courts can act only where their decisions will enjoy the finality demanded by Article III. The finality rule emerges from the judicial responses to pension claims collected in *Hayburn's Case*, which highlighted executive revision of judgments in the course of refusing to accept a judicial role. The Court has consistently reaffirmed the finality rule in various settings, particularly in the context of ex parte proceedings. Thus, finality concerns informed the Court's approach to naturalization proceedings in *Spratt v. Spratt*. Speaking through the Chief Justice, the Court emphasized that a decision granting a petition for citizenship was subject to review but was to be regarded as a binding judgment unless overturned through proper proceedings. Justice Brandeis made much the same argument in *Tutun*, emphasizing that a judgment conferring citizenship was conclusive, although subject to proper forms of judicial revision. Under the common law system, writs of *scire facias* and *coram nobis* were available to reopen proceedings and challenge matters of record. (Those writs no longer control in federal courts, having been superseded by the all-purpose Rule 60 motion.) So long as the courts themselves preside over the revision of their own decrees, no problem of executive revision would appear to arise, even where the government itself was the party seeking to reopen the judgment.[4]

Although justly regarded as essential to the exercise of judicial power, finality in the context of uncontested adjudication does not require final judicial resolution of an entire dispute. That is the office of contentious jurisdiction. Instead, finality simply requires the conclusive determination of the issue that has been assigned to the federal courts for decision (subject to appellate review in a higher Article III court). On this view, federal courts can determine a single issue in the context of a proceeding that will ultimately be resolved by a different institution. Consider the judicial role in the fact-finding that preceded the Treasury Secretary's ultimate authority to consider a petition for remission of penalties imposed on merchant shipping for violation of the navigation laws. In upholding the judicial role, Justice Story explained that it was upon the district court's "statement of the facts, and this only, that the secretary is authorized to proceed." Consider as well the enforcement of discovery requests, whether in support of a foreign proceeding (through letters rogatory) or in support of administrative investigations (through administrative subpoenas). In such matters, the federal court conclusively resolves the right to discovery, but does so in support of another judicial or administrative institution's proceeding.

This approach to finality helps to explain a longstanding puzzle: the role of the federal judiciary in extradition cases. In the typical case, a foreign government applies to the United States for the extradition of an individual, and the Department of Justice (DOJ) initiates the proceeding by filing an extradition complaint before a judge or magistrate. Following the issuance of a warrant for apprehension, the individual may contest the extradition claim. If the judge or magistrate agrees that the case for extradition has been made (after considering the treaty and assessing the case for probable cause), the magistrate certifies the propriety of detention to the Secretary of State, for a final determination as to whether extradition should be ordered. The target of extradition may seek limited review by petition for habeas corpus, but the system does not provide for direct appellate review of initial extradition decisions, and a variety of questions have arisen as to the nature of the tribunal's power at that stage. From a practical perspective, moreover, reliance on habeas review can result in duplicative proceedings.[5]

Yet modern decisions correctly recognize that, despite the ultimate decision-making authority of the Secretary of State, extradition presents no finality problem. Judge Frank Easterbrook, writing in *DeSilva v. DiLeonardi*, recognized that the Secretary of State does not have power to *revise* the judicial certificate but only to *refrain* from extraditing in cases where the judge has found just cause. As Easterbrook explained, the judicial decision finally determines the government's right to extradite and the Secretary simply decides whether to carry out the extradition (as she almost invariably does). But the Secretary cannot extradite without a judicial certificate and cannot overturn a judicial decision rejecting extradition on probable cause, treaty, or other grounds. Judge Easterbrook drew the logical conclusion: the government's application for an extradition certificate gives rise to a "case" within the meaning of Article III to which the judicial power extends. Such applications could be assigned to the district courts as courts, and subject to appellate review in the Article III hierarchy.[6]

11.1.3 The Line Between Judicial and Ministerial Work

The federal courts should accept assignments of uncontested adjudication only where the task at hand involves the exercise of judicial, rather than ministerial, judgment. Listen again to Chief Justice Marshall's description of the judicial role in naturalization:

> The [courts] are to receive testimony, to compare it with the law, and to judge on both law and fact. This judgment is entered on record as the judgment of the court.

Marshall's comment anticipates later comments from Story and Brandeis. In discussing petitions for remissions of forfeitures, Justice Story worked hard to defend the judicial quality of the proceeding: in taking evidence and making factual findings, "the judge exercises judicial functions, and is bound by the same rules of evidence, as in other cases."

Brandeis's comment in *Tutun* was similar: according to Brandeis, the applicant seeking naturalization

> must allege in his petition the fulfillment of all conditions upon the existence of which the alleged right is made dependent, and he must establish these allegations by competent evidence to the satisfaction of the court. In passing upon the application the court exercises judicial judgment.

In both instances, the Court confirmed the judicial quality of the judgment being exercised, and that quality is crucial to the propriety of the exercise of non-contentious jurisdiction.[7]

In emphasizing the judicial quality of the work, the Court suggested that while some administrative assignments were proper grist for the mill of the Article III judiciary, others might be considered ministerial in character and thus appropriate for assignment to another department or officer. The idea of ministerial action played an important and somewhat unsettled role in the early Republic: ministerial action was subject to judicial control through writs of mandamus, whereas the exercise of judicial discretion by a lower court was not typically subject to mandamus control. Similarly, officers acting in a judicial capacity typically enjoyed immunity from suit for actions taken within the scope of their jurisdiction, whereas officers acting in a ministerial capacity were subject to suit when they failed to perform duties required by law. Marshals, though assigned to serve process and execute the judgments of the federal courts, were officers of the executive branch of government and were subject to suit for the unlawful performance of their duties. Judicial clerks were also considered ministerial officers in the sense that individuals who claimed a legal entitlement to action by the clerk (copying a court record or entering a judgment) could apply to the court to compel performance of the duty.

The judicial/ministerial distinction allows the Court to reject administrative assignments that are improperly ministerial or that require the rote performance of a duty without calling for the exercise of judicial judgment. One can get a sense of the intuition underlying this admittedly somewhat blurry line by considering the initial judicial reaction to the pension law: the Pennsylvania circuit reportedly refused the assignment in part because the statute compelled the court to sit for five days to receive pension applications and thus overrode the court's discretion to close the court session when the work was complete. Obligatory work may have been viewed by some as not of a "judicial" nature. The nation's first copyright law furnishes an additional example. An author seeking a copyright on a "map, chart, or book" was obliged to lodge a copy with the Secretary of State and to "record" a printed copy of the title of the work with the federal district court of the district in which the author resided. In specifying the duty to record, no judicial judgment was contemplated. Congress instead provided that the "the clerk of such court is hereby directed and required to record the same forthwith, in a book to be kept by him for that purpose." Congress apparently shared the view that work of a clearly ministerial character was properly assigned to the clerk, leaving the court to enforce the duty (if necessary) through a proper judicial proceeding.[8]

The judicial/ministerial distinction provides a straightforward answer to the question of how the federal courts in the early Republic came to view themselves as empowered to hear ex parte matters. While the pension applications at issue in *Hayburn's Case* lacked the finality necessary to make them proper objects of the judicial power, the same criticism cannot be made of the naturalization process. Federal courts passing on naturalization applications were making conclusive determinations of the petitioner's entitlement to citizenship. They were also, as Chief Justice Marshall and Justice Brandeis later observed, exercising judicial judgment in determining whether the petition met the statute's parameters and was adequately supported by the factual record. The apparent tension between pension claims and naturalization petitions disappears; both sought uncontested adjudication, but the pension claims lacked the finality necessary to bring them within the judicial power.

Although the judicial/ministerial distinction provides the federal courts with authority to reject proceedings that do not call for the exercise of judicial judgment, the practice of the Court has been to defer to Congress and accept ex parte assignments in doubtful cases. This practice of deference poses a potential threat to the federal courts, given that Congress has control over the assignment of a truly staggering array of federal administrative chores as to which the federal courts could be called upon to conduct their own investigation of the facts. While a threat does exist, Congress for the most part values the dispute-resolution and law-elaboration roles of the federal judiciary and generally works to support those roles. Moreover, Congress can be expected to monitor the cost-effectiveness of its administrative systems and attend to arguments from the federal judiciary as to the budget implications of expanded ex parte assignments. It seems unlikely that a Congress already concerned with the cost, say, of administering Social Security benefit claims, would turn to the federal courts. However efficiently the courts might process such claims, the cost per claim would predictably far exceed that of the current administrative arrangement. Except where Congress decides that proper administration requires the high-powered (and -priced) judgment of the federal judiciary, as in the case of FISA courts, it will continue to rely on agencies instead.[9]

11.1.4 Due Process and Notice to Interested Parties

Due process guarantees play an important role in ensuring the protection of third-party interests. The Due Process Clause of the Fifth Amendment applies to all proceedings in federal court and requires that interested parties receive notice and an opportunity to be heard. While certain forms of in rem procedure remain intact (admiralty, bankruptcy, and certain forfeiture proceedings), the Court has long since held that in rem forms of notice by publication no longer suffice. Thus, in *Mullane v. Central Hanover Bank*, the Court rejected notice by publication in a newspaper and required instead notice "reasonably calculated" to inform known parties affected by the proceedings. Similarly, in *Shaffer v. Heitner*, the Court found that the power of a state court to adjudicate could no longer rest alone on the court's control over property located within the territorial boundaries of the state. In rem process can dramatically affect the rights of individuals and may call for measures aimed at safeguarding those rights. Thus, voluntary petitions for bankruptcy require notice to known creditors, just as many states now require that the petitioner in uncontested common form probate proceedings provide notice to those with an interest in the assets of the estate. Best practices in uncontested adjudication call upon courts to pay careful attention to the notification of possibly interested parties.[10]

Concerns with the importance of genuine contestation in cases such as *Lord v. Veazie* reflect an understandable attention to the interests of third parties but do not necessarily cast doubt on the propriety of uncontested adjudication. Notably, in *Lord*, the parties followed the forms of contested adjudication to secure a favorable precedent for use against an unrepresented party; they were not pursuing an original uncontested adjudication of a claim of right. To the extent that a single party pursues an original suit to register or claim a federal right or benefit, third-party rights are unlikely to be implicated. More for one, as with the award of naturalized citizenship or pension benefits, does not necessarily mean less for someone else (except for the taxpayer, of course, who generally cannot challenge congressional decisions to distribute such largesse). But in other circumstances, where the exercise of non-contentious jurisdiction does pose a potential threat to the rights of third parties (such as in the case of settlement class actions, the issuance of FISA warrants, and some bankruptcy proceedings), federal courts must be especially vigilant to ward off the entry of judgments that unfairly burden those who have not been brought before the court. Potential problems with third-party rights may not deprive the court of power to hear an uncontested case, but they certainly require a more searching investigation and may require separate justification. State courts face similar challenges when probate in the common form threatens the interests of third parties.[11]

11.2 Fact-Finding and Uncontested Adjudication

Among its most challenging features, uncontested adjudication requires the federal judiciary to conduct its own investigation of the facts and law on which the propriety of the proposed judgment will depend. Effective performance of this fact-finding role poses a problem for a federal judiciary that typically relies on adverse parties to develop and present the relevant facts and law. In some instances, the federal courts must adapt their procedures to perform their inquisitorial functions more effectively. That was the lesson of Justice Story's approach to prize cases in the nineteenth century; knowing that adverse parties might never appear, the admiralty court instituted a process that relied upon officers of the court (commissioners and the like) to collect the documentary evidence and witness testimony needed for a fair determination of the captor's prize claim. Although prize claims have disappeared from modern dockets, today's federal courts bear responsibility to test the factual and legal basis of a variety of claims.

Sometimes, the federal courts can rely on the presence of adverse interests to gain confidence about the fairness and accuracy of a proposed settlement or other agreed-upon disposition. Entry of a consent decree thus makes sense when it carries into effect the agreed-upon resolution of a dispute between adversaries who have the means to secure competent counsel. Similarly, judicial approval of guilty pleas makes sense when the defendant has been represented by an attorney who has the time and resources to conduct a full investigation and evaluate the likely outcome of a prosecution. Here, then, one finds a place for adverse interests in the evaluation of judicial practice. One sees this recognition of the importance of interest adversity reflected in early assessments of the fact-finding process in naturalization. As one nineteenth-century court observed in passing on an uncontested naturalization petition, an agreed-upon submission by parties with adverse interests provides a much more reliable basis for judicial action than the unilateral assertions of an interested party. Accordingly, the court demanded sworn affidavits from knowledgeable witnesses and proper documentation to support the claim for naturalization. Judges called upon to perform non-adversarial judicial fact-finding have long placed a burden on the petitioner to support the claim in fact and law.[12]

Notably, though, the inquisitorial duty imposed by uncontested adjudication does not represent a wholesale departure from existing judicial obligations. Consider the rules governing the entry of default judgments, which require the district court to determine if the well-pleaded facts in the complaint support the entry of judgment and to fix the amount of damages based on the court's own investigation. A similar inquisitorial duty attaches to the judicial role in overseeing class action settlements, bankruptcy orders of various kinds, guilty pleas, and consent decrees. The FISA court has taken important steps to improve the quality of its ex parte decisions, hiring a group of legal advisors to conduct thorough initial investigations of important petitions and inviting the DOJ to highlight and thoroughly brief any suggested changes in the law. Further reforms may be needed following reports that government attorneys had been less than fully candid about the facts in their zeal to secure FISA warrants for use against some U.S. persons.[13]

As the case of FISA litigation reveals, fact-finding practices in inquisitorial proceedings often impose special duties of candor on attorneys. The Court's dismay in *Lord v. Veazie* reflected its dissatisfaction with the attorneys' failure to disclose that the proceeding lacked true adversaries; the threat of contempt was meant to ensure that lawyers attended to their duty of candor to the court in the future. Rule 3.3 of the American Bar Association's Model Rules of Professional Conduct similarly recognizes a duty of candor in ex parte proceedings: "In an ex parte proceeding, a lawyer shall inform the tribunal of all material facts known to the lawyer that will enable the tribunal to make an informed decision, whether or not the facts are adverse." This duty of candor has been thought to apply with special force to proceedings before the FISA court, where the absence of an adversary and the secret nature of the proceedings imposes a particularly demanding duty on the government attorneys who appear before that court.[14]

11.3 The Importance of Appellate Review

From the earliest days of the Republic, federal courts have recognized the centrality of appellate review to the just operation of uncontested adjudication. In *Ex parte Fitzbonne*, for example, a petitioner sought review of a district court decision rejecting his application for citizenship under a statute that prohibited the naturalization of those from countries at war with the United States. Agreeing to review the district court decision by way of mandamus, the Supreme Court directed the naturalization to proceed on the theory that the undeclared war with France did not trigger the statute's application. Similarly, in *Hayburn's Case*, the attorney general sought mandamus review of the lower courts' refusal to adjudicate the pension claims of disabled veterans. While such proceedings might occasionally name the district court judge as a nominal defendant, they effectively sought uncontested appellate review of the denial of an original application seeking uncontested adjudication of a claim of right under federal law. No adverse parties appeared in the appellate court in either matter.

Appellate review seems particularly appropriate, as in *Fitzbonne* and *Hayburn's Case*, when the trial court bases its refusal to adjudicate on an issue of law. Trial court decisions that turn on the failure of the petitioner to make the requisite factual showing present a different problem. In some circumstances, where the trial court's rejection of the claim operates without prejudice, the petitioner remains free to submit a second or successive petition with a more complete factual record. So long as that option remains open to the petitioner as a way to cure an insufficient factual showing, it makes little sense for an appellate court to get involved. But if the petitioner cannot cure, and believes that the showing made to the trial court suffices as a legal matter, then appellate review sensibly follows.[15]

Current statutes seemingly make two forms of such review available. Circuit courts retain their power to issue writs of mandamus to district courts. In addition, the Supreme Court has quietly but consistently viewed the submission of original petitions for uncontested adjudication as "cases" in the district courts, thereby triggering provisions for appellate review of final district court decisions. That was the Court's approach in *Tutun v. United States*, involving a naturalization petition; in *Hohn v. United States*, a petition for a habeas-based certificate of appealability; and in *Ayestas v. Davis*, a petition for the approval of habeas investigation expenses. Today, of course, the jurisdiction of the appellate courts extends to the "decisions" of the district courts, a formulation that has been read to refer to "cases." All uncontested cases in the district courts thus, at least potentially, qualify for appellate review.[16]

Unconventional modes of appellate engagement do not deprive the matter of the case-like quality needed for the exercise of federal judicial power. In *Hohn*, for example, the statute calls for a successive habeas petitioner to seek leave to file before a three-judge appellate panel before bringing suit in district court. The appellate panel thus operates as an initial forum for the adjudication of a suit to establish a federal claim of right: the right to pursue a successive petition. It was that unconventional feature of the statute that led Justice Scalia, in dissent, to question the power of an appellate court to hear a non-adverse proceeding. But the majority shrugged off convention, concluding that Congress can structure the litigation by assigning it to lower federal courts as it sees fit. Similarly, in *Ayestas*, the unconventional assignment of some appellate review functions to the chief judge of the circuit, sitting alone, did not trouble the Court.[17]

Finality also plays a role in defining appellate court review of the issuance of uncontested judgments below. The applicable statute extends appellate review only to the "final" decisions of the district court. In circumstances in which the district court has denied an uncontested application, but intends to allow the petitioner to supplement the record with additional factual material, the district court can dismiss with leave to amend. Such a disposition would not normally qualify as a final decision for purposes of triggering a right to appellate review. Once the petitioner has amassed what evidence she has, the district can either grant the requested judgment or deny the petition in a final decision that would set the stage for appellate consideration. While the appellate court would presumably have access to the record in the district court, the logic of uncontested adjudication requires the appellate panel to conduct an appellate inquest, much like the ex parte inquiry in the district court. If adversarial briefing were thought necessary to the resolution of an important issue of law, the appellate court might appoint an amicus to brief the question.[18]

The D.C. Circuit's decision in *In re Flynn*, denying mandamus to overturn a district judge's ex parte inquiry into the dismissal of a prosecution, reveals the continuing value of appointed counsel and appellate review. After Michael Flynn pleaded guilty to making false statements to the FBI and was scheduled for sentencing, the DOJ in May 2020 moved to dismiss the indictment with prejudice. District court Judge Emmet Sullivan appointed an amicus to advise him in connection with his consideration of the proposed dismissal. Flynn sought immediate review, contending that the judge had no role to play in overseeing the DOJ's dismissal decision. A panel of the D.C. Circuit agreed with Flynn, ordering dismissal and reassignment of the case. Judge Sullivan, through counsel, filed a petition for rehearing en banc. That petition posed a tricky question: Was Sullivan a party to the mandamus proceeding in the appellate court, entitled to seek en banc review? If so, would that require his disqualification when the case reappeared on his docket below? And would the jurisdiction conferred in Article III extend to such oddly configured proceedings? Eventually, a judge of the D.C. Circuit urged en banc reconsideration sua sponte, mooting the questions raised by Sullivan's petition. Ultimately, the en banc court overturned the panel decision, vacated the mandamus, and returned the case to Sullivan for further proceedings.[19]

Judge Sullivan's actions illustrate the challenges associated with the judicial role in uncontested proceedings. When the DOJ and Flynn agreed as to the propriety of the indictment's dismissal, the proceeding lost its adversary character. But the applicable procedural rule did not clearly require Judge Sullivan to accept the agreed-upon disposition; Rule 48 of the Federal Rules of Criminal Procedure provides that "[t]he government may, with leave of court, dismiss an indictment, information, or complaint." In calling for leave of court, the Rule might be plausibly interpreted to contemplate a judicial role in assessing the proposed dismissal. Much of what Judge Sullivan and the appellate court have done in the meantime finds support in the history of inquisitorial proceedings. Judge Sullivan's decision to appoint an amicus to advise him, and to argue against the government's dismissal decision, resembles the efforts of other inquisitorial judges to inquire more fully into the facts and law relevant to an uncontested adjudication. Similarly, Sullivan's appearance through counsel on appeal in the mandamus action reflects the somewhat one-sided nature of mandamus petitions. Finally, the en banc appellate court's ultimate decision echoes that reached in one of the nation's first such proceedings. As did the Supreme Court in the *Barré* proceeding in 1795, rejecting the use of mandamus to compel Judge Laurance to decide a warrant proceeding in a particular way, the D.C. Circuit refused to compel a district court to decide "an *undecided* motion *in a particular way*." Once one considers the inquisitorial role into which the rules of criminal procedure were understood to have cast the district court judge, much of what came next makes more sense than when read against the backdrop of the presumptive judicial passivity that we associate with the adversary system.[20]

11.4 Handling Uncontested Pro Se Prisoner Petitions

According to the latest statistics from the Administrative Office of the U.S. Courts, prisoner petitions account for 55,000 of the 332,000 new cases that appeared on federal court dockets 2020, in the most recent year—or roughly 17 percent of the total. Prisoner petitions fall into several categories: some challenge the prisoner's conviction by way of habeas or by motion to vacate the sentence; others, some 30,000 in 2020, seek redress for unlawful conditions of confinement or for other violations of civil rights by the prison and its officials. In over 90 percent of these petitions, the prisoners appear without legal counsel and rely heavily on form complaints, made available through the federal courts. Commentators report that these forms sometimes elicit useless information, sometimes fail to elicit relevant information, and often call for legal knowledge to which many prisoners, for obvious reasons, do not have access. When coupled with the Prison Litigation Reform Act's (PLRA's) requirement of remedial exhaustion, and the PLRA's three-strikes provision, the form-based approach to prisoner litigation tends in the judgment of many to restrict access to needed prison reforms and remedies.[21]

One element of the PLRA brings much prisoner litigation squarely within the tradition of uncontested adjudication. The PLRA provides that the court "shall review" a prisoner complaint, either before docketing or "as soon as practicable" after docketing and shall dismiss the complaint if it is frivolous, malicious, fails to state a claim, or seeks monetary relief from a defendant that is immune from such relief. Such prescreening seeks to eliminate marginal claims and free both the courts and prison officials from the burden of undue prison litigation. A growing perception of such litigation as frivolous, wasteful, and burdensome animated the congressional adoption of the PLRA. Many courts must now conduct an initial screening of prisoner petitions and determine, without the benefit of adversarial briefing or argumentation, whether the claim qualifies for further litigation. The combined effect of the uncontested nature of the adjudication and the prisoners' attempt to represent themselves has been thought to pose a grave challenge to the ability of the federal courts to balance fairness and efficiency in the disposition of prison claims.[22]

This book's treatment of uncontested adjudication offers insights into many of the problems that have arisen in connection with the statutory obligation of the federal courts to screen prisoner petitions. For starters, one should note that Article III poses no barrier to this form of adjudication. Prisoner petitions, addressed to district courts, seek to establish the prisoner's right to pursue a claim for relief and thus satisfy the antebellum definition of a case as a claim in the form prescribed by law. As we have seen, ex parte applications for leave to proceed (whether by way of mandamus, certiorari, prohibition, or habeas corpus) have long been viewed as proceedings proper for the Article III judiciary. As a result, both the initial district court decision at the prescreening stage and any subsequent appellate review of the rejection of a prisoner complaint fall squarely within the scope of federal judicial power as defined in such cases as *Tutun* and *Hohn*. Such petitions qualify as cases under Article III even before the government joins as an adversary party.[23]

Yet perhaps inevitably, the prescreening function of the federal judiciary has been criticized as a departure from the adversarial model. One scholar focused on the tendency of federal courts to base screening dismissals on such defenses as exhaustion of remedies.

> Any kind of sua sponte action marks a departure from the common law's adversarial tradition. The default rule in federal civil litigation is that defendants raise their own affirmative defenses, and if they fail to do so, the defenses are waived. The PLRA's sua sponte dismissal provisions permit the federal district courts to do the work that is otherwise assigned to civil defendants, a shift in responsibility unique in federal litigation and the common law in general.

Many courts agree with this criticism of dismissal on the basis of an affirmative defense that the respondent has yet to raise. The court's initial determination should focus on the stated statutory criteria: failure to state a claim and the assertion of money claims against those with immunity. But the failure of some district courts to limit the scope of their screening inquiry to the matters specified in the statute does not imply that the uncontested nature of the initial screening decision presents a problematic departure from the adversarial system. As we have seen, federal courts have long been expected to conduct their own inquisitions into fact and law as part of their responsibilities for the fair disposition of uncontested litigation.[24]

In a more troubling assertion, some commentators have challenged the expanded judicial role that often accompanies the adjudication of claims brought by pro se litigants. Although the authors acknowledge decisional law that allows federal judges to give pro se litigants some measure of assistance, they nonetheless question the wisdom of any judicial departure from the adversarial norm:

> The effort to equalize adversarial ability is a futile endeavor, but the hopelessness of the task is not the greatest danger. Instead, the greater danger is the loosening of the well-designed constraints on the role of the judiciary in the adversarial process. Judges are not advocates or advisors. When judges adopt these roles, they violate deeply embedded legal principles. For example, advocacy runs afoul of the judge's duty of impartiality. Additionally, giving legal advice is prohibited by multiple canons of judicial conduct. Finally, warnings to litigants closely resemble the sort of "advisory opinions" prohibited in Article III of the United States Constitution.

In effect, then, the authors argue that any departure from the adversarial model in connection with the assessment of the claims of pro se litigants undermines the properly limited role of the Article III judiciary.[25]

But this argument presents serious problems. For starters, as we have seen, any court called upon to consider an ex parte assertion of a claim of right in the form prescribed by law should proceed on an inquisitorial, rather than an adversarial basis. District courts thus owe a duty to conduct a reasonable inquiry into fact and law in connection with the performance of their screening duties under the PLRA. Such an inquiry, as Justice Story reminded us in defending the inquisitorial practice of prize courts, differs sharply from the usual form of adversarial presentation. Rather than hold pro se litigants to a high standard of lawyerly competence, federal courts should put in place mechanisms designed to ensure a reasonable judicial determination based on the facts and applicable law. Judges can institute such procedures without running afoul of the rules of neutrality and passivity that govern judicial conduct in an adversary system. To be sure, the ABA Model Rules of Judicial Conduct require judges to perform their duties fairly and impartially. But a comment to the applicable rule explains that it "is not a violation of this Rule for a judge to make reasonable accommodations to ensure pro se litigants have the opportunity to have their matters fairly heard." Such accommodations might well be extended to pro se litigants in connection with the judicial assessment of ex parte prisoner petitions.[26]

Other questions have arisen in connection with the screening of prisoner petitions for which past practices provide some guidance. Some courts report that they have put in place procedures to investigate the allegations prior to ruling on the complaint's sufficiency during the screening process. Other courts should adopt similar practices, in keeping with an understanding that judges have a more active role to play in developing the facts underlying an uncontested submission. Some courts welcome the amendment and resubmission of prisoner complaints, following an initial dismissal. Such openness to resubmission finds support in antebellum practice on naturalization petitions, where applicants for citizenship were permitted to renew their claim after an initial denial. Unfortunately, some courts today treat the dismissal of prisoner petitions as adjudications on the merits that bar future submissions. Finally, some appellate courts conduct de novo review of a screening dismissal based on the failure of the prisoner's complaint to state a claim. Others continue to review such dismissals for an abuse of discretion. Here again, we might learn something from the practice of antebellum courts, which treated legal questions in uncontested adjudication as subject to de novo review but deferred to the trial court's handling of factual issues.[27]

11.5 Avoiding Uncontested Matters of State Law

Just as federal courts owe a duty responsibly to adjudicate uncontested matters of federal law as assigned by Congress, so too should they refrain from hearing such matters of state law. Chapter 3 explained that nineteenth-century jurists, having embraced federal adjudication of uncontested naturalization claims under federal law, nonetheless shied away from the issuance of constitutive decrees as to matters of probate and domestic relations law. Those nineteenth-century decisions have given rise to what the Supreme

Court has referred to as the probate and domestic relations exceptions to Article III. Scholars and jurists have raised important questions both about the origins of these exceptions and as to their proper application today, questions that a better understanding of uncontested adjudication and Article III can help to answer.

11.5.1 The Domestic Relations Exception

As for the origins of the domestic relations exceptions, critics worry that judges may respond to these cases with more than their usual desire to steer clear of a complex body of state law. For these critics, federal courts have "naturally" come to avoid domestic relations matters because they regard such issues of hearth and home as unfit for federal adjudication. In this telling, federal judges come to the bench with a conception of which disputes belong in the federal courts. Complex commercial disputes and disputes over federal law certainly qualify, but the tendency of federal judges to shy away from domestic relations work signals to some a subtle form of gender bias. Critics thus suggest that federal judges have consigned the gender-intensive issues that arise in family law to a separate domain.[28]

It does not slight the explanatory power of these accounts of gendered judicial diffidence to suggest that federal judges may have sought to avoid such matters for a range of additional reasons. For starters, the legal relations among family members who share a common domicile would ordinarily fall outside the scope of diversity jurisdiction. In addition, as explained in chapter 3, many matters of domestic relations and probate law would have arisen under state law as applications for constitutive orders in uncontested proceedings and thus have fallen outside the Article III definition of controversies. Along with their possible disinclination to entertain family law matters, federal judges may have viewed certain forms of uncontested adjudication as less deserving of a place on the federal docket than the resolution of prominent disputes. They may have also doubted the extent to which such matters qualified as controversies between citizens of different states for purposes of diversity jurisdiction.

Restating this body of nineteenth-century law, Supreme Court decisions narrowly define the domestic relations exception. Beginning in *Ankenbrandt v. Richards*, the Court has treated the exception as a matter of the interpretation of the diversity statute, 28 U.S.C. § 1332. Although one can quibble with its approach to statutory interpretation, *Ankenbrandt* achieved some notable goals. By basing the domestic relations exception squarely on the diversity statute, the Court freed Congress to assign the federal courts a role in any domestic relations issues that implicate federal law. And, by rejecting arguments that posited a constitutional foundation for the exception, the Court eliminated the possibility that the limits of Article III would deprive the federal courts of power to take up matters that Congress had chosen to assign to them. As we have seen, treaties address the problem of child custody across international borders; Congress may implement such a treaty by assigning custody issues to the federal courts. Still, by emphasizing that only the issuance of decrees of divorce, alimony, and custody lie beyond the diversity jurisdiction of the lower federal courts, the Court has reaffirmed the lesson of *Barber v. Barber*: former spouses with separate domiciles may invoke diversity to settle a jurisdictionally sufficient dispute over the terms of their former relationship.[29]

This book's account of the domestic relations exception would achieve some of the same goals but would come at the problem from a different angle. In contrast to the Court's emphasis on the terms of the diversity statute, one might well view the exception as constitutionally grounded in the federal courts' inability to administer the state law of domestic relations except in the context of a controversy between citizens of different states. That interpretation of Article III's reference to "controversies" means that the federal courts lack the power to entertain uncontested applications for constitutive decrees on such domestic relations matters as marriage, consensual separation and divorce, alimony, adoption, and surrogacy proceedings. At the same time, the federal courts would enjoy full authority to conduct such non-contentious proceedings when they implicate federal law and arrive on the docket as federal question "cases." Like *Ankenbrandt*, then, the interpretation advanced in this book achieves the goal of coextensivity by assuring that the federal courts can hear all domestic relations questions that arise under federal law.

The scope of disagreement with the Court thus seems quite modest. This book accepts the Court's narrow interpretation of the diversity statute and its holding as to the existence of jurisdiction over the tort claims of the former spouse. Still, the approach advanced here would leave Congress free to expand diversity if it chose to do so. Nothing in Article III would prevent the federal courts from entertaining a contested state-law divorce proceeding, so long as it arose between citizens of different states. Nor do the incidental issues that might arise in connection with such a proceeding, including alimony and child custody, necessarily lie beyond federal power. In general, federal courts that obtain jurisdiction on the basis of diversity can entertain the whole case, including such incidental questions. It's not obvious that the *Ankenbrandt* Court would disagree; having disavowed any constitutional underpinning, the Court recognized broad power in Congress to manage the scope of diversity jurisdiction. In the end, the Court was content to allow Congress to decide whether to expand the role of federal law, or the role of federal courts, sitting in diversity, over disputes arising in the family law realm.[30]

11.5.2 The Probate Exception

This book's account of uncontested adjudication and Article III also offers important insights into the Supreme Court's handling of the probate exception in its 2006 decision in *Marshall v. Marshall*. Emphasizing as it had done in *Ankenbrandt* the narrow scope of the exception and the importance of congressional control, the *Marshall* Court began by restating its view that federal courts have no statutory diversity jurisdiction to probate or annul a will, administer a decedent's estate, or otherwise "dispose of property that is in the custody of a state probate court." The Court also refused to credit the state's determination of the exclusivity of its own jurisdiction, reaffirming its earlier holdings that federal jurisdiction can "not be impaired by subsequent state legislation creating courts of probate." Recognizing that the case at hand did not "involve the administration of an estate, the probate of a will, or any other purely probate matter," the Court permitted the assertion of federal jurisdiction by the bankruptcy court. It explained its previously stated concern with "interference" as "a reiteration of the general principle that, when one court is exercising *in rem* jurisdiction over a *res*, a second court will not assume *in rem* jurisdiction over the same *res*." This principle of deference to prior custody explains why federal courts cannot "dispose of property that is in the custody of a state probate court." In *Marshall*, however, the tort claim did not threaten the probate court's custody but sought only to impose in personam liability on the beneficiary of the estate.[31]

The approach suggested in this book would not call for a different result in *Marshall*. To be sure, the *Marshall* Court based the probate exception entirely on statutory grounds, and one can regard the exception as rooted in

Article III of the Constitution. But the *Marshall* case did not implicate any constitutional limits. It was an *inter partes* dispute over tortious interference with a promised bequest and thus clearly satisfied the requirements of party adverseness. Everyone agreed that the initial submission of the will to probate was a subject for the Texas state court to handle. In the absence of any attempt on the part of the federal court to exercise jurisdiction over an *ex parte* proceeding grounded in state law, the probate exception does not come into play. Thus, a state court dispute implicating the estate of a wealthy decedent did not oust the federal bankruptcy court's jurisdiction. True, having properly federalized the law of probate, Congress could assign probate matters to federal courts for administration as "cases." But the existing federal bankruptcy statute does not make such an assignment.[32]

Congress would retain a great deal of control over the scope of the probate exception, notwithstanding its roots in the Constitution. And so long as Congress chooses to defer to the state role in probate matters, state court primacy in the administration of the probate estate will do much of the work in defining the practical workaday scope of the probate exception. The Court has long required the federal courts to tailor their decrees in diverse-party disputes so as to respect the primacy of the state courts in overseeing probate administration. That was the message of *Markham v. Allen*. After placing the probate exception on statutory grounds, the Court added that federal courts do have "jurisdiction to entertain suits in favor of creditors, legatees and heirs, and other claimants against a decedent's estate to establish their claims so long as the federal court does not interfere with the probate proceedings or assume general jurisdiction of the probate or control of the property in custody of state court." In warding off federal "control of the property in custody of a state court," the Court appears to have built on its earlier in rem analogy in an effort to protect the state's primacy in the administration of estates governed by state law.[33]

A second, and more fundamental, difference may separate the approach here from that of the *Marshall* Court. Congress may have power to authorize the federal courts to entertain a claim based on state law to annul a will, so long as the requisite diversity of citizenship appears between opposing parties. Consider suits to annul a will for fraud. *Marshall* was at pains to exclude such matters from federal cognizance, doing so on the basis of statutory considerations that enjoy a measure of historical support. After all, while equity generally entertained fraud claims of all sorts, a well-established rule prevented equity from taking jurisdiction of such claims in connection with disputes over the validity of wills. Joseph Story explained the rule as follows:

> In certain cases, as of fraud in obtaining a will, whether of personal estate or real estate, the proper remedy is exclusively vested in other Courts; in wills of personal estate in the Ecclesiastical Courts, in wills of real estate in the Courts of Common Law.

To the extent that one views the probate exception as an outgrowth of the limits of equity, in short, one can readily understand why suits to annul a will for fraud were thought to lie beyond the statutory power of federal courts vested with diversity jurisdiction over suits "in law and equity." The *Marshall* Court thus adopted an understandable version of an established rule in choosing to treat suits to annul a will as beyond the diversity jurisdiction statute as currently framed.[34]

However well supported as a matter of statutory interpretation, the *Marshall* Court's view of federal power over suits to annul a will has little foundation in Article III. Notably, as Judge Jack Weinstein observed in *Spindel v. Spindel*, the controversy bases of jurisdiction in Article III contain no "law and equity" restriction. So long as the suit to annul satisfies the elements of diversity as a "controversy" between citizens of different states, it would seem to qualify for federal jurisdiction under Article III. On this view, Congress could, if it chose, expand the diversity jurisdiction of the federal courts to encompass will contests between contending parties from different states. This book does not advocate such an expansion, supporting as a matter of policy restrictions in the scope of diversity jurisdiction. But the possibility highlights the difference, small but significant, between the broader, statutory probate exception defined in *Marshall v. Marshall* and the narrower, constitutional exception implicit in the idea of a controversy.[35]

With this background in place, consider the questions that have divided lower federal courts in the wake of *Marshall*. On the first question, whether the probate exception applies to cases arising under federal law, the answer is mixed. The principle of coextensivity suggests that the Court has the power to oversee on appeal all violations of federal law that occur in connection with state probate proceedings. What's more, Congress has the power, if it chooses to federalize the law of probate, to assign the *ex parte* chores of probate and administration to the federal judiciary. Uncontested federal adjudication extends to "cases" under Article III. But we do not think that most *current* federal jurisdictional statutes should be interpreted as conferring original jurisdiction on the federal district courts to conduct pure probate proceedings. Those statutes, unlike the naturalization laws and other sources of original uncontested federal jurisdiction, provide for the resolution of contentious disputes between adverse parties. We see little basis for concluding that these laws seek to displace state court administration of probate estates.[36]

In a second post-*Marshall* puzzle, federal courts have divided in their analysis of the probate exception's application to claims relating to the administration of an *inter vivos* trust and other "will substitutes." Tackling that problem in *Oliver v. Hines*, one district court emphasized the Court's narrow view of the probate exception:

> [T]he thrust of the *Marshall* decision makes clear that the scope of the probate exception is limited to actual probate matters. The Supreme Court rejected the repeated expansion of the exception to matters that were merely ancillary to probate. An *inter vivos* trust is not a will, and although it may, on occasion, serve as the functional equivalent of a will, the application of the probate exception to such trusts would mark an unwarranted expansion of the exception.

While acknowledging that *inter vivos* trusts and other legal devices may be the functional equivalent of wills that the probate exception would prevent federal courts from adjudicating, *Oliver* permitted federal jurisdiction because the trust was not technically a will. We agree with this reading of *Marshall* and simply add that we would not expect the probate exception to apply to a genuine controversy unless litigation over an *inter vivos* trust were to begin with an initial *ex parte* application to a state court that sought to prove or establish the trust.[37]

A similarly narrow view of the exception emerges from a series of *inter partes* disputes over assets claimed by or from a probate estate. In *United States v. Tyler*, the Third Circuit found that federal jurisdiction extended to an action to recover tax revenue from the sale of a decedent's property, notwithstanding that the property was under the administration of a state probate court. The "judgment was not against any *res* held by the state probate court; it was a judgment *in personam* . . . to pay the government its share of the proceeds." Probate exception decisions in other circuits have similarly turned on whether a state probate court already had control over the property at the center of the dispute, even if those cases do not use the vocabulary of in rem jurisdiction. Finally, in *Lefkowitz v. Bank of New York*, the Second Circuit acknowledged that *Marshall* narrowed the scope of the probate exception. The court accordingly blocked jurisdiction over claims that would wrest control of property from state probate courts but allowed claims that did not directly interfere with state court's possession, including those that "undoubtedly intertwine with the litigation proceeding in the probate courts." Overlapping and duplicative adversary proceedings, even those that happen to grow out of a decedent's estate, do not fall within the probate exception.[38]

Uncontested adjudication, this chapter shows, can fit comfortably on the docket of the Article III judiciary. To be sure, inquisitorial proceedings make special demands on federal judges, demands that may seem awkward or untoward when considered in relation to the practice of conducting adversarial trials. Judges may need to demand candor from advocates and sift through testimony and documents in an effort to test the sufficiency of the claim. Prisoner petitions may prove especially challenging, given the difficulty of gaining access to additional evidence. But many federal judges gain experience with inquisitorial judging, as they oversee class actions and multidistrict litigation, establish discovery schedules, and enter consent decrees and default judgments. Courts might draw on these experiences, confident that uncontested adjudication has been a part of the work of the Article III judiciary from its earliest days. Reviewing those proceedings, this chapter has identified a collection of best practices for courts to use in handling today's noncontentious assignments. In the end, the familiar judicial task remains: that of applying the law to the facts as found and deciding whether to grant proposed relief. By accepting the legitimacy and constitutionality of their role in resolving uncontested submissions, federal judges and magistrates might more effectively take up the responsibility of sifting through the stacks of prisoner petitions that arrive in federal courthouses every day.[39]

Notes

1. Marshall's definitions of a "suit" in *Weston v. City Council*, 27 U.S. 449, 464 (1829), "any proceeding in a court of justice by which an individual pursues that remedy which the law affords him," and in *Cohens v. Virginia*, 19 U.S. 264, 408 (1821), "all cases where the party suing claims to obtain something to which he has a right," echo these elements.

2. On the adverse interests that underlie the nominally uncontested application for entry of a consent decree or class action settlement, *see* Redish & Kastanek at 589–92; Avery at 409–10.
3. On the use of "alchemy" to describe a particularly aggressive form of statutory interpretation, *see* Textile Workers Union v. Lincoln Mills, 353 U.S. 448 (1957) (Frankfurter, J., dissenting) (concluding that Justice William Douglas's majority opinion had attempted to accomplish more than could fairly be achieved through the "alchemy" of statutory interpretation). *Cf.* James E. Pfander, *Judicial Purpose and the Scholarly Process: The* Lincoln Mills *Case*, 69 WASH. U. L.Q. 243 (1991) (arguing that Frankfurter's claim was based on a selective and ultimately unpersuasive evaluation of the statute's text and legislative history). For the Court's skeptical view of implied rights of action, *see* Stoneridge Inv. Partners, LLC v. Scientific-Atlanta, Inc., 552 U.S. 148 (2008).
4. *See* Plaut v. Spendthrift Farm, Inc., 514 U.S. 211 (1995) (invalidating congressional legislation because it violated the finality rule). *See* HART & WECHSLER at __.
5. For an overview of extradition process, *see* Lindstrom v. Graber, 203 F.3d 470, 472–74 (7th Cir. 2000). *See generally* John T. Parry, *The Lost History of International Extradition Litigation*, 43 VA. J. INT'L L. 93 (2002) (outlining the history of extradition in the United States). For a critique of duplicative process in extradition litigation, *see* DeSilva v. DiLeonardi, 181 F.3d 865, 870 (7th Cir. 1999) (decrying delay and multiplicity of proceedings in an extradition matter pending in the federal system for seven years).
6. *DeSilva*, 125 F.3d at 1110. *Id.* at 1113 (characterizing an extradition certificate as one that "authorizes but does not compel" the executive to carry out an extradition and concluding that federal courts have the constitutional authority to certify for extradition). *See id.* at 870 (excoriating the multiple levels of review occasioned by the current structure of extradition litigation and calling upon Congress to set matters right through the usual practice of initial district court decision followed by appellate review).
7. *See also* Hohn v. United States, 524 U.S. 236 (1998).
8. *See* Copyright Act of 1790, ch. 15, §§ 3–4, 1 Stat. 124, 125. Thus, the statute specifically provided that the clerk shall give a copy of the copyright record to the author upon request. *Id.* § 3.
9. Tara Leigh Grove, *The Exceptions Clause as a Structural Safeguard*, 113 COLUM. L. REV. 929 (2013).
10. *See Mullane*, 339 U.S. 306. *See* Shaffer v. Heitner, 433 U.S. 186 (1977). Sheldon Levy reports that by 1952, only seventeen states still permitted probate in the common form without notice to parties interested in the decedent's estate. *See* Levy, *Probate in the Common Form*, at 422–25.
11. On the whole, the Fifth Amendment's Due Process Clause may provide a more effective instrument for moderating non-contentious forms than a strict adherence to an adverse-party rule that would foreclose the exercise of all judicial power over such matters. Non-contentious practice frequently occurs in connection with the assertion of what was once called in rem jurisdiction over such estates as those in probate, prize,

and bankruptcy. The Supreme Court has long since ruled that the due process rights to notice and an opportunity to be heard apply with equal force to such proceedings as to in personam proceedings, thereby limiting the potential threat to third-party rights. *See Mullane*, 339 U.S. at 314 (requiring notice "reasonably calculated . . . to apprise interested parties of the pendency of the action and afford them an opportunity to present their objections"). For an argument that *Mullane* casts doubt on the validity of common-form probate proceedings, *see* Levy, *Probate in the Common Form in the United States: The Problem of Notice in Probate Proceedings*, 1952 WIS. L. REV. 420 (1952). On *Lord v. Veazie*, 49 U.S. (8 How.) at 252–55 (stating that "such amicable actions . . . are always approved and encouraged, because they facilitate greatly the administration of justice," but that "there must be an actual controversy, and adverse interests"), *see* Robertson at 255, 262–63. Contempt was commonly used by the superior courts in England to punish lawyers for bringing improper feigned proceedings. *See* Bethany R. Berger at 2000–01 (2004) (citing Hoskins v. Berkeley, 100 Eng. Rep. 1086, 1086 (K.B. 1791)).

12. On the comment by nineteenth-century judge, *see In re* an Alien, 7 Hill 137, 138 (N.Y. 1845): "As between parties litigant, their admissions and agreement may satisfy a court of the existence or non-existence of material facts: but in applications for naturalization there are no hostile parties who can adjust or establish any thing by way of stipulation. The court cannot take the mere statement of any person unsupported by an oath."
13. *See* chapter 7.5 for preceding discussion on the FISA court.
14. ABA Model Rule 3.3(d). As the comment to ABA Model Rule 3.3 cmt. 14 explains, "Ordinarily, an advocate has the limited responsibility of presenting one side of the matters that a tribunal should consider in reaching a decision; the conflicting position is expected to be presented by the opposing party. However, in any ex parte proceeding, such as an application for a temporary restraining order, there is no balance of presentation by opposing advocates. The object of an ex parte proceeding is nevertheless to yield a substantially just result." *See* David S. Kris, *On the Bulk Collection of Tangible Things*, 7 J. NAT'L SEC. L. & POL'Y 209 (2014).
15. In some instances, petitioners were permitted to bring more than one petition. *See, e.g., Ex parte* Walton, 29 F. Cas. 125 (C.C.D.C. 1804) (No. 17,127) (discussed in chapter 2). Successive petitions for habeas relief were historically permissible, until qualified in the contest of state post-conviction review. *See* McClesky v. Zant, 499 U.S. 467, 479 (1991) (collecting authority for the proposition that, at common law, res judicata did not attach to a decision denying relief on a petition for habeas corpus). The Court qualified that common law rule by adopting an abuse-of-the-writ doctrine that limited second or successive petitions. *Id.* at 488–89.
16. 28 U.S.C. § 1651(a) permits "[t]he Supreme Court and all courts established by Act of Congress" to issue "all writs necessary or appropriate in aid of their respective jurisdictions," which extends to writs of mandamus. *See* Cheney v. U.S. Dist. Court for Dist. of Columbia, 542 U.S. 367, 380 (2004) (affirming appellate authority to issue writs to lower courts). 28 U.S.C. § 1291 (2018) (appellate jurisdiction over "all final decisions of the district courts of the United States"). This grant of "final decisions" was

found to map at a minimum onto district court jurisdiction over "cases." *See* Mohawk Indus., Inc. v. Carpenter, 558 U.S. 100, 106 (2009) (quoting Swint v. Chambers Cty. Comm'n, 514 U.S. 35, 42 (1995), in stating that a "final decision" is one "by which a district court disassociates itself from a case.").

17. The statute in *Hohn*, the Antiterrorism and Effective Death Penalty Act of 1996, 110 Stat. 1214 § 102, required "state prisoners to obtain a certificate of probable cause before appealing the denial of a habeas petition" which were reviewed by a three-judge panel. *Hohn*, 524 U.S. at 239–40. The majority concluded that there was "little doubt that Hohn's application for a certificate of appealability constitutes a case" within the scope of the Court's appellate review. *Id.* at 241. In *Ayestas*, the Court concluded, "Nothing in the constitution ties Congress to the typical structure of appellate review established by statute." *Ayestas*, 138 S. Ct. at 1092.
18. 28 U.S.C. § 2253(c)(1)(A), (B) (2018) (allowing appeal from "the final order in a habeas corpus proceeding" or "the final order" in a constitutional or statutory challenge to the sentence).
19. *See In re* Flynn, 973 F.3d 74 (D.C. Cir. 2020).
20. For the text of the applicable rule, *see* FED. R. CRIM. P. 48. For a discussion of *Laurance*, *see* chapter 2.2. The quote appears in *In re Flynn*, 973 F.3d at 79. The urgency with which the two dissenting judges attacked Judge Sullivan's role in reviewing the DOJ dismissal decision appears to have reflected both a failure to appreciate the inquisitorial setting in which Judge Sullivan was operating and a sense of partisan grievance. *See In re* Flynn, 973 F.3d at 85 (Griffith, J., concurring) (implicitly rejecting the dissent's view of the judicial process as a "skirmish in a partisan battle" and defending the majority opinion as an application of well-settled principles of mandamus review). In the end, the resolution of the question may turn on whether the power of the DOJ to drop a prosecution ends when the prosecution enters the sentencing phase of the proceeding, as it had done in Flynn's case. If so, then Flynn might still be granted relief in the form of a pardon.
21. Prison Litigation Reform Act, 42 U.S.C. § 1997(e) (2018). For the most recent federal court statistics, *see* U.S. DISTRICT COURTS, TABLE C-2, CIVIL CASES FILED, BY JURISDICTION AND NATURE OF SUIT, https://www.uscourts.gov/statistics/table/c-2/federal-judicial-caseload-statistics/2020/03/31 (last visited July 27, 2020). On pro se litigation and the use of form complaints for prisoner petitions, *see* Richard H. Frankel & Alistair E. Newbern, *Prisoners and Pleading*, 94 WASH. U. L. REV. 899 (2017) (reporting that in 92% of civil rights suits, the prisoner proceeds pro se). *See also* Russell Engler, *And Justice for All-Including the Unrepresented Poor: Revisiting the Roles of the Judges, Mediators, and Clerks*, 67 FORDHAM L. REV. 1987, 2015 (1999). For a critique of the Prison Litigation Reform Act's preliminary requirements, *see* Molly Guptill Manning, *Trouble Counting to Three: Circuit Splits and Confusion in Interpreting the Prison Reform Act's "Three Strikes Rule," 28 U.S.C. § 1915(G)*, 28 CORNELL J.L. & PUB. POL'Y 207 (2018).
22. *See* 28 U.S.C. § 1915A (2018) (calling for screening of prisoner complaints and declaring that a district court may dismiss *sua sponte* a complaint if it is "frivolous,

malicious, or fails to state a claim upon which relief may be granted."). *Id.* at § 1915A(b)(1). On the public concern with "frivolous" pro se prisoner litigation leading to the adoption of the PLRA, *see* Manning at 212–15. Although we do not subscribe to the author's view that district court ex parte jurisdiction is unconstitutional by nature, Michael J. Donaldson highlights the challenges posed by the uncontested screening process in *Justice in Full Is Time Well Spent: Why the Supreme Court Should Ban Sua Sponte Dismissals*, 36 Quinnipac L. Rev. 25 (2017).

23. *See* chapters 7.1 and 7.2 for discussion of judicial consideration of ex parte writs, and contrast between *Tutun* and *Hohn*.
24. For the quote, *see* Katherine A. Macfarlane, *Procedural Animus*, 71 Ala. L. Rev. 1185, 1208–10 (2020). For courts that have refused to consider affirmative defenses during prescreening, *see* Aquilar-Avellaveda v. Terrell, 478 F.3d 1223 (10th Cir. 2007); Anderson v. XYZ Corr. Health Servs., 407 F.3d 674, 682 (4th Cir. 2005).
25. Robert Bacharach & Lyn Entzeroth, *Judicial Advocacy in Pro Se Litigation: A Return to Neutrality*, 42 Ind. L.J. 19 (2009). Bacharach served as a federal magistrate before being confirmed as a judge on the U.S. Court of Appeals for the Tenth Circuit. Dean Entzeroth leads the University of Tulsa College of Law.
26. ABA Model Rules of Judicial Conduct (2020), cmt. 4 to Rule 2.2.
27. For cases applying the abuse-of-discretion standard to dismissals for failure to state a claim, *see, e.g.*, Edler v. Hockley Cty. Comm'rs Court, 589 Fed. App'x 664, 666 (5th Cir. 2014) (applying abuse of discretion review to dismissal of in forma pauperis complaint and citing Denton v. Hernandez, 504 U.S. 25, 33 (1992)); Nagy v. FMC Butner, 376 F.3d 252, 254 (4th Cir. 2004) (same). For those applying de novo review, *see* Wershe v. Combs, 763 F.3d 500, 504–05 (6th Cir. 2014). Most courts agree that an abuse-of-discretion standard applies to appellate review of the dismissal of complaints as frivolous. *See* Miller v. Donald, 541 F.3d 1091, 1100 (11th Cir.2008). For the practice of requiring investigative reports, *see* Lamb v. Norwood, 895 F.3d 756 (10th Cir. 2018) (reporting that district courts in the Tenth Circuit frequently require investigative reports and stay discovery until the filing of these reports). For an account of the importance of attending carefully to all submissions, even those that lack merit, *see* Alexander A. Reinert, *Screening Out Innovation: The Merits of Meritless Litigation*, 89 Ind. L.J. 1191 (2014).
28. *See, e.g.*, Barbara Freedman Wand, *A Call for the Repudiation of the Domestic Relations Exception to Federal Jurisdiction*, 30 Vill. L. Rev. 307, 385–86 (1985) ("Although not expressly articulated in federal court opinions, there is a persistent undercurrent in many cases involving the domestic relations exception: federal courts have a distaste for domestic relations disputes."); Barbara Ann Atwood, *Domestic Relations Cases in Federal Court: Toward a Principled Exercise of Jurisdiction*, 35 Hastings L.J. 571, 627 (1984) (concluding that the domestic relations exception saves the courts "from a distasteful category of litigation"); Naomi R. Cahn, *Family Law, Federalism, and the Federal Courts*, 79 Iowa L. Rev. 1073, 1116 (1994) (noting federal courts' reluctance to hear domestic relations cases); Judith Resnik, *"Naturally" Without Gender: Women, Jurisdiction, and the Federal Courts*, 66 N.Y.U. L. Rev. 1682, 1739–50 (1991) (arguing that, despite clear federal involvement in family law issues, "when

possible, federal courts divest themselves of 'family issues'"). Because the federal courts are "understood as the place in which the national agenda is debated and enforced," excluding family law issues and thereby women from federal adjudication labels both women and family law issues as undeserving of a place in public debate. *Id.* at 1699. *See also* Michael Ashley Stein, *The Domestic Relations Exception to Federal Jurisdiction: Rethinking an Unsettled Federal Courts Doctrine*, 36 B.C. L. Rev. 669, 708–10 (1995) (discussing the judiciary's bias against family law issues for being considered "beneath" the proper scope of the federal courts' jurisdiction).

29. *See* Ankenbrandt v. Richards, 504 U.S. 689 (1992). Many commentators have noted the Court's "shaky foundation" for the domestic relations exception. *See, e.g.*, Cahn at 1085 (noting the Court's "questionable reasoning" in relying on the diversity statute for the exception). Chapter 3 discusses the decision in *Barber v. Barber*, 62 U.S. 582 (1859).
30. On the power to hear incidental questions, *see* 28 U.S.C. § 1367 (defining federal courts' supplemental jurisdiction). On congressional authority, *see* Ankenbrandt v. Richards, 504 U.S. 689, 700 (1992) (stating that Congress "remains free to alter what [the Court] has done"). *See also* Cahn at 1083 (stating that *Ankenbrandt* "does not preclude Congress from enacting legislation to . . . allow federal courts to hear these [domestic relations] cases").
31. *See* Marshall v. Marshall, 547 U.S. 293 (2006). For the quoted portions, *see Marshall*, 547 U.S. at 311–14. As for the *Marshall* Court's suggestion that the power of a federal court does not extend to suits between diverse parties that seek to annul a will, consider *Gaines v. Fuentes*, 92 U.S. 10, 20 (1875). The *Gaines* Court squarely held that the diversity jurisdiction of the federal courts extended to the removal of a "suit" brought in state court to annul a will "as a muniment of title, and to limit the operation of the decree admitting it to probate." *Id.* As the Court explained:

    > [W]henever a controversy in a suit between such parties arises respecting the validity or construction of a will, or the enforcement of a decree admitting it to probate, there is no more reason why the Federal courts should not take jurisdiction of the case than there is that they should not take jurisdiction of any other controversy between the parties.

    Id. at 22. As *Marshall* observed, however, the *Gaines* decision was apparently limited by later cases that treated a suit to annul as supplemental to the probate court's power to establish the will. *See Marshall*, 547 U.S. at 311 (citing Sutton v. English, 246 U.S. 199, 208 (1918)). Yet both *Gaines* and *Sutton* were decided at a time when the Court looked to the structure of state court proceedings to define the scope of the district court's *inter partes* authority. Having correctly concluded that state law cannot oust a district court of its diversity jurisdiction over a genuine dispute, the Court should not give much weight to the *Sutton* Court's finding that Texas did not permit *inter partes* disputes to annul a will.
32. *See* Marshall v. Marshall, 547 U.S. at 308–09 (linking probate exception to federal jurisdiction to language in Judiciary Act of 1789).
33. *See* Markham v. Allen, 326 U.S. 490 (1946).

34. Suits to annul a will can arise as diverse-party controversies and should qualify for federal adjudication. That's the message of cases from the nineteenth century. 1 JOSEPH STORY, COMMENTARIES ON EQUITY JURISPRUDENCE AS ADMINISTERED IN ENGLAND AND AMERICA 194 (1836). On reviewing Story and other authorities, Professor Langbein accordingly concluded that, when the claim was fraud, "the Chancery was without authority to determine the validity of the execution of a will." John H. Langbein, *Fact Finding in the English Court of Chancery: A Rebuttal*, 83 YALE L.J. 1620, 1623 (1974). For the quote, *see* Marshall v. Marshall, 547 U.S. 293, 311–12 (2006).
35. *See* Spindel v. Spindel, 283 F. Supp. 797, 800–01 (E.D.N.Y. 1968).
36. One question, whether the probate exception applies to claims under federal law, the Court deliberately sidestepped. *See Marshall*, 547 U.S. at 308 ("Federal jurisdiction in this case is premised on 28 U.S.C. § 1334, the statute vesting in federal district courts jurisdiction in bankruptcy cases and related proceedings"). For other evaluations, *compare In re* Goerg, 844 F.2d 1562, 1565 (11th Cir. 1988) (holding that the probate exception does not apply to federal question jurisdiction), *with* Jones v. Brennan, 465 F.3d 304, 307 (7th Cir. 2006) (Posner, J.) (holding that the probate exception does apply to federal jurisdiction), *and In re* Marshall, 392 F.3d 1118, 1131–32 (9th Cir. 2004), *rev'd on other grounds*, *Marshall*, 547 U.S. at 311 (extending the probate exception to federal question cases). One might ask if Congress could simply confer probate jurisdiction on the federal courts so that any claim for probate would arise under the grant of jurisdiction. Such a jurisdictional statute would run afoul of the principle that cases arise under federal law only when a federal question "forms an ingredient of the original cause." *See* Osborn v. Bank of U.S., 22 U.S. 738, 823 (1824). Jurisdictional grants alone do not supply the requisite ingredient. *See, e.g.*, Mesa v. California, 489 U.S. 121, 138–39 (1989) (construing the federal officer removal statute to confer jurisdiction only when the official raises a substantive federal question). On annulment, consider *In re* Brown, 484 B.R. 322, 330–32 (Bankr. E.D. Ky. 2012). There, a federal bankruptcy court assumed that the probate exception applied with equal force to bankruptcy proceedings and blocked the approval of a settlement agreement that contained a provision nullifying a will, citing *Marshall* for the proposition that federal courts cannot annul a will.
37. *Compare* Curtis v. Brunsting, 704 F.3d 406, 409–10 (5th Cir. 2013) (holding that the probate exception does not apply to trust property because that property never came under the control of a probate court), *with* Evans v. Pearson Enters., Inc., 434 F.3d 839, 849 (6th Cir. 2006) (holding that refusing to hear cases regarding "will substitutes" is consistent with the probate exception). For the quote, *see* Oliver v. Hines, 943 F. Supp. 2d 634, 638 (E.D. Va. 2013). *But see* Chabot v. Chabot, No. 4:11-CV-217-BLW, 2011 WL 5520927, at *4 (D. Idaho 2011) (concluding that "the probate exception analysis applies to trusts that act as will substitutes"); Leskinen v. Halsey, No. CV 12-623(JFB)(ETB), 2013 WL 802915 (E.D.N.Y. Jan. 28, 2013) (broadly interpreting the probate exception as intended to prohibit federal involvement in the administration of decedent's estates).

38. *See* United States v. Tyler, 528 Fed. App'x 193, 197 (3d Cir. 2013). The First and Seventh Circuits have each held that federal courts may adjudicate claims that will add to an estate in probate without running afoul of the probate exception because such a dispute does not require a federal court to usurp control over property already under the control of a state probate court. *See* Jimenez v. Rodriguez-Pagan, 597 F.3d 18, 24 (1st Cir. 2010) ("Indeed, the very relief sought here is enlargement of the decedent's estate through assets not currently within it. While divvying up an estate falls squarely within the probate exception, merely increasing it does not."); Gustafson v. zumBrunnen, 546 F.3d 398, 400 (7th Cir. 2008):

> The suit, though based ultimately on the will, is not within the probate exception to federal jurisdiction. The judgment sought would just add assets to the decedent's estate; it would not reallocate the estate's assets among contending claimants or otherwise interfere with the probate court's control over and administration of the estate.

For the view of the Second Circuit, *see* Lefkowitz v. Bank of New York, 528 F.3d 102, 105 (2d Cir. 2007) ("Before *Marshall*, most federal courts, including ours, had interpreted the probate exception more broadly than the Supreme Court has now defined it."). *See also* Moser v. Pollin, 294 F.3d 335, 340 (2d Cir. 2002) (describing a conjunctive test used to determine whether application of the probate exception to federal diversity jurisdiction is appropriate). For the order, *see Lefkowitz*, 528 F.3d at 107–08.

39. *See* Jon O. Newman, *Pro Se Prisoner Litigation: Looking for Needles in Haystacks*, 62 BROOK. L. REV. 519, 520 (1996) (likening the process of evaluating prisoner petitions to the search for the proverbial needle in a haystack and questioning accounts of such petitions as invariably frivolous).

12
Toward a Constructive Constitutional History

How should we read and interpret our eighteenth-century Constitution as the pace of social and legal change makes it increasingly difficult to recover the unwritten assumptions, tacit understandings, unspoken commitments, and background legal norms of the founding generation? Some try to understand old ways on their own terms; others look at them with an eye for modern doctrine. That modern vision has informed leading recent treatments of the adverse-party and injury-in-fact requirements that we encountered in chapters 7 and 10. Looking at uncontested proceedings in bankruptcy in the 1980s, some found them impossible to defend as part of a system of adversarial contestation.

Authors of a recent edition of a leading casebook, *Hart & Wechsler's Federal Courts and the Federal System*, took the same view of naturalization practice in the nineteenth century. Viewing naturalization as flatly incompatible with standing and adverse-party requirements, *Hart & Wechsler*'s authors asked (in a rhetorical question pregnant with doubt) whether pedigree alone could justify the exercise of federal judicial power over similar obligations today. As chapter 7 recounted, other scholars and jurists have questioned such well-pedigreed practices as habeas corpus proceedings, warrant applications, consent decrees, fee petitions, and immunized testimony approval orders. This chapter explores the challenges of integrating text, history, and practice in the development of a coherent and constructive body of constitutional law.[1]

12.1 The Role of Pedigree in Debates over Article III

With the authors of *Hart & Wechsler*, Justice Scalia shared a skeptical view that pedigree could justify practices that did not conform to modern justiciability norms. Justice Scalia tackled the problem of pedigree in *Vermont Agency*, *qui tam* litigation brought to recover a penalty against an agency

Cases Without Controversies. James E. Pfander, Oxford University Press. © James E. Pfander 2021.
DOI: 10.1093/oso/9780197571408.003.0013

of the state government for the benefit of the United States and the informer, Jonathan Stevens. Under the terms of the False Claims Act, first enacted in 1863 and reinstated in 1986, informers were required to notify the Department of Justice that a prospective defendant had defrauded the government through the assertion of false claims. On notification, the government could pursue the claim itself or defer to the private litigant. If the action was successful under either scenario, the private informer would keep a share of the penalties assessed against the defendant, and would recover her attorney's fees as well. The action thus presented a challenge to the coherence of standing law. The plaintiff clearly had a concrete stake in the action with the opportunity to secure a bounty as a result of successful litigation. But while it created a concrete stake, the bounty was not necessarily designed to remedy any personal injury to the plaintiff, as the modern law of standing had been interpreted to require.[2]

Or at least that's how Justice Scalia understood the problem. His opinion explained that "[a]n interest unrelated to injury in fact is insufficient to give a plaintiff standing." Instead, the "interest must consist of obtaining compensation for, or preventing, the violation of a legally protected right." Justice Scalia found that this crucial connection was missing:

> A *qui tam* relator has suffered no such invasion—indeed, the "right" he seeks to vindicate does not even fully materialize until the litigation is completed and the relator prevails. This is not to suggest that Congress cannot define new legal rights, which in turn will confer standing to vindicate an injury caused to the claimant. As we have held in another context, however, an interest that is merely a "byproduct" of the suit itself cannot give rise to a cognizable injury in fact for Article III standing purposes.

Something, it seemed, would have to give.[3]

Justice Scalia resolved the tension between the undoubted pedigree of *qui tam* litigation and the Court's injury-in-fact requirement with a workaround. He chose to treat the informer as the assignee of the government's interest in recovering penalties for false claims. The government had doubtless suffered an injury in fact and doubtless had standing to sue. The provisions of the False Claims Act could "reasonably be regarded as effecting a partial assignment of the Government's damages claim." Although the Court had not previously recognized the representational standing of assignees, Justice Scalia identified cases that assumed the viability of such litigation including that brought by subrogees. In the end, then, Justice Scalia found "that the United States' injury in fact suffices to confer standing on respondent Stevens."[4]

Having located an injury in fact, Justice Scalia turned to the history of *qui tam* litigation both in England and in the courts of the United States:

> *Qui tam* actions appear to have been as prevalent in America as in England, at least in the period immediately before and after the framing of the Constitution. Although there is no evidence that the Colonies allowed common-law *qui tam* actions (which, as we have noted, were dying out in England by that time), they did pass several informer statutes expressly authorizing *qui tam* suits. . . . Moreover, immediately after the framing, the First Congress enacted a considerable number of informer statutes. Like their English counterparts, some of them provided both a bounty and an express cause of action; others provided a bounty only.

That answered the standing puzzle. Justice Scalia found the history "well-nigh conclusive" as to the question whether *qui tam* actions were "cases and controversies" of the sort traditionally amenable to, and resolved by, the judicial process. But he was careful to add that it was the history combined with the plaintiff's assigned injury that left "no room for doubt" as to Article III standing. Pedigree alone would not suffice.[5]

Assessed by the standards set forth by *Hart & Wechsler* and Justice Scalia, uncontested adjudication would seem to violate latter-day Article III strictures; its pedigree alone would not assure its continuing validity. Indeed, many contemporary scholars who have encountered such forms view them as the quaint and likely simple-minded products of an earlier day. In a paper on the role of the attorney general and the forms of adjudication, one scholar described early assignments of uncontested matters to the federal courts as instances of pragmatism. On this view, by authorizing federal circuit courts to hear pension benefit claims (and other judicial work that moderns find unconventional), early Congresses made unprincipled but expedient judicial assignments. Such assignments likely violated the adverse-party requirement of Article III as well as other possible limitations. By treating them as "pragmatic," this account tends to deny early practices any persuasive power in the evaluation of the nature of judicial authority.[6]

If one sees the early practices recounted in this book as less a matter of pedigree alone and more a reflection of the way the history of uncontested litigation informs the distinction between cases and controversies, then the "problem" of how to explain early instances of uncontested adjudication largely disappears. That observation teaches important lessons about constitutional interpretation: that text, theory, and practice can together provide a persuasive account of the meaning of the judicial power that text or theory or practice alone cannot. In a sense, that lesson coheres with Justice Scalia's instinct in *Vermont Agency*, where he coupled practice and theory to justify bounty claims. But Scalia's theoretical justification for bounty claims—that they represented the assignment of the government's injury to a private litigant—likely departs from the understanding of the legislators in the early Republic who first enacted such provisions into federal law. Public actions were (as we have seen) a recognized feature of the inherited view of the judicial role and no thoroughgoing injury requirement was applied to condition the right of individuals to institute judicial proceedings. Just as Justice Field used the term "controversy" to import a measure of contestation into his definition of "cases," Justice Scalia used the same language to import an injury requirement into his conception of the legality of bounty claims.[7]

Vermont Agency suggests that practice alone (or pedigree in the terms chosen by *Hart & Wechsler*) cannot solve interpretive problems without being integrated into a conceptual framework that explains the judicial role. When old practices encounter a very different modern conceptual framework, they look odd and out of place. The modern Supreme Court may find it tempting to discard such practices, in much the same way *Hart & Wechsler* would apparently discard the naturalization practices of the nineteenth century and others would discard bankruptcy administration, consent decrees, and warrant proceedings. But that response to the seeming anomalies of the past only underscores the problem with an interpretive approach that assumes the explanatory power of the modern conceptual framework and treats past practice as out of step. A more sensible approach, or so this book argues, would be to understand past practices on their own terms and to develop a conceptual framework that helps to make sense of those practices. The more widespread the practice, the more insistently it demands understanding and accommodation rather than rejection.

The conflict between modern conceptions of the case-or-controversy rule and the past understandings described in this book reveals something important about the accessibility of the past. Modern lawyers and jurists may overestimate their ability to make sense of what the Constitution meant to those who ratified its terms. Article III was written and ratified by lawyers steeped in the eighteenth-century legal practices and institutions of England,

Scotland, and the colonies of British North America. Originalists often assume that modern understandings of the Constitution's terms run in an unbroken line back to the meanings understood by those who participated in drafting the document. But the changing content of cases and controversies, as revealed in this book, casts doubt on the easy assumption that texts written more than two centuries ago will readily yield their meaning to modern readers. Cases differed from controversies until those terms were fused in the late nineteenth century and came to operate as placeholders for a variety of twentieth-century concerns about the proper exercise of the judicial function. Yet today, we read those terms through twentieth-century eyes and scarcely recognize the world of adjudication they were meant to accommodate and set in motion.

Apart from counseling a modest, careful, and practice-driven approach to claims about the textual meaning of an aging document's reference to the judicial power, the book suggests that arguments from longstanding tradition have an important role to play in constitutional argument. In some ways, the invocation of tradition as an argument in constitutional discourse may strike the reader as mundane, hackneyed, or worse. Judicial decisions abound with arguments from tradition. Justice Scalia's majority opinion in *Grupo Mexicano*, as Sam Bray has observed, invokes the term "tradition" as often as the opening song in *Fiddler on the Roof*. Even cases like *Spokeo*, which apply new conceptual limits on judicial power, do so in the name of fealty to a supposed tradition. Yet arguments from tradition that would invalidate a right to pursue claims "in the form prescribed by law," such as that in *Spokeo*, seem much harder to justify than those that invoke tradition in the course of upholding a longstanding practice. Continuing practices, based on longstanding tradition, enjoy a claim of presumptive constitutionality and courts should hesitate to declare them invalid. Even a court with a bold new understanding of original meaning should proceed cautiously when asked to apply that meaning to invalidate established practices. The very boldness and novelty of the interpretation may count heavily against its implementation.[8]

12.2 Pedigree and Constructive Constitutionalism

How then should courts incorporate the lessons of pedigree into the modern constitutional law of judicial power? True, almost everyone would agree with originalists that history can *help* answer *some* modern interpretive questions.

But just about everyone also recognizes that relevant history does not always point in one direction: well-informed observers may dispute the historical meaning of a constitution's text, and their views may conflict with the way the text has been applied by the federal courts. The context of a modern dispute might differ from that in which the issue first arose, making past applications an uncertain guide to current questions.[9]

If methodological problems abound among originalists, they persist for those who do not subscribe to originalist precepts. Even if the text and original meaning seem unusually clear, interpreters (originalist and non-originalist alike) must reckon with the claims of intervening decisions and historical eras. Further, non-originalists display some continuing devotion to the idea that federal courts should fashion a body of law that fits tolerably well with the nation we once were and the nation we have become. With so much room for argument about the many relevant histories that inform constitutional decisions, why bother to conduct serious constitutional history at all except within an originalist framework? What can constitutional history contribute to non-originalist constitutional discourse, and what guideposts mark the path of persuasive constitutional history in a world of constant change?[10]

Constructive constitutional history can provide an approach to constitutional history for non-originalists. Use of the term "constructive" to describe a constitutional history for non-originalists reflects a variety of considerations. First, a constructive history portrays the Framers as they saw themselves: as builders. They sought to create a "new order for the ages," a machine that would "go of itself," a complex set of government institutions that would doubtless develop in new and unexpected ways. Second, the term "constructive" conveys the idea, common among constitutional historians, that the meaning of the Constitution reflects the constructions, practices, and layers of meaning that lawyers, judges, legislators, and presidents have adopted over the decades. Third, the idea of a constructive constitutional history calls to mind the constructivist approach to constitutional interpretation that Professor Richard Fallon has advanced and refined over a brilliant career. For Fallon, interpreters must offer an interpretation that takes account of—that coheres or "fits" with—a whole range of interpretive considerations, including the lessons of text, history, prior decisional law, and institutional developments.[11]

Finally, *constructive* constitutional history offers a form of historical discourse that attempts to make a positive contribution to the interpretive enterprise. Constructive, in this sense, means useful and forward-looking; it contrasts with destructive or oppositional. The Anti-Federalists struggled in the ratification debates in part because, busy opposing the Federalist project, they neglected to offer a positive account of the form of government they would embrace. Perhaps it makes sense for those who doubt the wisdom of exclusively originalist interpretive modalities to frame their contributions in positive terms. Better to put forward a constructive vision of the Constitution's meaning than to stand in opposition as anti- or non-originalists, or as supporters of an unwritten Constitution.[12]

12.3 A Constructive Account of Cases and Controversies

Within the organizing framework of constructive constitutionalism, the history of uncontested adjudication may provide broader insights into the interpretive enterprise. For starters, a constructive approach would emphasize the importance of synthesis, of bringing all of the interpretive materials together in an effort to fashion a body of law that takes account of text, history, past practice, and fits tolerably with today's jurisprudential commitments. The construct of the "litigable interest"—as explained more fully in chapter 10—illustrates how such a synthetic approach might work. The litigable interest can accommodate uncontested adjudication, make sense of the textual distinction between cases and controversies, and leave the Court free to insist upon concrete interests and a measure of adverseness when claims come to the federal courts as disputes. Contestation, in short, can still play a central role in a system of federal adjudication that accepts jurisdiction over some uncontested matters.

The instinct toward accommodation and synthesis reflected in the construct of the litigable interest acknowledges that legal ideas must fit well in the surrounding judicial ecosystem. Fit, of course, has long been a key element of non-originalist approaches to the interpretive enterprise. Existing doctrinal assumptions create a framework within which courts operate in resolving new disputes; past practice creates patterns and habits of judicial mind that suggest analogies and possible solutions. Originalists, depending on how faint- or stout-hearted they consider themselves to be, sometimes proceed as if they care little for how well their ideas fit within the surrounding ecosystem. Indeed, for the most stout-hearted, originalism may demand destruction of the existing framework in service to a conception of legality based on a real or imagined past. Justice Clarence Thomas, for example, has sometimes proclaimed himself willing to adhere to originalist outcomes even where that would uproot much of the modern administrative state. One can discern an almost righteous zeal in the words of some stout-hearted originalists—they call to mind the abolitionist idea that one must "[l]et justice be done, though the heavens fall."[13]

However understandable in support of the cause of abolition, constitutional interpretations that threaten to bring down the firmament will prove difficult for jurists facing the more mundane questions in this book to adopt and justify. One can see Justice Scalia's faint-hearted originalism at work in *Vermont Agency*: the pedigree of bounty claims suggested a traditional understanding of judicial power not lightly to be cast aside. In bringing the practice within Article III, Justice Scalia located an otherwise-missing injury in the fictional idea that the plaintiff had been assigned responsibility for seeking redress of the government's injury. Justice Scalia thus sought to accommodate the traditional practice of informer litigation, rather than overthrowing the practice in light of his conception of the demands of originalism. To Justice Scalia's way of thinking, the case-or-controversy requirement inflexibly demands concrete injuries and party contestation, but it did not deprive the federal courts of power to hear bounty claims.

Justice Scalia's instinct toward the accommodation of past practice or pedigree represents one possible approach to problems of constitutional adjustment. Concern with pedigree, tradition, precedent, and fit—however one might choose to characterize a jurist's natural tendency to accommodate existing practices—represents a form of epistemic humility. The need for epistemic humility flows from what philosophers of science characterize as the fragility of epistemic confidence—that is, "confidence invested in activities aimed at the acquisition, assessment, and application of knowledge." Jurists, needless to say, engage in an epistemic enterprise: they acquire, assess, and apply knowledge in the resolution of disputes over constitutional meaning. Humility in such an enterprise begins with the recognition that any one judge or court cannot know everything. Epistemic humility, then, accepts "an acute sense of the fact that epistemic confidence is conditional, complex, contingent, and therefore *fragile*." In relying on pedigree, precedent, and fit, judges in our constitutional tradition display the virtue of epistemic humility.[14]

Stout-hearted originalists, by contrast, sometimes operate from a position of epistemic hubris. In their willingness to invalidate broad swaths of accumulated practice in service of a particular conception of constitutional meaning, originalists sometimes display great confidence in their ideas. But that very confidence may make it harder to recognize the fragility of knowledge. And without such a recognition, originalists may grow so attached to their ideas that they lack the ability to reflect, to evaluate new sources of knowledge, and to update their understandings in light of new discoveries. In other words, epistemic confidence may make it particularly difficult for some stout-hearted originalists to incorporate new accounts of text, history, and practice into their conception of the proper interpretation any particular constitutional provision.

The debate over the references to cases and controversies in Article III may illustrate the challenges of updating for the epistemically confident. Having committed themselves to the idea that the case-or-controversy requirement inflexibly limits the federal courts to the redress of injuries inflicted by opposing parties, the Justices (and some scholars) may find it difficult to incorporate the construct of uncontested adjudication. One sees some signs of that epistemic confidence in Justice Scalia's insistence on rigorous adherence to the adverse-party rule in such cases as *Windsor* and *Hohn*. So far, however, the Court has been unwilling to overthrow past practice in service of a full-throated embrace of the adverse-party ideal. Use of the idea of prudence in *Windsor* and the idea of adverse interests in *Ayestas v. Davis* served as temporizing measures that allowed the Court to uphold a judicial role in uncontested matters without threatening or uprooting the Court's justiciability doctrine. The Court's approach thus resembles Justice Scalia's reliance in *Vermont Agency* on an assignment of interests to solve the injury problem posed by bounty litigation, thereby accommodating practice without overthrowing existing doctrinal categories.

Epistemic humility thus supports the use of temporizing measures that allow the Court to reaffirm traditional practices without embracing a rigid adversarialism that might threaten much settled law. For some of the same reasons, an epistemically humble Court might refrain from too quickly adopting this book's litigable interest construct as a new synthesis of Article III's provision for the adjudication of cases and controversies. Rather than commit to the new interpretation advanced in the book, the twin counsels of prudence and humility may encourage the Court to adopt minimalist or temporizing measures. Through such measures, the Court can preserve much settled law for use in future cases and can refrain from unleashing the potentially disruptive force of a new interpretation. Something like that conception of the judicial role appears to have underlain the Court's decision in *McDonald v. City of Chicago* to continue to rely on the Fourteenth Amendment's Due Process Clause as the provision that incorporates and makes the Bill of Rights applicable to state actors. Stout-hearted originalists had unsuccessfully urged a switch to reliance on the privileges and immunities clause, a switch with potentially radical implications.[15]

Nonetheless, by documenting uncontested adjudication in nineteenth-century practice and connecting that practice to the distinctive meaning of cases and controversies, this book may lend support to the Court's use of temporizing measures. With a standing doctrine that takes account of the context in which the dispute arises and prudential doctrines of contestation that it can trim to fit the needs of the particular case, the Court has the capacity to tailor its justiciability law to the contested or uncontested nature of the underlying proceeding. In short, the Court might achieve the functional equivalent of a litigable interest approach without firmly or openly embracing the lessons of this book. Epistemic humility might encourage the Court both to adapt its doctrine to authorize uncontested adjudication and to refrain from openly adopting the litigable interest construct as the measure of what constitutes a case arising under federal law within the meaning of Article III. The Court's conclusion in *Ayestas v. Davis* that ex parte habeas fee applications were cases within the appellate jurisdiction of the federal courts may present one example of such temporizing measures.

Indeed, the adverse-interest theory discussed in chapter 9 may offer the Court a way to uphold some uncontested forms of adjudication without fully embracing the distinct meanings of cases and controversies. One can see the Court in *Ayestas* gesturing toward the existence of adverse interests in its discussion of the state's opposition to any habeas relief for the petitioner. Similar gestures appear in other temporizing decisions, such as that in *Hohn* upholding appellate jurisdiction over petitions for the issuance of certificates of appealability. There, the Court similarly explained that an adverse-party dispute lurked in the background of the petitioner's ex parte application for habeas review. Such decisions allow the Court to resolve the case at hand without committing itself to what it may perceive as a revolutionary restatement of existing law.

But such humility, like the temporizing fictions of an earlier day, comes with a cost—the cost of obscuring the content of the law. Scholars working in the realist tradition understood that fictions threaten the clarity of the law; they pushed for candor in the identification of the underlying factors that explain the results achieved through fictions and workarounds. Some of the most powerful works of legal imagination in the twentieth century challenged the conceptual clarity of certain formal categories, urging courts to abandon their fictions and focus instead on the factors that appear to have driven the decisions. The lessons of realism suggest that lower courts may not fully understand the limits of the Court's fictional requirement of party contestation. They may instead adhere to the letter of formal doctrine and continue to insist on adverse-party presentations; they may doubt their capacity to entertain uncontested proceedings originally or on appeal; and they may misunderstand the qualified nature of the injury-in-fact requirement. Such errors can cause important dislocations, as when appellate courts refuse to entertain appeals from parties with an obvious stake in securing review of the denial of their ex parte application for a waiver of fees, or when commentators call into question the constitutionality of longstanding practices.

The Court can surely continue to correct such errors on a case-by-case basis without overthrowing the received case-or-controversy wisdom. Unless the Court faces the relatively pure form of uncontested adjudication that Justice Brandeis considered in *Tutun*, temporizing references to potential adversaries may adequately serve its purpose. In such a world, the litigable interest may help to structure our understanding of the Court's decisions even if it fails to secure an explicit place in them. But as the Court grows more confident in decisions upholding uncontested adjudication and less patient with the disruptive consequences of lower court misapprehensions, a new synthesis may become possible. If and when it arrives at such a synthesis, perhaps by invoking the litigable interest, the Court will have implemented a form of constructive constitutionalism. Messier, perhaps, than the clean lines often suggested by formalists, such constructive solutions offer the virtue of taking into account much of the accumulated wisdom of the past.

Notes

1. Hart & Wechsler at 86 ("When if ever should a deep historical pedigree sustain a practice if the Court would otherwise find it unconstitutional?").
2. *See* Vermont Agency of Nat. Res. v. United States *ex rel.* Stevens, 529 U.S. 725 (2000).
3. *Vermont Agency*, 529 U.S. at 772. *Id.* at 772–73. For the byproduct quote, *see* Steel Co. v. Citizens for a Better Env't, 523 U.S. 83, 107 (1998). Justice Scalia had previously suggested that a bounty would suffice to give the plaintiff a concrete interest in the outcome of litigation, thereby satisfying that portion of justiciability law. *See* *Lujan*, 504 U.S. at 572–73 (distinguishing the injury claims of the plaintiffs from the

"unusual case in which Congress has created a concrete private interest in the outcome of a suit against a private party for the government's benefit, by providing a cash bounty for the victorious plaintiff"). But he was later to reject a bounty as the basis for standing. *See Vermont Agency*, 529 U.S. at 773.

4. *Id.* at 773–74. On this point, the Court was unanimous. But Justice Scalia was unable to locate any prior decisions upholding the right of Congress to provide for an assignment of injuries in fact. Some language in prior opinions had assumed that the injury in fact must be personal to the plaintiff. *See, e.g., Lujan*, at 581 (Kennedy, J., concurring) (observing that "the party bringing suit must show that the action injures him in a concrete and personal way.").
5. Block quotation appears in *id.* at 776–77. *Id.* at 777. *Id.* at 778.
6. Bloch at 563 (describing the Framers' approach as "neither rigid nor doctrinaire. On the contrary, it was remarkably subtle and pragmatic."). *See* Morley, *Consent of the Governed*, at 647 n.40, 666–67 (noting the Supreme Court's inconsistent and unpersuasive justification for consent decrees in *Swift & Co. v United States*, 276 U.S. 311, 313–15 (1928), and *Pope v. United States*, 323 U.S. 1, 3–5 (1944)).
7. *Vermont Agency*, 529 U.S. 765. *See* chapter 5.1 for a discussion of the Field theory.
8. Samuel L. Bray, *The Supreme Court and the New Equity*, 68 VAND. L. REV. 997, 1022 (2015) (noting that "the word tradition or a cognate appears fourteen times. That is the same number of times tradition appears in the first song of Fiddler on the Roof."). *Spokeo, Inc.*, 136 S. Ct. at 1547 ("Standing to sue is a doctrine rooted in the traditional understanding of a case or controversy.").
9. *See, e.g.*, Mitchell N. Berman, *Originalism Is Bunk*, 84 N.Y.U. L. REV. 1, 24–25 (2009) (noting that non-originalists agree that original meaning has a bearing on constitutional interpretation); Richard H. Fallon Jr., *The Political Function of Originalist Ambiguity*, 19 HARV. J.L. & PUB. POL'Y 487, 488 (1996) (acknowledging the importance of history and emphasizing that scholars differ as to the weight to ascribe to historical meanings). Consider, for example, the problem of whether Congress has power to incorporate a national bank, an issue that divided Alexander Hamilton and Thomas Jefferson and featured plausible constitutional arguments on both sides. President Andrew Jackson's view of constitutionality departed from the meaning that President James Madison viewed as having been established through practice. For a brief sketch of the issue and the interpretive puzzles to which it gave rise, *see* PAUL BREST, PROCESSES OF CONSTITUTIONAL DECISIONMAKING: CASES AND MATERIALS 8–58 (4th ed. 2000) (collecting and interrogating sources on the bank's constitutionality and reprinting Jackson's veto message). *See* Richard H. Fallon Jr., *"The Rule of Law" as a Concept in Constitutional Discourse*, 97 COLUM. L. REV. 1, 45 (1997) (noting that normative consensus may erode between enactment and application of law, and questions may arise in an altered "factual or normative" context). Many have contributed to the ongoing debate over the role of history in constitutional interpretation. For particularly insightful contributions, *see* CHARLES A. MILLER, THE SUPREME COURT AND THE USES OF HISTORY 27 (1969) (emphasizing the wisdom of history understood "not only as contemporaneous meaning but also as potential for growth");

Paul Brest, *The Misconceived Quest for the Original Understanding*, 60 B.U. L. REV. 204 (1980); Martin S. Flaherty, *The Most Dangerous Branch*, 105 YALE L.J. 1725 (1996).

10. *See* Thomas B. Colby & Peter J. Smith, *Living Originalism*, 59 DUKE L.J. 239, 239–40 (2009) (arguing that "originalism is not a single, coherent unified theory of constitutional interpretation"). *See* Richard H. Fallon Jr., *The Many and Varied Roles of History in Constitutional Adjudication*, 90 NOTRE DAME L. REV. 1753, 1788–89 (2015) (analyzing the relevance of such intervening events and observing that "more history" may be needed to assess "when precedent should trump original meanings"). *See id.* at 1758 (stating that "claims of constitutional validity and authority depend on current agreement manifest in the judgments of officials, judges, lawyers, and others concerning the contemporary legal significance of past events. This agreement begins with foundational matters."); *see also* Larry Kramer, *Fidelity to History—And Through It*, 65 FORDHAM L. REV. 1627, 1651–52 (1997) (treating the founding era as establishing a textual framework within which our institutions began to evolve and emphasizing the importance of fidelity to institutional history over time).
11. The Framers frequently embraced constructive imagery in their discussion of the constitutional project. Later generations picked up such themes. *See generally* MICHAEL KAMMEN, A MACHINE THAT WOULD GO OF ITSELF: THE CONSTITUTION IN AMERICAN CULTURE 125 (1987) (quoting an 1888 statement by James Russell Lowell saying to the effect that in drafting the Constitution, "we had invented a machine that would go of itself"); *cf.* JILL LEPORE, THESE TRUTHS: A HISTORY OF THE UNITED STATES (2018), *passim*, (invoking the Framers' metaphor of the machine). No single moment of history necessarily decides the meaning of the document; instead, it has layers of sedimentary meaning that build up over time. *See* Barry Friedman & Scott B. Smith, *The Sedimentary Constitution*, 147 U. PA. L. REV. 1, 6 (1998) (arguing in favor of an interpretive approach in which "the relevant history is not just that of the Founding, it is that of *all* American constitutional history"). That sedimentary conception of meaning explains the lasting appeal of Justice Oliver Wendell Holmes's observation in *Missouri v. Holland*, 252 U.S. 416, 433 (1920), inviting us to consult our entire history as a nation in deciding how to read the Constitution. *See also* Ernest A. Young, *Our Prescriptive Judicial Power: Constitutive and Entrenchment Effects of Historical Practice in Federal Courts Law*, 58 WM. & MARY L. REV. 535, 540 (2016) (arguing that history properly attends to the practices that help to constitute the powers of government that have been incompletely specified in the Constitution's text and linking this conception of history to Burkean values of customary practice and prescriptive wisdom). On Fallon's use of constructivist constitutionalism to describe his conception of the interpretive process, *see* Richard H. Fallon Jr., *Arguing in Good Faith about the Constitution: Ideology, Methodology, and Reflective Equilibrium*, 84 U. CHI. L. REV. 123 (2017); Fallon, *Legitimacy and the Constitution*, 118 HARV. L. REV. 1787 (2005); Fallon, *A Constructivist Coherence Theory of Constitutional Interpretation*, 100 HARV. L. REV. 1189 (1987).
12. *See generally* HERBERT J. STORING, WHAT THE ANTI-FEDERALISTS WERE FOR: THE POLITICAL THOUGHT OF THE OPPONENTS OF THE CONSTITUTION (1981) (providing a comprehensive look at the role the Anti-Federalists played in shaping the country's

principles). *Cf.* Thomas C. Grey, *Origins of the Unwritten Constitution: Fundamental Law in American Revolutionary Thought*, 30 STAN. L. REV. 843 (1978) (examining the origins and legitimacy of unwritten constitutionalism during the founding period).

13. Justice Scalia long described himself as a faint-hearted originalist, as an originalist but not a nut. Justice Thomas, by contrast, would appear a good deal less faint hearted. Thomas, for example, has argued for a narrow interpretation of the Commerce Clause to exclude federal authority to regulate "manufacturing and agriculture." United States v. Lopez, 514 U.S. 549, 586 (1995) (Thomas, J., concurring). If realized in practice, such a position might invalidate—as a starting place—much of Title 21 of the United States Code, including regulations of meat inspection (21 U.S.C. §§601–26 (2018)) and narcotic drugs (*id.* §§ 171–200b, among others). *See also* Dep't of Transp. v. Ass'n of Am. R.R.s., 575 U.S. 43, 76–82 (2015) (Thomas, J., concurring) (urging the reconsideration of Congress's ability to create administrative agencies). The quote, "let justice be done," was famously used by Lord Mansfield in declaring slavery to be inconsistent with the principles of the common law. Somerset v. Stewart (1772) 98 Eng. Rep. 499, 509 (K.B.) ("If the parties will have judgment, fiat Justitia, ruat coelum, let justice be done whatever be the consequence."). It was a commonplace of abolitionist rhetoric. *See, e.g.*, CLAUDINE L. FERRELL, GREENWOOD GUIDES TO HISTORICAL EVENTS, 1500–1900: THE ABOLITIONIST MOVEMENT 42 (2005) (noting that this phrase was the masthead of the abolitionist paper *Genius of Universal Emancipation*).
14. For an account of epistemic humility, *see* Ian James Kidd, *Confidence, Humility, and Hubris in Victorian Scientific Naturalism*, *in* EPISTEMIC VIRTUES IN THE SCIENCES AND THE HUMANITIES 11 (Jeroen van Dongen & Herman Paul eds., 2017). Other legal scholars have brought the principle of humility to bear in contrast to more hubristic models of epistemic certainty. *See, e.g.*, Michael W. McConnell, *The Importance of Humility in Judicial Review: A Comment on Ronald Dworkin's "Moral Reading" of the Constitution*, 65 FORDHAM L. REV. 1269 (1997); Suja A. Thomas, *Judicial Modesty and the Jury*, 76 U. COLO. L. REV. 767 (2005) (discussing judicial "modesty" in reviewing jury findings).
15. *See* McDonald v. City of Chicago, 561 U.S. 742, 758–59 (2010) (Alito, J.) (reaffirming use of the Due Process Clause as the vehicle for incorporation of enumerated rights against the states); *cf. id.* at 805 (Thomas, J., concurring) (urging use of the privileges and immunities clause as the vehicle for incorporation). The radical potential of the privileges and immunities clause would be moderated by a clear indication that it incorporates only enumerated rights. *See* KURT T. LASH, THE FOURTEENTH AMENDMENT AND THE PRIVILEGES AND IMMUNITIES OF AMERICAN CITIZENSHIP (2014) (reading the incorporating force of the clause as limited to rights enumerated elsewhere in the Constitution).

PART IV
CONCLUSION

So far, in the cases surveyed in this book, the Court has mostly deferred to Congress and to long-standing tradition, even in circumstances where tradition conflicts with some modern conceptions of the judicial power. Indeed, in many of the most interesting decisions upholding non-contentious jurisdiction, the challenge to the federal judicial role was based on the perceived demands of modern case-or-controversy rules. The pattern was set in *Tutun*, where Justice Brandeis rejected the government's argument that uncontested naturalization petitions did not qualify as cases within the appellate jurisdiction of the federal circuit courts. Brandeis had embraced and powerfully restated the Court's adverse-party rhetoric in the early twentieth century as a way to prevent feigned and collusive suits brought to challenge social legislation under *Lochner*. Apparently recognizing that the fact-intensive practice of naturalization did not present the same concerns he and the Court would come to associate with collusive suits to procure judicial review of the constitutionality of state and federal laws, Justice Brandeis invoked tradition in upholding federal judicial power to hear non-adverse naturalization claims.

Notably, however, Brandeis did not rest on traditional practice alone. Rather, he relied on the nineteenth-century conception of cases as claims of right, touching federal subjects, in the form prescribed by law. He thus brought the practice of naturalization squarely within the framework of Article III adjudication by offering a synthesis of text, pedigree, and theory. Drawing conclusions that anticipate the lessons of this book, Brandeis followed the nineteenth century's leading jurists in concluding that not all cases within the meaning of the Constitution must seek to redress injuries inflicted by opposing parties. Brandeis thus strongly reaffirmed the principle that Congress has the authority, as it may deem appropriate from time to time, to assign matters to the federal courts for uncontested adjudication.

Nearly one hundred years after Brandeis wrote, nineteenth-century practice has further receded from view, but the lessons of his *Tutun* decision remain vitally alive. While controversies require contestation, cases within the meaning of Article III arise under federal law whenever a party sets up a claim of right in the form prescribed by law. Such claims of right surely include contested claims against party opponents. But they also include ex parte claims of right to secure a benefit or status as provided in federal law. The resulting judgments create or constitute a new legal status or invest a party with new legal rights. The Supreme Court could contribute much to the coherence of our law of justiciability by recognizing that, in this important sense, Article III allows the federal courts to hear cases without controversies.

Table of Authorities

Aloe, Paul H., *Civil Practice*, 60 Syr. L. Rev. 717 (2010)—**§ 2.5.1.**

Alschuler, Albert W., *Plea Bargaining and Its History*, 13 Law & Soc'y Rev. 11 (1979)—**§ 2.5.3.**

Amar, Akhil Reed, *Fourth Amendment First Principles*, 107 Harv. L. Rev. 757 (1994)—**§ 2.2.**

Amar, Akhil Reed, *The Two-Tiered Structure of the Judiciary Act of 1789*, 138 U. Pa. L. Rev. 1499 (1990)—**§ 9.3.**

Andrews, Charles, The Colonial Period of American History (1938)—**§§ 2.3.1, 2.4.**

Arlyck, Kevin, *Forged by War: The Federal Courts and Foreign Affairs in the Age of Revolution* (Sept. 2014) (unpublished Ph.D. dissertation, New York University) (on file with author)—**§§ 2.3.1, 8.2, 9.1.**

Atwood, Barbara Ann, *Domestic Relations Cases in Federal Court: Toward a Principled Exercise of Jurisdiction*, 35 Hastings L.J. 571 (1984)—**§ 11.5.1.**

Avery, Ralph, *Article III and Title 11: A Constitutional Collision*, 12 Bankr. Dev. J. 397 (1996)—**Introduction; §§ 7.3, 9, 9.3, 11.1.1.**

Bacharach, Robert & Entzeroth, Lyn, *Judicial Advocacy in Pro Se Litigation: A Return to Neutrality*, 42 Ind. L.J. 19 (2009)—**§ 11.4.**

Baker, Steven N. & Fesak, Matthew Lee, *Who Cares About the Counterfeiters? How the Fight Against Counterfeiting Became an In Rem Process*, 83 St. John's L. Rev. 735 (2009)—**§ 7.7.**

Barron, David & Lederman, Martin S., *The Commander-in-Chief at Lowest Ebb—A Constitutional History*, 121 Harv. L. Rev. 941 (2008)—**§ 7.5.**

Bayard, Samuel, An Abstract of those Laws of the United States Which Relate Chiefly to the Duties and Authority of the Judges of the Inferior State Courts and Justices of the Peace Throughout the Union (1804)—**Introduction.**

Bederman, David J., The Classical Foundations of the American Constitution (2008)—**§ 1.3.**

Bee, Thomas, Reports of Cases Adjudged in the District Court of South Carolina—**§ 2.3.1.**

Bellia, Anthony J., Jr., *Article III and the Cause of Action*, 89 Iowa L. Rev. 777 (2004)—**§ 3.2.**

Berger, Adolf, *Encyclopedic Dictionary of Roman Law*, *in* 43 Transactions of the Am. Phil. Soc'y 333 (1953)—**§ 1.1.**

Berger, Bethany R., *"Power over This Unfortunate Race": Race, Politics and Indian Law in* United States v. Rogers, 45 Wm. & Mary L. Rev. 1957 (2004)—**§§ 7.6, 11.1.4.**

Berger, Raoul, *Intervention by Public Agencies in Private Litigation in the Federal Courts*, 50 Yale L.J. 65 (1940)—**§ 8.2.**

Berger, Raoul, *Standing to Sue in Public Actions: Is It a Constitutional Requirement?*, 78 Yale L.J. 816 (1969)—**§ 9.5.**

Berman, Mitchell N., *Originalism Is Bunk*, 84 N.Y.U. L. Rev. 1 (2009)—**§ 12.2.**

Billings, Warren M., *Pleading, Procedure, and Practice: The Meaning of Due Process of Law in Seventeenth-Century Virginia*, 47 J.S. Hist. 569 (1981)—**§ 1.3.**

Bishop, Joel Prentiss, New Commentaries on Marriage, Divorce, and Separation as to the Law, Evidence, Pleading, Practice, Forms and the Evidence of Marriage in All Issues on a New System of Legal Exposition (Chi., T.H. Flood & Co. 1891)—**§ 3.3.**

Blackstone, William, Commentaries on the Laws of England—**Introduction, §§ 3.2, 9.5.**

Bloch, Susan Low, *The Early Role of the Attorney General in Our Constitutional Scheme: In the Beginning There Was Pragmatism*, 1989 Duke L.J. 561 (1989)—**§§ 2.2, 4, 7.6, 12.1.**

Bogert, George T, Trusts (6th ed. 1987)—**§ 7.4.**

Bonfield, Lloyd, Devising, Dying and Dispute: Probate Litigation in Early Modern England (2012)—**§ 3.1.**

Borchard, Edwin M., *The Constitutionality of Declaratory Judgments*, 31 Colum. L. Rev. 561 (1931)—**§ 6.3.**

Borchard, Edwin M., Convicting the Innocent: Errors of Criminal Justice (1932)—**§ 6.3.**

Borchard, Edwin M., Declaratory Judgments (2d ed. 1941)—**§ 1.2.**

Borchard, Edwin M., *Government Liability in Tort*, 34 Yale L.J. 129 (1924)—**§ 6.3.**

Borchard, Edwin M., *Justiciability*, 4 U. Chi. L. Rev. 1 (1936)—**§ 6.3.**

Borchard, Edwin M., *The Next Step beyond Equity: The Declaratory Action*, 13 U. Chi. L. Rev. 145 (1946)—**§ 6.3.**

Borchard, Edwin M., *Treaty-Making Power as Support for Federal Legislation*, 29 Yale L.J. 445 (1920)—**§ 6.3.**

Borchard, Edwin M., *Shall the Executive Agreement Replace the Treaty?*, 53 Yale L.J. 664 (1944)—**§ 6.3.**

Bourguignon, Henry J., The First Federal Court: The Federal Appellate Prize Court of the American Revolution, 1775–1787 (1977)—**§ 2.3.**

Bray, Samuel, *The Supreme Court and the New Equity*, 68 Vand. L. Rev. 997 (2015)—**§ 12.1.**

Brest, Paul, *The Misconceived Quest for the Original Understanding*, 60 B.U. L. Rev. 204 (1980)—**§ 12.2.**

Brest, Paul, Processes of Constitutional Decisionmaking: Cases and Materials (4th ed. 2000)—**§ 12.2.**

Briggs, Herbert W., *In Memoriam: Edwin M. Morchard, 1884–1951*, 45 Am. J. Int'l L. 708 (1951)—**§ 6.3.**

Briggs, William K., *Deconstructing "Just and Proper": Arguments in Favor of Adopting the "Remedial Purpose" Approach to Section 10(j) Labor Injunction*, 110 Mich. L. Rev. 127 (2011)—**§ 6.**

Brubaker, Ralph, *On the Nature of Federal Bankruptcy Jurisdiction: A General Statutory and Constitutional Theory*, 41 Wm. & Mary L. Rev. 743 (2000)—**§ 7.3.**

Burbank, Stephen B. & Farhang, Sean, Rights and Retrenchment: The Counterrevolution against Federal Litigation (2017)—**§ 10.3.**

Burdick, William L., The Principles of Roman Law and Their Relation to Modern Law (1938)—**§§ 1.1, 1.3.**

Cahn, Naomi R., *Family Law, Federalism, and the Federal Courts*, 79 Iowa L. Rev. 1073 (1994)—**§ 11.5.1.**

Capelletti, Mauro, *Fundamental Guarantees of the Parties in Civil Litigation*, 25 Stan. L. Rev. 651 (1973)—**§ 1.2.**

Cappelletti, Mauro et al., The Italian Legal System: An Introduction (1967)—**§§ 1.1, 1.2.**

Capelletti, Mauro, *Fundamental Guarantees of the Parties in Civil Litigation: Comparative Constitutional, International and Social Trends*, 25 Stan. L. Rev. 651 (1973)—**§ 1.2.**

Casto, William, *America's First Independent Counsel: The Planned Criminal Prosecution of Chief Justice John Jay*, 1 Green Bag 353 (1998)—**§ 2.2.**

Casto, William R., *The Origins of Federal Admiralty Jurisdiction in an Age of Privateers, Smugglers, and Pirates*, 37 Am. J. Legal Hist. 123 (1993)—**§ 2.3.1.**

Chayes, Abram, *The Role of the Judge in Public Law Litigation*, 89 Harv. L. Rev. 1281 (1976)—**§§ 10, 10.2.**

Chitty, Joseph, Jr., A Treatise on the Law of the Prerogatives of the Crown; and the Relative Duties and Rights of the Subject (London, Joseph Butterworth & Son 1820)—**§ 3.3.**

Clark, Charles E., *Edwin Borchard*, 60 Yale L.J. 1071 (1951)—**§ 6.3.**

CLARK, HOMER H., JR., THE LAW OF DOMESTIC RELATIONS IN THE UNITED STATES (2d ed. 1987)—**§ 3.3.**

CLYDE, LORD & EDWARDS, DENIS J., JUDICIAL REVIEW (2000)—**§ 10.2.**

Coffee, John C. & Schwartz, Donald E., *The Survival of the Derivative Suit: An Evaluation and a Proposal for Legislative Reform*, 81 COLUM. L. REV. 261 (1981)—**§ 8.2.**

Colby, Thomas B. & Smith, Peter J., *Living Originalism*, 59 DUKE L.J. 239 (2009)—**§ 12.2.**

Comment, *The Case-Concept and Some Recent Indirect Procedures for Attacking the Constitutionality of Federal Regulatory Statutes*, 45 YALE. L.J. 469 (1936)—**§ 7.6.**

Comment, *Immunization of Congressional Witnesses Under the Compulsory Testimony Act: Constitutionality of the Function of the District Courts*, 22 U. CHI. L. REV. 657 (1955)—**§ 7.8.1.**

Coquillette, Daniel R., *Justinian in Braintree: John Adams, Civilian Learning, and Legal Elitism, 1758–1775*, *in* 62 PUBL'NS OF THE COLONIAL SOC'Y OF MASS., LAW IN COLONIAL MASSACHUSETTS 1630–1800 (Daniel R. Coquillette et al. eds., 1984)—**§ 1.3.**

COTT, NANCY F., PUBLIC VOWS: A HISTORY OF MARRIAGE AND THE NATION (2000)—**§ 3.3.**

Crane, Charlotte, *Before* Marbury: Hylton v. United States *and the Origins of Judicial Review*, J. SUP. CT. HIST. 1 (2003)—**§ 7.6.**

CUDDIHY, WILLIAM J., THE FOURTH AMENDMENT: ORIGINS AND ORIGINAL MEANING 1602–1791 (2009)—**§ 2.2.**

Curtis, Benjamin R., *The Colonial County Court, Social Forum and Legislative Precedent: Accomack County, Virginia, 1633–1639*, 85 VA. MAG. HIST. & BIOGRAPHY 274 (1977)—**§ 1.3.**

CURTIS, BENJAMIN R., JURISDICTION, PRACTICE, AND PECULIAR JURISPRUDENCE OF THE COURTS OF THE UNITED STATES (2d ed. 1896)—**§ 5.1.**

DALRYMPLE, JAMES, THE INSTITUTIONS OF THE LAW OF SCOTLAND (3d ed. 1759)—**§ 10.2.**

Daskal, Jennifer, *The Geography of the Battlefield: A Framework for Detention and Targeting Outside the "Hot" Conflict Zone*, 161 U. PA. L. REV. 1165 (2013)—**§ 7.5.**

Davies, Thomas Y., *Recovering the Original Fourth Amendment*, 98 MICH. L. REV. 547 (1999)—**§ 2.2.**

Davis, Kevin E. & Hershkoff, Helen, *Contracting for Procedure*, 53 WM. & MARY L. REV. 507 (2011)—**§ 7.6.**

Day, Alan F., *Lawyers in Colonial Maryland, 1660–1715*, 17 AM. J. LEGAL HIST. 145 (1973)—**§ 1.3.**

De Bujan, Antonio Fernandez, Jurisdiccion Voluntaria en Derecho Romano [Voluntary Jurisdiction in Roman Law] (1986)—**§ 1.1.**

Deans, Mungo, Scots Public Law (1995)—**§ 10.2.**

DeSipio, Louis & Pachon, Harry P., *Making Americans: Administrative Discretion and Americanization*, 12 Chicano-Latino L. Rev. 52 (1992)—**§ 2.1.**

Digest of Justinian (Alan Watson et al. eds., 1985)—**§ 10.1.**

diGiacomantonio, William C., *Petitioners and Their Grievances: A View from the First Federal Congress, in* The House and Senate in the 1790s (Kenneth R. Bowling & Donald R. Kennon eds., 2002)—**§ 2.4.**

Dixon, Robert G., Jr., *The Doctrine of Separation of Powers and Federal Immunity Statutes*, 23 Geo. Wash. L. Rev. 501 (1955)—**§ 7.8.1.**

The Documentary History of the Supreme Court (Maeva Marcus ed., 2007)—**§§ 2.1, 2.2, 7.1, 9.2.**

Donahue, Charles, Jr., *Ius Commune, Canon Law, and Common Law in England*, 66 Tul. L. Rev. 1745 (1992)—**§ 1.3.**

Donaldson, Michael J., *Justice in Full Is Time Well Spent: Why the Supreme Court Should Ban Sua Sponte Dismissals*, 36 Quinnipac L. Rev. 25 (2017)—**§ 11.4.**

Dunlap, Andrew, A Treatise on the Practice of the Courts of Admiralty in Civil Causes of Maritime Jurisdiction; with an Appendix Containing Rules in the Admiralty Courts of the United States, and a Full Collection of Practical Forms (2d ed. 1850)—**§ 2.3.1.**

Elliot, Heather, *The Functions of Standing*, 61 Stan. L. Rev. 459 (2008)—**§ 8.2.**

Encyclopedia of the War of 1812: A Political, Social and Military History (Spencer C. Tucker ed., 2012)—**§ 2.3.1.**

Engdahl, David, *Intrinsic Limits of Congress' Power Regarding the Judicial Branch*, 1999 B.Y.U. L. Rev. 75 (1999)—**§ 8.4.**

Engler, Russell, *And Justice for All—Including the Unrepresented Poor: Revisiting the Roles of the Judges, Mediators, and Clerks*, 67 Fordham L. Rev. 1987 (1999)—**§ 11.4.**

The English Law Courts VI: The Ecclesiastical Courts, 8 Green Bag 330 (1896)—**§ 1.3.**

Epstein, David G., Bankruptcy (1993)—**§ 7.3.**

Epstein, David G. & Nickles, Steven H., Principles of Bankruptcy Law (2007)—**§ 7.4.**

Erichson, Howard M., *Mass Tort Litigation and Inquisitorial Justice*, 87 Geo. L.J. 1983 (1999)—**Introduction.**

Erskine, John, An Institute of the Law of Scotland (James Badenach Nicolson ed., Edinburgh, Bell & Bradfute 1871) (1773)—**§ 1.2.**

Fairfax, Roger A., Jr., *The Jurisdictional Heritage of the Grand Jury Clause*, 91 Minn. L. Rev. 398 (2006)—**§ 5.1.**

Fallon, Richard H., Jr., *Arguing in Good Faith about the Constitution: Ideology, Methodology, and Reflective Equilibrium*, 84 U. Chi. L. Rev. 123 (2017)—**§ 12.2.**

Fallon, Richard H., Jr., *A Constructivist Coherence Theory of Constitutional Interpretation*, 100 Harv. L. Rev. 1189 (1987)—**§ 12.2.**

Fallon, Richard, Jr., *The Fragmentation of Standing*, 93 Tex. L. Rev. 1061 (2015)—**§ 10.1.**

Fallon, Richard H., Jr., *Legitimacy and the Constitution*, 118 Harv. L. Rev. 1787 (2005)—**§ 12.2.**

Fallon, Richard, Jr., *The Many and Varied Roles of History in Constitutional Adjudication*, 90 Notre Dame L. Rev. 1753 (2015)—**§ 12.2.**

Fallon, Richard, Jr., *The Political Function of Originalist Ambiguity*, 19 Harv. J.L. & Pub. Pol'y 487 (1996)—**§ 12.2.**

Fallon, Richard, Jr., *"The Rule of Law" as a Concept in Constitutional Discourse*, 97 Colum. L. Rev. 1 (1997)—**§ 12.2.**

Fallon, Richard, Jr. et al., Hart & Wechsler's Federal Courts and the Federal System (7th ed. 2015)—**Introduction; §§ 5.2, 7.1, 9.3, 11.1, 12.**

Farrand, Max, The Records of the Federal Convention of 1787 (1911)—**§§ 1.3, 3.2.**

Ferrell, Claudine L., Greenwood Guides to Historical Events, 1500–1900 The Abolitionist Movement (2005)—**§ 12.3.**

Fisher, George, *Plea Bargaining's Triumph*, 109 Yale L.J. 857 (2000)—**§ 2.5.3.**

Flaherty, Martin S., *The Most Dangerous Branch*, 105 Yale L.J. 1725 (1996)—**§ 12.2.**

Fletcher, William A., *The "Case or Controversy" Requirement in State Court Adjudication of Federal Questions*, 78 Cal. L. Rev. 263 (1990)—**§ 8.4.**

Force, Robert, Admiralty and Maritime Law (2d ed. 2013)—**§§ 2.3.1, 2.3.2.**

Frankel, Richard H. & Newbern, Alistair E. Newbern, *Prisoners and Pleading*, 94 Wash. U. L. Rev. 899 (2017)—**§ 11.4.**

Frankel, Robert P., Jr., *Before* Marbury: Hylton v. United States *and the Origins of Judicial Review*, J. Sup. Ct. Hist. 1 (2003)—**§ 7.6.**

Frankfurter, Felix & Greene, Nathan, The Labor Injunction (1930)—**§ 6.**

Franklin, Frank G., The Legislative History of Naturalization in the United States from the Revolution War to 1861 (1906)—**§ 2.1.**

Friedman, Barry & Smith, Scott B., *The Sedimentary Constitution*, 147 U. Pa. L. Rev. 1 (1998)—**§ 12.2.**

Frost, Amanda, *The Limits of Advocacy*, 59 Duke L.J. 447 (2009)—**Introduction.**

Fuller, Lon L., *The Forms and Limits of Adjudication*, 92 Harv. L. Rev. 353 (1978)—**Introduction.**

Funk, Kellen, *The Union of Law and Equity: The United States, 1800–1938*, *in* LAW AND EQUITY: FUSION AND FISSION (John C.P. Goldberg et al. eds., 2019)—**§ 5.1.**

GAREIS, KARL, INTRODUCTION TO THE SCIENCE OF LAW: SYSTEMATIC SURVEY OF THE LAW AND PRINCIPLES OF LEGAL STUDY (Albert Kocourek trans., 1911)—**§ 1.2.**

Golman, Eric, Ex Parte *Seizures and the Defend Trade Secrets Act*, 72 WASH. & LEE L. REV ONLINE 284 (2015)—**§ 7.7.**

Sanger, David E., & Perlroth, Nicole, *Microsoft Takes Down a Risk to the Election, and Finds U.S. Doing the Same*, N.Y. TIMES (Oct. 12, 2020)—**§ 7.7.**

GREEN'S ENCYCLOPAEDIA OF THE LAW OF SCOTLAND (John Chisholm ed., 1912)—**§ 10.2.**

Grey, Thomas C., *Origins of the Unwritten Constitution: Fundamental Law in American Revolutionary Thought*, 30 STAN. L. REV. 843 (1978)—**§ 12.2.**

Grobman, Daniel, Note, *Preemptive* Ex Parte *Seizure Orders and Substantive Relief: A Far Cry From Congressional Intent*, 33 CARDOZO L. REV. 1185 (2012)—**§ 7.7.**

GROSSBERG, MICHAEL, GOVERNING THE HEARTH: LAW AND THE FAMILY IN NINETEENTH-CENTURY AMERICA (1985)—**§ 3.3.**

Grove, Tara Leigh, *The Exceptions Clause as a Structural Safeguard*, 113 COLUM. L. REV. 929 (2013)—**§ 11.1.3.**

HAMLIN, PAUL M., LEGAL EDUCATION IN COLONIAL NEW YORK (1939)—**§ 1.3.**

Harrington, Matthew P., *The Legacy of the Colonial Vice-Admiralty Courts*, 27 J. MAR. L. & COM. (1996)—**§ 2.3.1.**

Harrison, John, *The Power of Congress to Limit the Jurisdiction of Federal Courts and the Text of Article III*, 64 U. CHI. L. REV. 203 (1997)—**§ 8.4.**

HART, HENRY M. & WECHSLER, HERBERT, THE FEDERAL COURTS AND THE FEDERAL SYSTEM (1st ed. 1953)—**§ 6.2.**

Hartnett, Edward A., *Questioning Certiorari: Some Reflections Seventy-Five Years After the Judges' Bill*, 100 COLUM. L. REV. 1643 (2000)—**§ 8.2.**

HARTOG, HENDRIK, MAN AND WIFE IN AMERICA: A HISTORY (2000)—**§ 3.3.**

Hartog, Hendrik, *The Public Law of a County Court: Judicial Government in Eighteenth Century Massachusetts*, 20 AM. J. LEGAL HIST. 282 (1976)—**§ 1.3.**

HASDAY, JILL ELAINE, FAMILY LAW REIMAGINED (2014)—**§ 3.3.**

Haskins, George B., *The Beginnings of the Recording System in Massachusetts*, 21 B.U. L. REV. 281 (1941)—**§ 1.3.**

Hazard, Geoffrey C., Jr., *Forms of Action Under the Federal Rules of Civil Procedure*, 63 NOTRE DAME L. REV. 628 (1988)—**§ 10.1.**

Heins, Matthew, *An Appeal to Common Sense: Why "Unappealable" District Court Decisions Should Be Subject to Appellate Review*, 109 NW. U. L. REV. 773 (2015)—**§ 7.8.2.**

HELMHOLZ, R.H., CANON LAW AND THE LAW OF ENGLAND (1987)—**§ 3.3.**

HELMHOLZ, R.H., THE OXFORD HISTORY OF THE LAWS OF ENGLAND: THE CANON LAW AND ECCLESIASTICAL JURISDICTION FROM 597 TO THE 1640S (2004)—**Introduction; § 3.2.**

Hessick, F. Andrew, *Standing, Injury in Fact, and Private Rights*, 93 CORNELL L. REV. 275 (2008)—**§ 10.1.**

HIGH, JAMES L., A TREATISE OF THE LAW OF RECEIVERS (Chicago, Callaghan & Co. 3d ed. 1894)—**§ 7.4.**

HIGHMORE, A., A TREATISE ON THE LAW OF IDIOCY AND LUNACY (Exeter, N.H., G. Lamson 1822)—**§ 1.3.**

HOEFLICH, M.H., ROMAN AND CIVIL LAW AND THE DEVELOPMENT OF ANGLO-AMERICAN-JURISPRUDENCE IN THE NINETEENTH CENTURY (1997)—**§ 1.3.**

HOLDSWORTH, WILLIAM S., HISTORY OF ENGLISH LAW (1926)—**Introduction; §§ 1.3, 3.2, 3.3.**

HOME, HENRY, LORD KAMES, ELUCIDATIONS RESPECTING THE COMMON AND STATUTE LAW OF SCOTLAND (1777)—**§ 10.2.**

HOME, HENRY, LORD KAMES, HISTORICAL LAW-TRACTS (2d ed., Lawbook Exch. Ltd. 2000) (1758)—**§ 10.2.**

House, Lolabel, *The County Court in the Thirteenth Century*, 49 AM. L. REGISTER 284 (1901)—**§ 1.3.**

JOHNSON, ALVIN W. & YOST, FRANK H., SEPARATION OF CHURCH AND STATE IN THE UNITED STATES (2d ed. 1948)—**§ 3.2.**

KAMMEN, MICHAEL, A MACHINE THAT WOULD GO OF ITSELF: THE CONSTITUTION IN AMERICAN CULTURE (1987)—**§ 12.2.**

KETTNER, JAMES H., THE DEVELOPMENT OF AMERICAN CITIZENSHIP, 1607–1870 (1978)—**§ 2.1.**

Kidd, Ian James, *Confidence, Humility, and Hubris in Victorian Scientific Naturalism*, *in* EPISTEMIC VIRTUES IN THE SCIENCES AND THE HUMANITIES (Jeroen van Dongen & Herman Paul eds., 2017)—**§ 12.3.**

Koniak, Susan, *Feasting While the Widow Weeps:* Georgine v. AmChem Products, Inc., 80 CORNELL L. REV. 1045 (1995)—**§ 7.6.**

Kramer, Larry, *Fidelity to History—And Through It*, 65 FORDHAM L. REV. 1627 (1997)—**§ 12.2.**

Kris, David S., *On the Bulk Collection of Tangible Things*, 7 J. NAT'L SEC. L. & POL'Y 209 (2014)—**§ 11.2.**

LANDSMAN, STEPHAN, READINGS ON ADVERSARIAL JUSTICE: THE AMERICAN APPROACH TO ADJUDICATION (1988)—**Introduction.**

Langbein, John H., *The German Advantage in Civil Procedure*, 52 U. Chi. L. Rev. 823 (1985)—**Introduction; § 2.3.1.**

Langbein, John H., *Fact Finding in the English Court of Chancery: A Rebuttal*, 83 Yale L.J. 1620 (1974)—**§ 11.5.2.**

Langdell, C.C., A Summary of Equity Pleading (2d ed. 1883)—**§ 10.1.**

Lash, Kurt T., The Fourteenth Amendment and the Privileges and Immunities of American Citizenship (2014)—**§ 12.3.**

Lasson, Nelson B., The History and Development of the Fourth Amendment to the United States Constitution (1937)—**§ 2.2.**

The Law Practice of Alexander Hamilton: Documents and Commentary (Julius Goebel Jr. & Joseph H. Smith eds., 1980)—**§ 1.3.**

Lawson, F.H., Remedies of English Law (2d ed. 1980)—**§§ 1.2, 3.3.**

Layton, C.M., *Canadian Refugee Lands in Ohio*, 24 Can. Hist. Rev. 377 (1943)—**§ 5.1.**

Lee, Evan Tsen, Judicial Restraint in America: How the Ageless Wisdom of the Federal Courts Was Invented (2011)—**§ 5.2.**

Lee, Evan Tsen & Ellis, Josephine Mason, *The Standing Doctrine's Dirty Little Secret*, 107 Nw. U. L. Rev. 169 (2012)—**§ 10.1.**

Leiter, Brian, *Positivism, Formalism, Realism*, 99 Colum. L. Rev. 1138 (1999)—**§ 10.3.**

Lepore, Jill, These Truths: A History of the United States (2018)—**§ 12.2.**

Lettow, Renee B., Note, *Reviving Federal Grand Jury Presentments*, 103 Yale L.J. 1333 (1994)—**§ 5.1.**

Levack, Brian P., The Civil Lawyers in England 1603–1641: A Political Study (1973)—**§ 1.3.**

Levy, Sheldon S., *Probate in the Common Form in the United States: The Problem of Notice in Probate Proceedings*, 1952 Wis. L. Rev. 420 (1952)—**§§ 1.2, 11.1.4.**

Lipka, Lawrence J., Note, *Abandoned Property at Sea: Who Owns the Salvage "Finds"?*, 12 Wm. & Mary L. Rev. 97 (1970)—**§ 2.3.2.**

Liverant, Spencer R. & Hitchler, Walter H., *A History of Equity in Pennsylvania*, 37 Dick. L. Rev. 156 (1933)—**§ 1.3.**

Lynch, Gerald E., *Our Administrative System of Criminal Justice*, 66 Fordham L. Rev. 2117 (1998)—**§ 2.5.3.**

Lynch, Gerald E., *Screening Versus Plea Bargaining: Exactly What Are We Trading Off?*, 55 Stan. L. Rev. 1399 (2003)—**Introduction, § 2.5.3.**

Macfarlane, Katherine A., *Procedural Animus*, 71 Ala. L. Rev. 1185 (2020)—**§ 11.4.**

MacKenzie, George, The Institutions of the Law of Scotland (1694)—**§ 10.2.**

Manning, John F., *Foreword: The Means of Constitutional Power*, 128 Harv. L. Rev. 1, 73 (2014)—**§ 10.3.**

Manning, Molly Guptill, *Trouble Counting to Three: Circuit Splits and Confusion in Interpreting the Prison Reform Act's "Three Strikes Rule," 28 U.S.C. § 1915(G)*, 28 CORNELL J.L. & PUB. POL'Y 207 (2018)—**§ 11.4.**

Marcus, Maeva & Teir, Robert, Hayburn's Case: *A Misinterpretation of Precedent*, 1988 WIS. L. REV. 527 (1988)—**§ 9.2.**

Marsden, R.G., *Early Prize Jurisdiction and Prize Law in England*, 26 ENG. HIST. REV. 34 (1911)—**§ 1.3.**

MCCARTHY, CONOR, MARRIAGE IN MEDIEVAL ENGLAND: LAW, LITERATURE AND PRACTICE (2004)—**§ 3.3.**

McConnell, Michael W., *Establishment and Disestablishment at the Founding, Part I: Establishment of Religion*, 44 WM. & MARY L. REV. 2105 (2003)—**§ 3.2.**

McConnell, Michael W., *The Importance of Humility in Judicial Review: A Comment on Ronald Dworkin's "Moral Reading" of the Constitution*, 65 FORDHAM L. REV. 1269 (1997)—**§ 12.3.**

MCDONALD, FORREST, NOVO ORDUS SECLORUM: THE INTELLECTUAL ORIGINS OF THE AMERICAN CONSTITUTION (1985)—**§ 1.3.**

MCDOUALL, ANDREW, LORD BANKTON, AN INSTITUTE OF THE LAWS OF SCOTLAND IN CIVIL RIGHTS (R. Fleming 1751)—**§ 10.2.**

Merrill, Thomas W., *Article III, Agency Adjudication, and the Origins of the Appellate Review Model of Administrative Law*, 111 COLUM. L. REV. 939 (2011)—**§ 5.2.**

Mikos, Robert, *Can the States Keep Secrets from the Federal Government?*, 161 U. PA. L. REV. 103 (2012)—**§ 5.1.**

MILLER, CHARLES A., THE SUPREME COURT AND THE USES OF HISTORY (1969)—**§ 12.2.**

Mitchell, J.D.B., *The Royal Prerogative in Modern Scots Law*, *in* PUBLIC LAW 304 (J.A.G. Griffith ed., 1957)—**§ 10.2.**

Monaghan, Henry P., *Antisuit Injunctions and Preclusion Against Absent Nonresident Class Members*, 98 COLUM. L. REV. 1148 (1998)—**§ 7.6.**

Monaghan, Henry Paul, *On Avoiding Avoidance, Agenda Control, and Related Matters*, 112 COLUM. L. REV. 665 (2012)—**§ 8.2.**

Morawetz, Nancy, *Citizenship and the Courts*, 2007 U. CHI. LEGAL F. 447 (2007)—**§ 2.1.**

MORISON, WILLIAM MAXWELL, THE DECISIONS OF THE COURT SESSION FROM ITS INSTITUTION UNTIL THE SEPARATION OF COURT INTO TWO DIVISIONS IN THE YEAR 1808, DIGESTED UNDER PROPER HEADS, IN THE FORM OF A DICTIONARY (1811)—**§ 10.3.**

Morley, Michael T., *Consent of the Governed or Consent of the Government? The Problems with Consent Decrees in Government-Defendant Cases*, 16 U. PA. J. CONST. L. 637 (2014)—**Introduction; §§ 7.6, 9, 9.3, 12.1.**

Morley, Michael T., *Non-Contentious Jurisdiction and Consent Decrees*, 19 U. Pa. J. Const. L. Online 1 (2016)—**Introduction.**

Morrison, Alan & Wolfman, Brian, *What the* Shutts *Opt-Out Right Is and What It Ought to Be*, 74 U.M.K.C. L. Rev. 729 (2006)—**§ 7.6.**

Mulligan, Lumen & Staszewski, Glen, *The Supreme Court's Regulation of Civil Procedure: Lessons from Administrative Law*, 59 UCLA L. Rev. 1188 (2012)—**§ 10.3.**

Murray, Peter L. & Stürner, Rolf, German Civil Justice (2004)—**§ 1.2.**

Neitzel, Walter, *Non-Contentious Jurisdiction in Germany*, 21 Harv. L. Rev. 476 (1908)—**§§ 1.1, 1.2.**

Nelson, Caleb, *"Standing" and Remedial Rights in Administrative Law*, 105 Va. L. Rev. 703 (2019)—**§ 8.1.**

Newman, Jon O., *Pro Se Prisoner Litigation: Looking for Needles in Haystacks*, 62 Brook. L. Rev. 519 (1996)—**§ 11.5.2.**

Newmyer, R. Kent, Supreme Court Justice Joseph Story: Statesman of the Old Republic (1985)—**§ 8.2.**

Note, *Confessions of Judgment*, 102 U. Pa. L. Rev. 524 (1954)—**§ 7.6.**

Note, *Executors' and Trustees' Bills for Instructions*, 44 Yale L.J. 1433 (1935)—**§ 7.4.**

Note, *Shifting the FISA Paradigm: Protecting Civil Liberties by Eliminating Ex Ante Judicial Approval*, 121 Harv. L. Rev. 2200 (2008)—**Introduction.**

Note, *A Survey of the Qualifications of Magistrates Authorized to Issue Warrants*, 9 Val. U. L. Rev. 443 (1975)—**§ 7.5.**

Oldham, James, The Seventh Amendment: Trial by Jury and Anglo-American Special Juries (2006)—**§ 2.5.1.**

Parry, John T., *The Lost History of International Extradition Litigation*, 43 Va. J. Int'l L. 93 (2002)—**§ 11.1.2.**

Pfander, James E., *The Contested History of Article III's Case-or-Controversy Requirement*, 65 UCLA L. Rev. 170 (2018)—**Foreword.**

Pfander, James E., *Judicial Compensation and the Definition of Judicial Power in the Early Republic*, 107 Mich. L. Rev. 1 (2008)—**§ 2.4.**

Pfander, James E., *Judicial Purpose and the Scholarly Process: The* Lincoln Mills *Case*, 69 Wash. U. L.Q. 243 (1991)—**§ 11.1.1.**

Pfander, James E., *Jurisdiction-Stripping and the Supreme Court's Power to Supervise Inferior Tribunals*, 78 Tex. L. Rev. 1433 (2000)—**§ 7.2.**

Pfander, James E., *Rethinking the Supreme Court's Original Jurisdiction in State-Party Cases*, 82 Cal. L. Rev. 555 (1994)—**§§ 8.4, 9.4.**

Pfander, James E., *Scalia's Legacy: Originalism and Change in the Law of Standing*, 6 Brit. J. Am. Legal Stud. 85 (2017)—**Foreword.**

Pfander, James E., *Standing to Sue: Lessons from Scotland's Actio Popularis*, 66 Duke L.J. 1493 (2017)—**§§ 10.1, 10.2.**

Pfander, James E. & Birk, Daniel D., *Adverse Interests and Article III: A Reply*, 111 Nw. U.L. Rev. 1067 (2017)—**Foreword.**

Pfander, James E. & Birk, Daniel D., *Article III and the Scottish Judiciary*, 124 Harv L. Rev. 1613 (2011)—**Introduction, §§ 1.3, 10.2.**

Pfander, James E. & Birk, Daniel D., *Article III Judicial Power, the Adverse-Party Requirement, and Non-Contentious Jurisdiction*, 124 Yale L.J. 1346 (2015)—**§§ 2.3.1, 4.2, 8.2, 9, 9.1, 9.2, 9.3, 9.4, 9.5, 10.3.**

Pfander, James E. & Hunt, Jonathan, *Public Wrongs and Private Bills: Indemnification and Government Accountability in the Early Republic*, 85 N.Y.U. L. Rev. 1862 (2010)—**§ 7.6.**

Pfander, James E. & Nazemi, Nassim, *The Anti-Injunction Act and the Problem of Federal-State Jurisdictional Overlap*, 92 Tex. L. Rev. 1 (2013)—**§§ 2.5.2, 4.2.**

Pfander, James E. & Wardon, Theresa R., *Reclaiming the Immigration Constitution of the Early Republic: Prospectivity, Uniformity, and Transparency*, 96 Va. L. Rev. 359 (2010)—**§ 2.1.**

Pfander, James E. with Damrau, Emily, *A Non-Contentious Account of Article III's Domestic Relations Exception*, 92 Notre Dame L. Rev. 117 (2016)—**§§ 3.2, 9.2, 9.4, 9.5.**

Pfander, James E. with Downey, Michael J.T., *In Search of the Probate Exception*, 67 Vand. L. Rev. 1533 (2014)—**§§ 8.3, 9.2, 9.4, 9.5.**

Plous, Harold J. & Baker, Gordon E., McCulloch v. Maryland: *Right Principle, Wrong Case*, 9 Stan. L. Rev. 710 (1957)—**§ 7.6.**

Purcell, Edward A., Brandeis and the Progressive Constitution: *Erie*, the Judicial Power, and the Politics of the Federal Courts in Twentieth-Century America (2000)—**§ 6.**

Pushaw, Robert J., Jr., *Article III's Case/Controversy Distinction and the Dual Functions of Federal Courts*, 69 Notre Dame L. Rev. 447 (1994)—**Introduction; §§ 8.4, 9.4.**

Pushaw, Robert J., Jr., *Congressional Power over Federal Court Jurisdiction: A Defense of the Neo-Federalist Interpretation of Article III*, 1997 B.Y.U. L. Rev. 847—**§ 8.4.**

Pushaw, Robert J., Jr., *Justiciability and Separation of Powers: A Neo-Federalist Approach*, 81 Cornell L. Rev. 393 (1996)—**§§ 7.1, 9.5.**

R.S., *The Scotch Action of Declarator*, 10 L. Mag. 173 (1849)—**§ 10.2.**

Redish, Martin H., *Class Actions, Litigant Autonomy, and the Foundations of Procedural Due Process*, 95 Cal. L. Rev. 1573 (2007)—**§ 7.6.**

Redish, Martin H. & Kastanek, Andrianna D., *Settlement Class Actions, the Case-or-Controversy Requirement, and the Nature of the Adjudicatory Process*, 73 U. Chi. L. Rev. 545 (2006)—**Introduction; §§ 7.6, 11.1.1.**

Register, Layton B., *Spanish Courts*, 27 YALE L.J. 769 (1918)—**§ 8.4.**

Reinert, Alexander A., *Screening Out Innovation: The Merits of Meritless Litigation*, 89 IND. L.J. 1191 (2014)—**§ 11.4.**

REPPY, ALISON & TOMPKINS, LESLIE, HISTORICAL AND STATUTORY BACKGROUND OF THE LAW OF WILLS: DESCENT AND DISTRIBUTION, PROBATE AND ADMINISTRATION (1928)—**§ 3.1.**

Resnik, Judith, *Managerial Judges*, 96 HARV. L. REV. 374 (1982)—**Introduction.**

Resnik, Judith, *"Naturally" Without Gender: Women, Jurisdiction, and the Federal Courts*, 66 N.Y.U. L. REV. 1682 (1991)—**§ 11.5.1.**

Resnik, Judith & Dilg, Lane, *Responding to a Democratic Deficit: Limiting the Powers and the Term of the Chief Justice of the United States*, 154 U. PA. L. REV. 1575 (2006)—**§ 7.5.**

RESTATEMENT (THIRD) OF TRUSTS—**§ 7.4.**

Robertson, Lindsay, *"A Mere Feigned Case": Rethinking the* Fletcher v. Peck *Conspiracy and Early Republican Legal Culture*, 2000 UTAH L. REV. 249 (2000)—**§§ 7.6, 11.1.4.**

Rogge, O. John, *The New Federal Immunity Act and the Judicial Function*, 45 CAL. L. REV. 109 (1957)—**§ 7.8.1.**

Ruger, Theodore, *The Judicial Appointment Power of the Chief Justice*, 7 U. PA. J. CONST. L. 341 (2004)—**§ 7.5.**

Sandler, Ross & Schoenbrod, David, *From Status to Contract and Back Again: Consent Decrees in Institutional Reform Litigation*, 27 REV. LITIG. 115 (2007)—**§ 7.6.**

Savage, Charlie, *Court Orders F.B.I. to Fix National Security Wiretaps after Damning Report*, N.Y. TIMES (Dec. 17, 2019)—**§ 7.5.**

Scalia, Antonin, *The Doctrine of Standing as an Essential Element of the Separation of Powers*, 17 SUFFOLK U.L. REV. 881 (1983)—**§ 6.2.**

SCALIA, ANTONIN & GARNER, BRYAN A., READING LAW: THE INTERPRETATION OF LEGAL TEXTS (2012)—**§ 8.4.**

SCHLEGEL, JOHN HENRY, AMERICAN LEGAL REALISM AND EMPIRICAL SOCIAL SCIENCE (1995)—**§ 10.3.**

Scrutton, Thomas Edward, *Roman Law Influence in Chancery, Church Courts, Admiralty, and Law Merchant*, *in* 1 SELECT ESSAYS IN ANGLO-AMERICAN LEGAL HISTORY 208 (1907)—**§ 1.3.**

Seipp, David J., *The Reception of Canon Law and Civil Law in the Common Law Courts Before 1600*, 13 OXFORD J. LEGAL STUD. 388 (1993)—**§ 1.3.**

Silvestri, Elisabetta, *Non-Contentious Jurisdiction in Italy*, *in* VOLUNTARY (NON-CONTENTIOUS) JURISDICTION AROUND THE WORLD 133 (V.V. Argounov ed., 2017)—**§§ 1.1, 1.2.**

Simes, Lewis M., *The Administration of a Decedent's Estate as a Proceeding In Rem*, 43 MICH. L. REV. 675 (1945)—**§ 2.3.**

Simes, Lewis M., *The Function of Will Contests*, 44 MICH. L. REV. 503 (1945)—**§ 1.3.**

SINGER, NORMAN J., SUTHERLAND'S STATUTES AND STATUTORY CONSTRUCTION (7th ed. 2010)—**§ 8.4.**

SMITH, JOHN W., THE LAW OF RECEIVERSHIPS (2d ed. 1900)—**§ 7.4.**

SNELL, STEVEN L., COURTS OF ADMIRALTY AND THE COMMON LAW: ORIGINS OF THE AMERICAN EXPERIMENT IN CONCURRENT JURISDICTION (2007)—**§ 2.3.1.**

Sosnov, Leonard N., *Separation of Powers Shell Game: The Federal Witness Immunity Act*, 73 TEMPLE L. REV. 171 (2000)—**§ 7.8.1.**

SPECIAL AND GENERAL REPORTS MADE TO HIS MAJESTY BY THE COMMISSIONERS APPOINTED TO INQUIRE INTO THE PRACTICE AND JURISDICTION OF THE ECCLESIASTICAL COURTS OF ENGLAND AND WALES (London et al. eds., 1832)—**§ 3.2.**

Stahr, Walter B., *Discovery Under 28 U.S.C. § 1782 for Foreign and International Proceedings*, 30 VA. J. INT'L L. 597 (1990)—**§ 2.5.4.**

Stein, Peter, *The Attraction of the Civil Law in Post-Revolutionary America*, 52 VA. L. REV. 403 (1966)—**§ 1.3.**

Stein, Peter G., *Roman Law, Common Law, and Civil Law*, 66 TUL. L. REV. 1591 (1992)—**§ 1.3.**

STONE, LAWRENCE, ROAD TO DIVORCE: ENGLAND 1530–1987 (1990)—**§ 3.3.**

Stein, Michael Ashley, *The Domestic Relations Exception to Federal Jurisdiction: Rethinking an Unsettled Federal Courts Doctrine*, 36 B.C. L. REV. 669 (1995)—**§ 11.5.1.**

STORING, HERBERT J., WHAT THE ANTI-FEDERALISTS WERE FOR: THE POLITICAL THOUGHT OF THE OPPONENTS OF THE CONSTITUTION (1981)—**§ 12.2.**

STORY, JOSEPH, COMMENTARIES ON EQUITY JURISPRUDENCE (photo. reprint 2006) (London, Stevens & Hayes 1884)—**§§ 1.3, 11.5.2.**

STORY, JOSEPH, COMMENTARIES ON THE CONSTITUTION (Thomas M. Cooley ed., 4th ed. 1873)—**Introduction, § 4.1.**

Strauss, David A., *Common Law Constitutional Interpretation*, 63 U. CHI. L. REV. 877 (1996)—**§ 9.2.**

Subrin, Stephen N., *How Equity Conquered Common Law: The Federal Rules of Civil Procedure in Historical Perspective*, 135 U. PA. L. REV. 909 (1987)—**§ 10.1.**

Summers, Clyde W., *Frankfurter, Labor Law and the Judge's Function*, 67 YALE L.J. 266 (1957)—**§ 6.**

The Supreme Court, 2015 Term—Leading Cases, 130 HARV. L. REV. 437 (2016)—**§ 10.3.**

Surrency, Erwin C., *The Evolution of an Urban Judicial System: The Philadelphia Story, 1683 to 1968*, 18 AM. J. LEGAL HIST. 95 (1974)—**§ 1.3.**

TAMANAHA, BRIAN Z., BEYOND THE FORMALIST-REALIST DIVIDE: THE ROLE OF POLITICS IN JUDGING (2010)—**§ 10.3.**

Tamanaha, Brian Z., *Understanding Legal Realism*, 87 TEX. L. REV. 731 (2009)—**§ 10.3.**

Thomas, Suja A., *Judicial Modesty and the Jury*, 76 U. COLO. L. REV. 767 (2005)—**§ 12.3.**

Thompson, Karen, Note, *Luddites No Longer: Adopting the Technology Tutorial at the Supreme Court*, 91 TEX. L. REV. 199 (2012)—**§ 10.3.**

THOMSON, STEPHEN, THE NOBILE OFFICIUM: THE EXTRAORDINARY EQUITABLE JURISDICTION OF THE SUPREME COURTS OF SCOTLAND (2015)—**§ 10.2.**

Vinogradoff, Paul, *Transfer of Land in Old English Law*, 20 HARV. L. REV. 532 (1907)—**§ 1.3.**

Wand, Barbara Freedman, *A Call for the Repudiation of the Domestic Relations Exception to Federal Jurisdiction*, 30 VILL. L. REV. 307 (1985)—**§ 11.5.1.**

WARREN, CHARLES, THE SUPREME COURT IN UNITED STATES HISTORY (1926)—**§ 7.6.**

WHEATON, HENRY, A DIGEST OF THE LAW OF MARITIME CAPTURES AND PRIZES (1815)—**§ 8.2.**

WHEATON, HENRY, REPORTS OF CASES ARGUED AND ADJUDGED IN THE SUPREME COURT OF THE UNITED STATES (Frederick C. Blightly ed., 4th ed. 1883)—**§ 2.3.1.**

Wieacker, Franz, *The Importance of Roman Law for Western Civilization and Western Legal Thought*, 4 B.C. INT'L & COMP. L. REV. 257 (1981)—**§ 1.2.**

Wiener, Frederick Bernays, *Notes on the Rhode Island Admiralty, 1727-1790*, HARV. L. REV. 44 (1932)—**§ 2.3.1.**

Winkler, John F., *The Probate Jurisdiction of the Federal Courts*, 14 PROB. L.J. 77 (1997)—**§§ 3.1, 7.3.**

Winter, Steven L., *The Metaphor of Standing and the Problem of Self-Governance*, 40 STAN. L. REV. 1371 (1988)—**§ 9.5.**

WOOD, THOMAS, A NEW INSTITUTE OF THE IMPERIAL OR CIVIL LAW (4th ed., J. & J. Knapton et al. eds., 1730)—**§§ 1.2, 9.5.**

Woolhandler, Ann, *Adverse Interests and Article III*, 111 NW. U. L. REV. 1025 (2017)—**§§ 9.1, 9.2, 9.3, 9.4, 9.5.**

Woolhandler, Ann & Nelson, Caleb, *Does History Defeat Standing Doctrine?*, 102 MICH. L. REV. 689 (2004)—**Introduction; §§ 9.5, 10.**

WRIGHT, CHARLES ALAN ET AL., FEDERAL PRACTICE AND PROCEDURE (3d ed. 2008)—**§§ 2.5.1, 7.8.2.**

WRIGHT, CHARLES ALAN & KANE, MARY KAY, LAW OF FEDERAL COURTS (8th ed. 2017)—**§§ 2.3.1, 9.1.**

Wroth, L. Kinvin, *The Massachusetts Vice Admiralty Court and the Federal Admiralty Jurisdiction*, 6 AM. J. LEGAL HIST. 250 (1962)—**§ 2.3.1.**

YEAZELL, STEPHEN C., CIVIL PROCEDURE (6th ed. 2004)—**§ 7.6.**

Young, Ernest A., *Our Prescriptive Judicial Power: Constitutive and Entrenchment Effects of Historical Practice in Federal Courts Law*, 58 WM. & MARY L. REV. 535 (2016)—**§ 12.2.**

Zalman, Marvin, *Edwin Borchard's Innocence Project: The Origin and Legacy of His Wrongful Conviction Scholarship*, 1 WRONGFUL CONVICTION L.R. 124 (2020)—**§ 6.3.**

Table of Cases

Department of Transportation v. Ass'n of American Railroads, 575 U.S. 43 (2015)—**§ 12.3.**

DeSilva v. DiLeonardi, 181 F.3d 865 (7th Cir. 1999)— **§ 11.1.2.**

Edler v. Hockley County Commissioners Court, 589 Fed. App'x 664 (5th Cir. 2014)— **§ 11.4.**

Ellis v. Davis, 109 U.S. 485 (1883)—**§§ 4.2, 8.3.**

Ellis v. Gallatin Steel Co., 390 F.3d 461 (6th Cir. 2004)— **§ 10.2.**

Erie v. Tompkins, 304 U.S. 64 (1938)—**§ 6.**

Evans v. Pearson Enterprises, Inc., 434 F.3d 839 (6th Cir. 2006)— **§ 11.5.2.**

Ex parte Fitzbonne (1800) (unreported)—**§ 2.1.**

Ex parte Milligan, 71 U.S. (4 Wall.) 2 (1866)—**§ 7.2.**

Ex parte Newman, 18 F. Cas. 96 (C.C.D. Ma. 1814) (No. 10,174)—**§ 2.1.**

Ex parte Pasqualt, 18 F. Cas. 1283 (C.C.D.C. 1805) (No. 10,788)—**§ 2.1.**

Ex parte Pic, 19 F. Cas. 580 (C.C.D.C. 1808) (No. 11,118)—**§ 2.1.**

Ex parte Quirin, 317 U.S. 1 (1942)—**§ 7.2.**

Ex parte Saunderson, 21 F. Cas. 540 (C.C.D.D.C. 1804) (No. 12,378)—**§ 2.1.**

Ex parte Walton, 29 F. Cas. 125 (C.C.D.C. 1804) (No. 17,127)—**§§ 2.1, 11.3.**

Ex parte Young, 209 U.S. 123 (1908)—**§§ 5.2, 10.2.**

Federal Election Commission v. Akins, 524 U.S. 11 (1998)—**§ 6.2.**

Federal Radio Commission v. General Electric Co., 281 U. S. 461 (1930)—**§ 5.2.**

First National Bank v. A.M. Castle & Co. Employee Trust, 180 F.3d 814 (7th Cir. 1999)— **§ 7.4.**

First Technology Safety Systems, Inc. v. Depinet, 11 F.3d 641 (6th Cir.1993)—**§ 7.7.**

Fouvergne v. City of New Orleans, 59 U.S. 470 (1855)—**§ 3.2.**

Frew v. Hawkins, 540 U.S. 431 (2004)—**§ 7.6.**

Friends of the Earth, Inc. v. Laidlaw Environmental Services (TOC), Inc., 528 U.S. 167 (2000)—**§ 10.2.**

Frothingham v. Mellon, 262 U.S. 447 (1923)—**§ 5.2.**

Gaines v. Fuentes, 92 U.S. 10 (1875)—**§§ 4.2, 8.3, 11.5.2.**

Gerstein v. Pugh, 420 U.S. 103 (1975)—**§ 2.2.**

Greenlaw v. United States, 554 U.S. 237 (2008)—**Introduction.**

Grignon's Lessee v. Astor, 43 U.S. (2 How.) 319 (1844)—**§ 2.3.**

Gustafson v. zumBrunnen, 546 F.3d 398 (7th Cir. 2008)— **§ 11.5.2.**

Hanover National Bank v. Moyses, 186 U.S. 181 (1902)—**§ 7.3.**

Harris Trust & Savings Bank v. E-II Holdings, Inc., 926 F.2d 636 (7th Cir.1991)—**§ 7.4.**

Hayburn's Case, 2 U.S. (2 Dall.) 411 (1792)—**§§ 2.1, 2.4, 7.1, 9.2.**

Headwaters Inc. v. U.S. Forest Service, 399 F.3d 1047 (9th Cir. 2005)— **§ 10.2.**

Hindry v. The Priscilla, 12 F. Cas. 201 (D.S.C. 1792) (No. 6,515)—**§ 2.3.1.**

Index

For the benefit of digital users, indexed terms that span two pages (e.g., 52–53) may, on occasion, appear on only one of those pages.